GHOST®

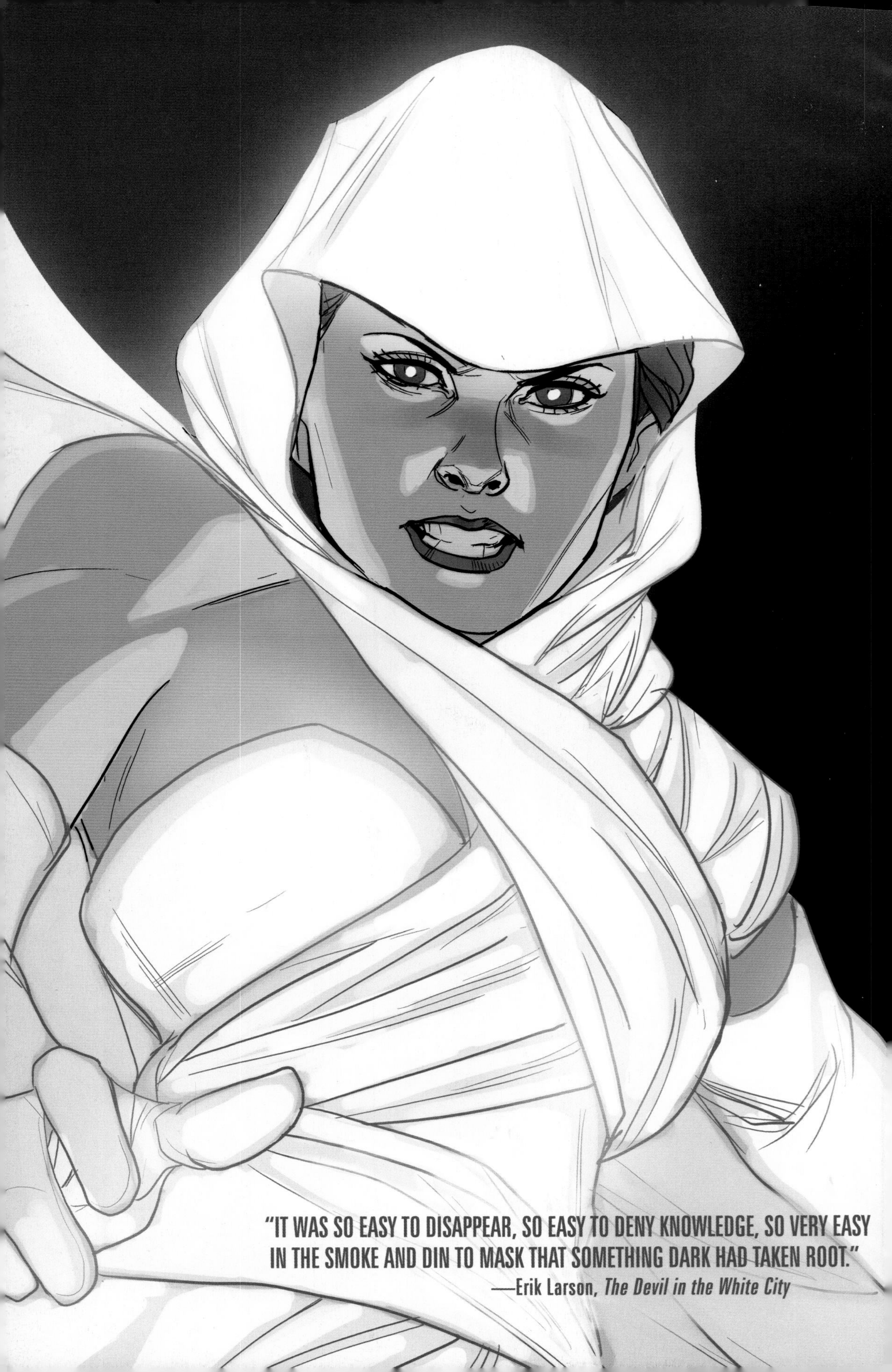

"IT WAS SO EASY TO DISAPPEAR, SO EASY TO DENY KNOWLEDGE, SO VERY EASY IN THE SMOKE AND DIN TO MASK THAT SOMETHING DARK HAD TAKEN ROOT."

—Erik Larson, *The Devil in the White City*

GHOST ®

VOLUME ONE
IN THE SMOKE AND DIN

STORY KELLY SUE **DECONNICK**

ART PHIL **NOTO**

COLORS ON CHAPTERS 3 AND 4 LEE LOUGHRIDGE
LETTERS RICHARD STARKINGS & COMICRAFT
COVER ALEX ROSS
CHAPTER 0 BREAK JENNY FRISON   *CHAPTERS 1–4 BREAKS* PHIL NOTO

DARK HORSE BOOKS

PUBLISHER MIKE RICHARDSON

EDITOR PATRICK THORPE

ASSISTANT EDITOR EVERETT PATTERSON

DESIGNER TINA ALESSI

PRODUCTION JASON HVAM & ALLYSON HALLER

GHOST VOLUME 1: IN THE SMOKE AND DIN

This book collects issues #0–#4 of Dark Horse Comics' miniseries *Ghost: In the Smoke and Din.*

Dark Horse Books
A division of Dark Horse Comics, Inc.
10956 SE Main Street
Milwaukie, OR 97222

DarkHorse.com

International Licensing (503) 905-2377
Comic Shop Locator Service (888) 266-4226

First edition: July 2013
ISBN 978-1-61655-121-6

10 9 8 7 6 5 4 3 2 1

Printed in China

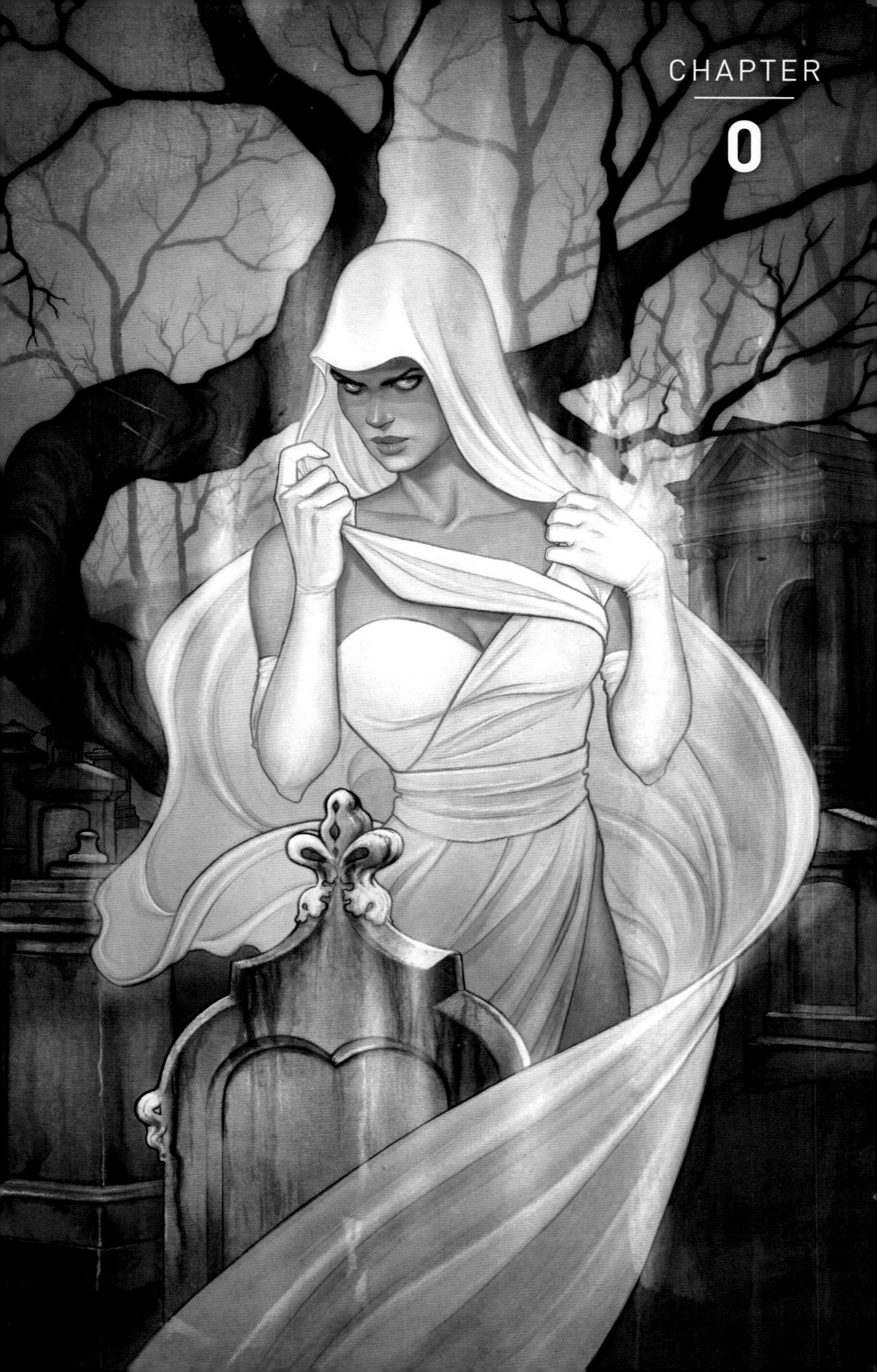
CHAPTER
0

"HEAVEN DID NOT SEEM TO BE MY HOME, AND I BROKE MY HEART WITH WEEPING . . . THE ANGELS WERE SO ANGRY THAT THEY FLUNG ME OUT . . ."

—Emily Brontë, *Wuthering Heights*

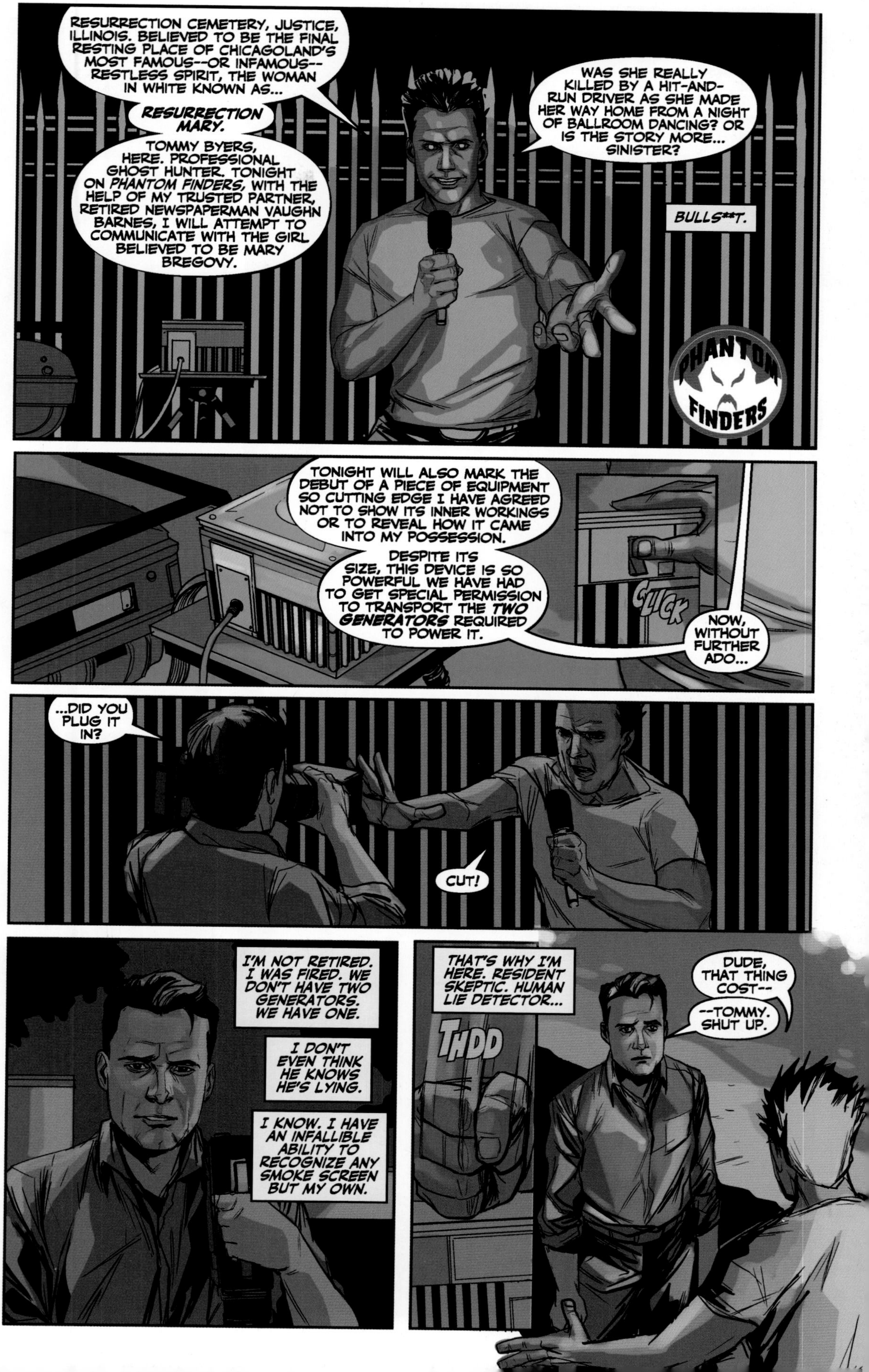

RESURRECTION CEMETERY, JUSTICE, ILLINOIS. BELIEVED TO BE THE FINAL RESTING PLACE OF CHICAGOLAND'S MOST FAMOUS--OR INFAMOUS--RESTLESS SPIRIT, THE WOMAN IN WHITE KNOWN AS...
RESURRECTION MARY.
TOMMY BYERS, HERE. PROFESSIONAL GHOST HUNTER. TONIGHT ON PHANTOM FINDERS, WITH THE HELP OF MY TRUSTED PARTNER, RETIRED NEWSPAPERMAN VAUGHN BARNES, I WILL ATTEMPT TO COMMUNICATE WITH THE GIRL BELIEVED TO BE MARY BREGOVY.
WAS SHE REALLY KILLED BY A HIT-AND-RUN DRIVER AS SHE MADE HER WAY HOME FROM A NIGHT OF BALLROOM DANCING? OR IS THE STORY MORE... SINISTER?
BULLS**T.
PHANTOM FINDERS
TONIGHT WILL ALSO MARK THE DEBUT OF A PIECE OF EQUIPMENT SO CUTTING EDGE I HAVE AGREED NOT TO SHOW ITS INNER WORKINGS OR TO REVEAL HOW IT CAME INTO MY POSSESSION.
DESPITE ITS SIZE, THIS DEVICE IS SO POWERFUL WE HAVE HAD TO GET SPECIAL PERMISSION TO TRANSPORT THE TWO GENERATORS REQUIRED TO POWER IT.
CLICK
NOW, WITHOUT FURTHER ADO...
...DID YOU PLUG IT IN?
CUT!
I'M NOT RETIRED. I WAS FIRED. WE DON'T HAVE TWO GENERATORS. WE HAVE ONE.
I DON'T EVEN THINK HE KNOWS HE'S LYING.
I KNOW. I HAVE AN INFALLIBLE ABILITY TO RECOGNIZE ANY SMOKE SCREEN BUT MY OWN.
THAT'S WHY I'M HERE. RESIDENT SKEPTIC. HUMAN LIE DETECTOR...
THDD
DUDE, THAT THING COST--
--TOMMY. SHUT UP.

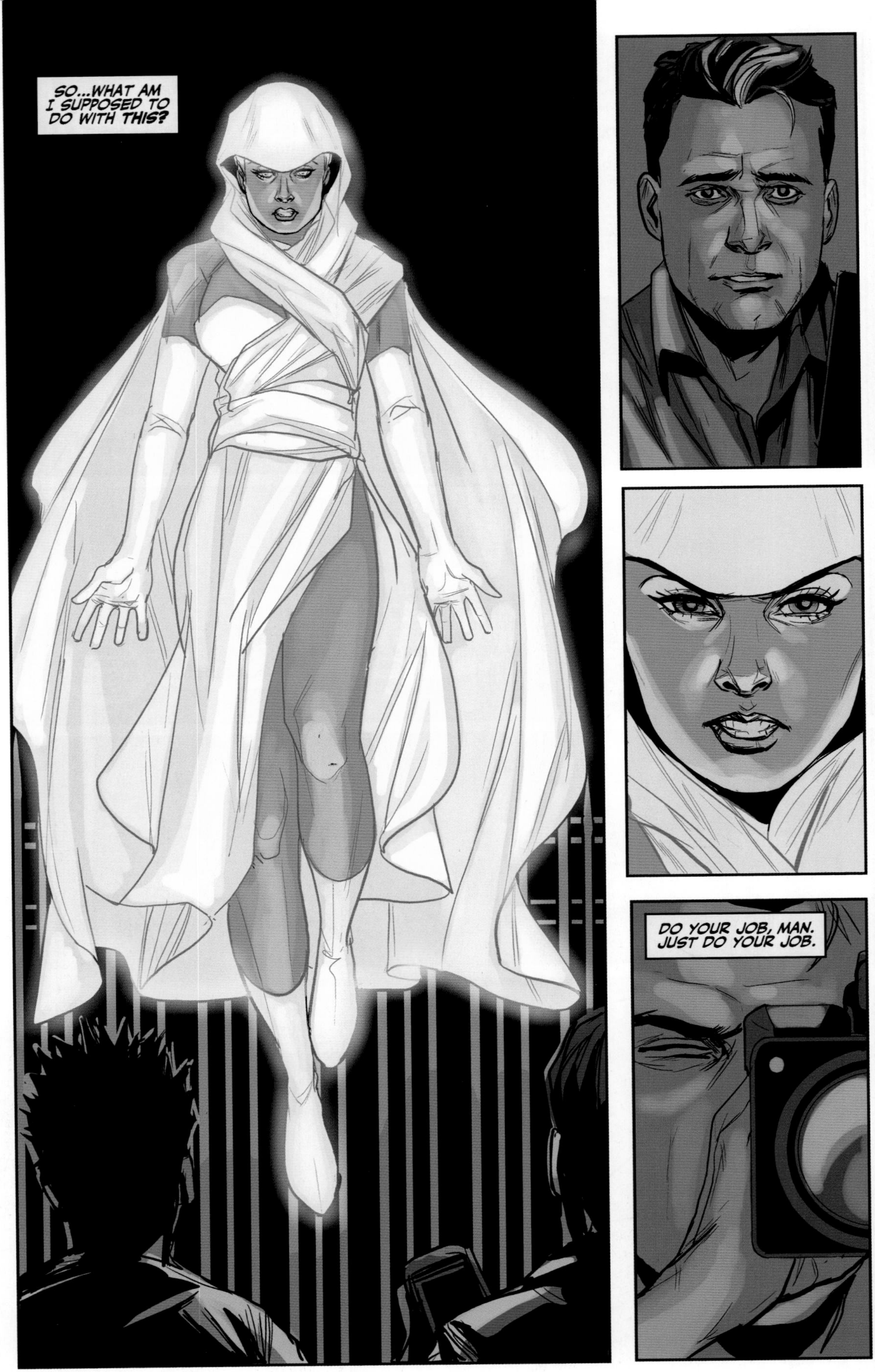
SO...WHAT AM I SUPPOSED TO DO WITH THIS?
DO YOUR JOB, MAN. JUST DO YOUR JOB.

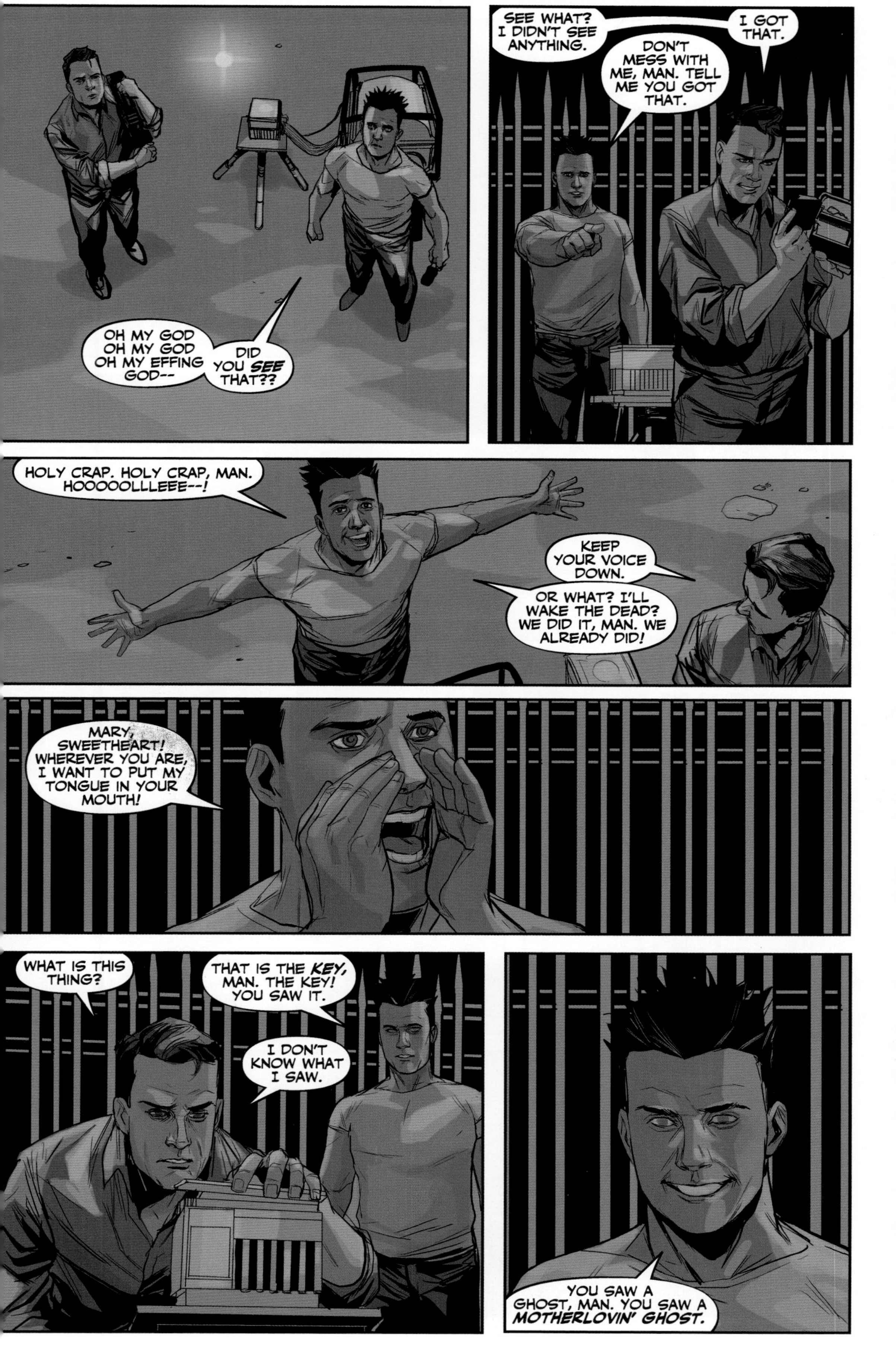
OH MY GOD OH MY GOD OH MY EFFING GOD--
DID YOU SEE THAT??
SEE WHAT? I DIDN'T SEE ANYTHING.
DON'T MESS WITH ME, MAN. TELL ME YOU GOT THAT.
I GOT THAT.
HOLY CRAP. HOLY CRAP, MAN. HOOOOOLLLEEE--!
KEEP YOUR VOICE DOWN.
OR WHAT? I'LL WAKE THE DEAD? WE DID IT, MAN. WE ALREADY DID!
MARY, SWEETHEART! WHEREVER YOU ARE, I WANT TO PUT MY TONGUE IN YOUR MOUTH!
WHAT IS THIS THING?
THAT IS THE KEY, MAN. THE KEY! YOU SAW IT.
I DON'T KNOW WHAT I SAW.
YOU SAW A GHOST, MAN. YOU SAW A MOTHERLOVIN' GHOST.

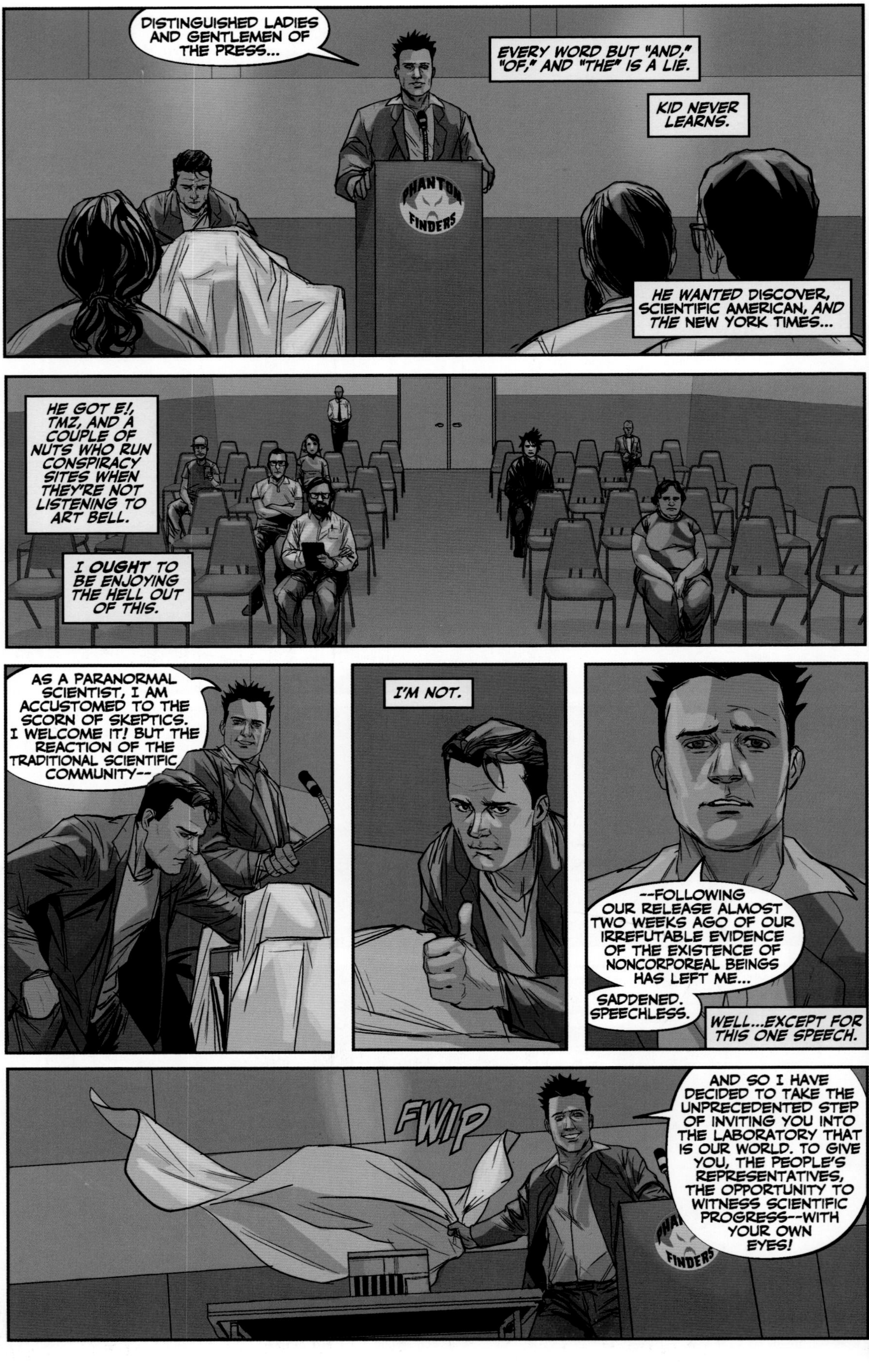
DISTINGUISHED LADIES AND GENTLEMEN OF THE PRESS...
EVERY WORD BUT "AND," "OF," AND "THE" IS A LIE.
KID NEVER LEARNS.
PHANTOM FINDERS
HE WANTED DISCOVER, SCIENTIFIC AMERICAN, AND THE NEW YORK TIMES...
HE GOT E!, TMZ, AND A COUPLE OF NUTS WHO RUN CONSPIRACY SITES WHEN THEY'RE NOT LISTENING TO ART BELL.
I OUGHT TO BE ENJOYING THE HELL OUT OF THIS.
AS A PARANORMAL SCIENTIST, I AM ACCUSTOMED TO THE SCORN OF SKEPTICS. I WELCOME IT! BUT THE REACTION OF THE TRADITIONAL SCIENTIFIC COMMUNITY--
I'M NOT.
--FOLLOWING OUR RELEASE ALMOST TWO WEEKS AGO OF OUR IRREFUTABLE EVIDENCE OF THE EXISTENCE OF NONCORPOREAL BEINGS HAS LEFT ME...
SADDENED. SPEECHLESS.
WELL...EXCEPT FOR THIS ONE SPEECH.
FWIP
AND SO I HAVE DECIDED TO TAKE THE UNPRECEDENTED STEP OF INVITING YOU INTO THE LABORATORY THAT IS OUR WORLD. TO GIVE YOU, THE PEOPLE'S REPRESENTATIVES, THE OPPORTUNITY TO WITNESS SCIENTIFIC PROGRESS--WITH YOUR OWN EYES!

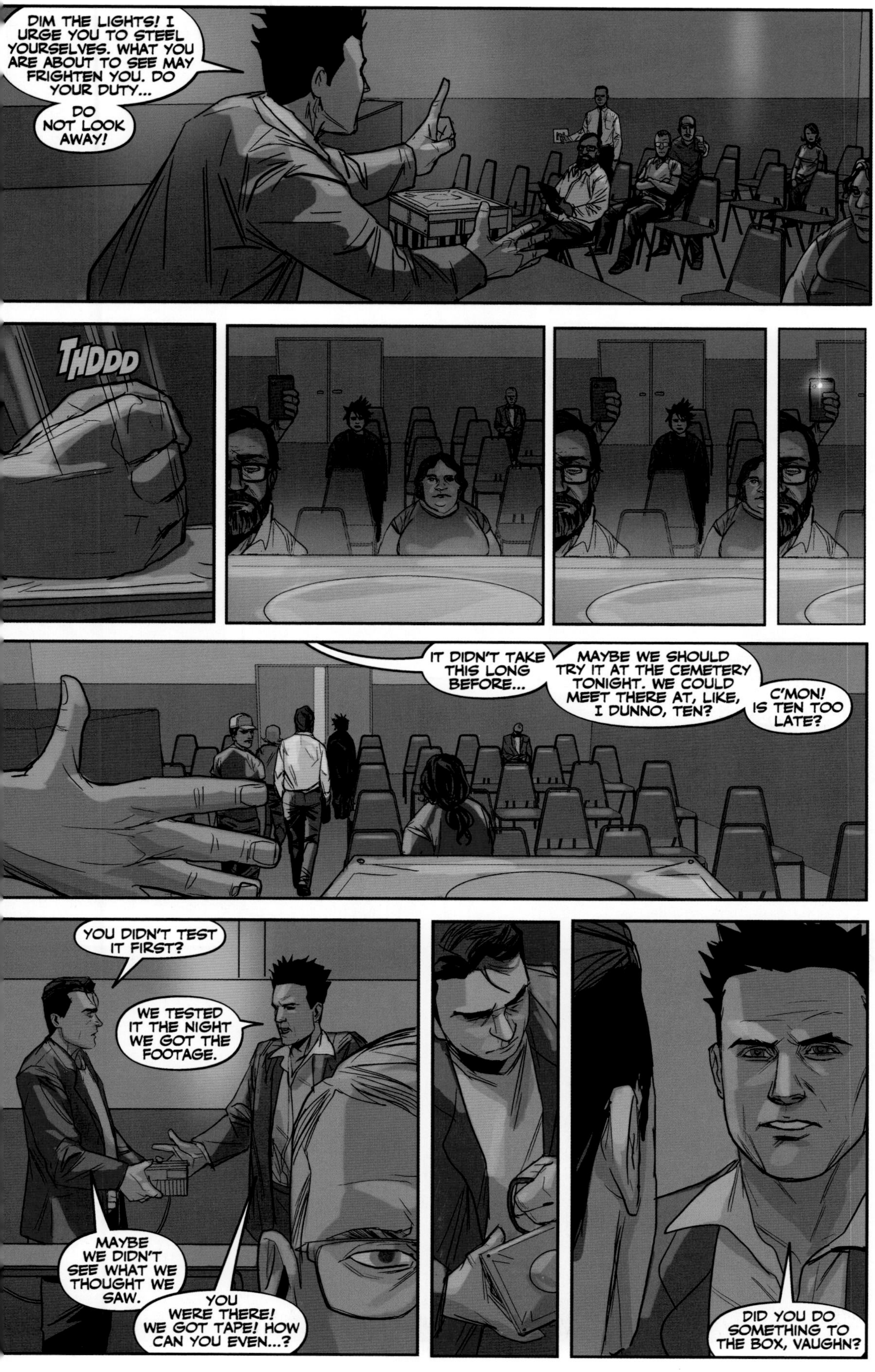
DIM THE LIGHTS! I URGE YOU TO STEEL YOURSELVES. WHAT YOU ARE ABOUT TO SEE MAY FRIGHTEN YOU. DO YOUR DUTY...
DO NOT LOOK AWAY!
THDDD
IT DIDN'T TAKE THIS LONG BEFORE...
MAYBE WE SHOULD TRY IT AT THE CEMETERY TONIGHT. WE COULD MEET THERE AT, LIKE, I DUNNO, TEN?
C'MON! IS TEN TOO LATE?
YOU DIDN'T TEST IT FIRST?
WE TESTED IT THE NIGHT WE GOT THE FOOTAGE.
MAYBE WE DIDN'T SEE WHAT WE THOUGHT WE SAW.
YOU WERE THERE! WE GOT TAPE! HOW CAN YOU EVEN...?
DID YOU DO SOMETHING TO THE BOX, VAUGHN?

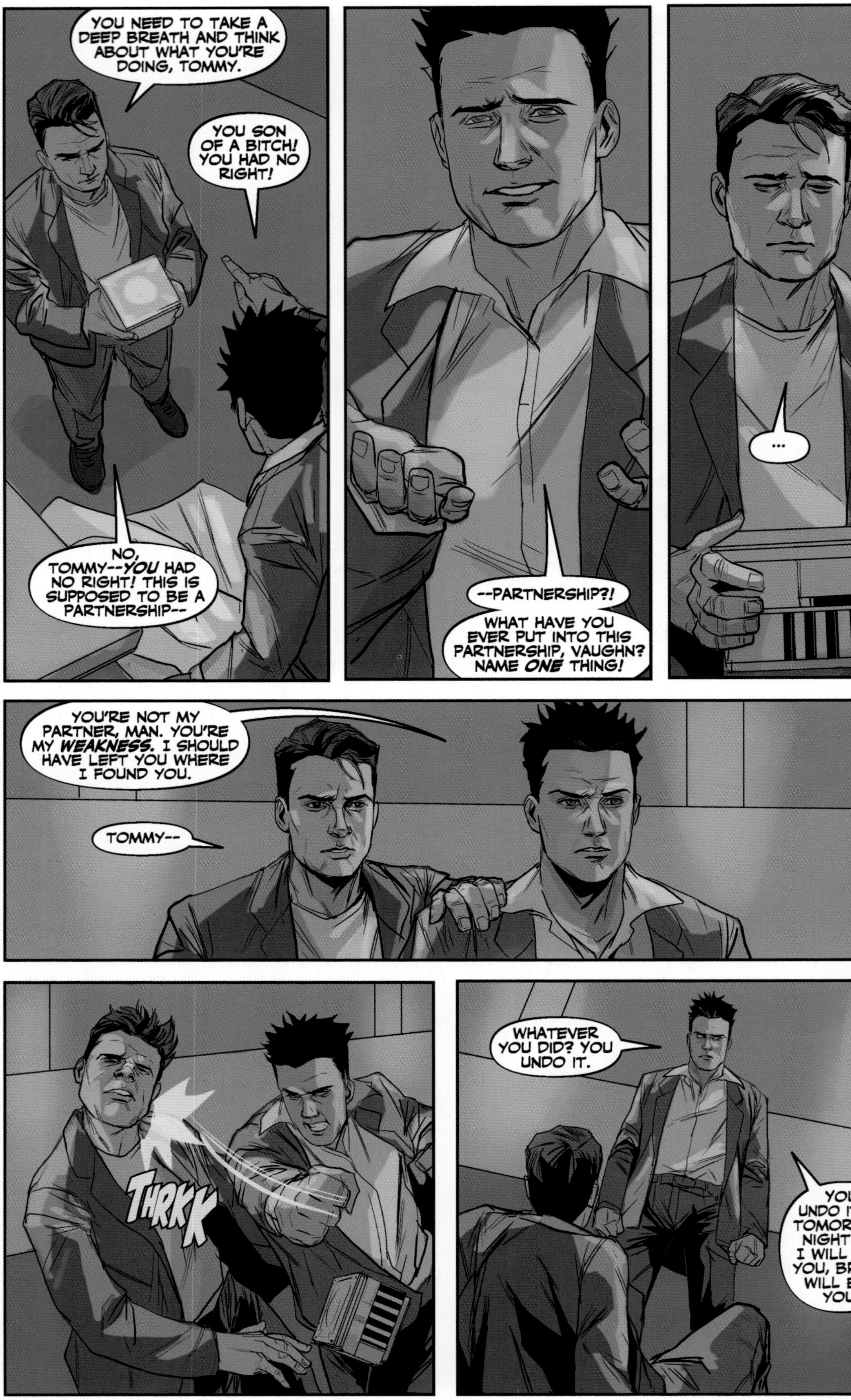
YOU NEED TO TAKE A DEEP BREATH AND THINK ABOUT WHAT YOU'RE DOING, TOMMY.
YOU SON OF A BITCH! YOU HAD NO RIGHT!
NO, TOMMY--*YOU* HAD NO RIGHT! THIS IS SUPPOSED TO BE A PARTNERSHIP--
--PARTNERSHIP?!
WHAT HAVE YOU EVER PUT INTO THIS PARTNERSHIP, VAUGHN? NAME *ONE* THING!
...
YOU'RE NOT MY PARTNER, MAN. YOU'RE MY *WEAKNESS.* I SHOULD HAVE LEFT YOU WHERE I FOUND YOU.
TOMMY--
THRKK
WHATEVER YOU DID? YOU UNDO IT.
YOU UNDO IT BY TOMORROW NIGHT OR I WILL END YOU, BRO. I WILL END YOU.

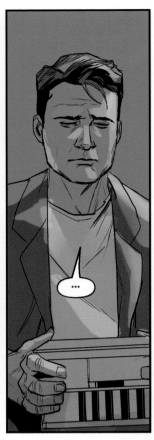

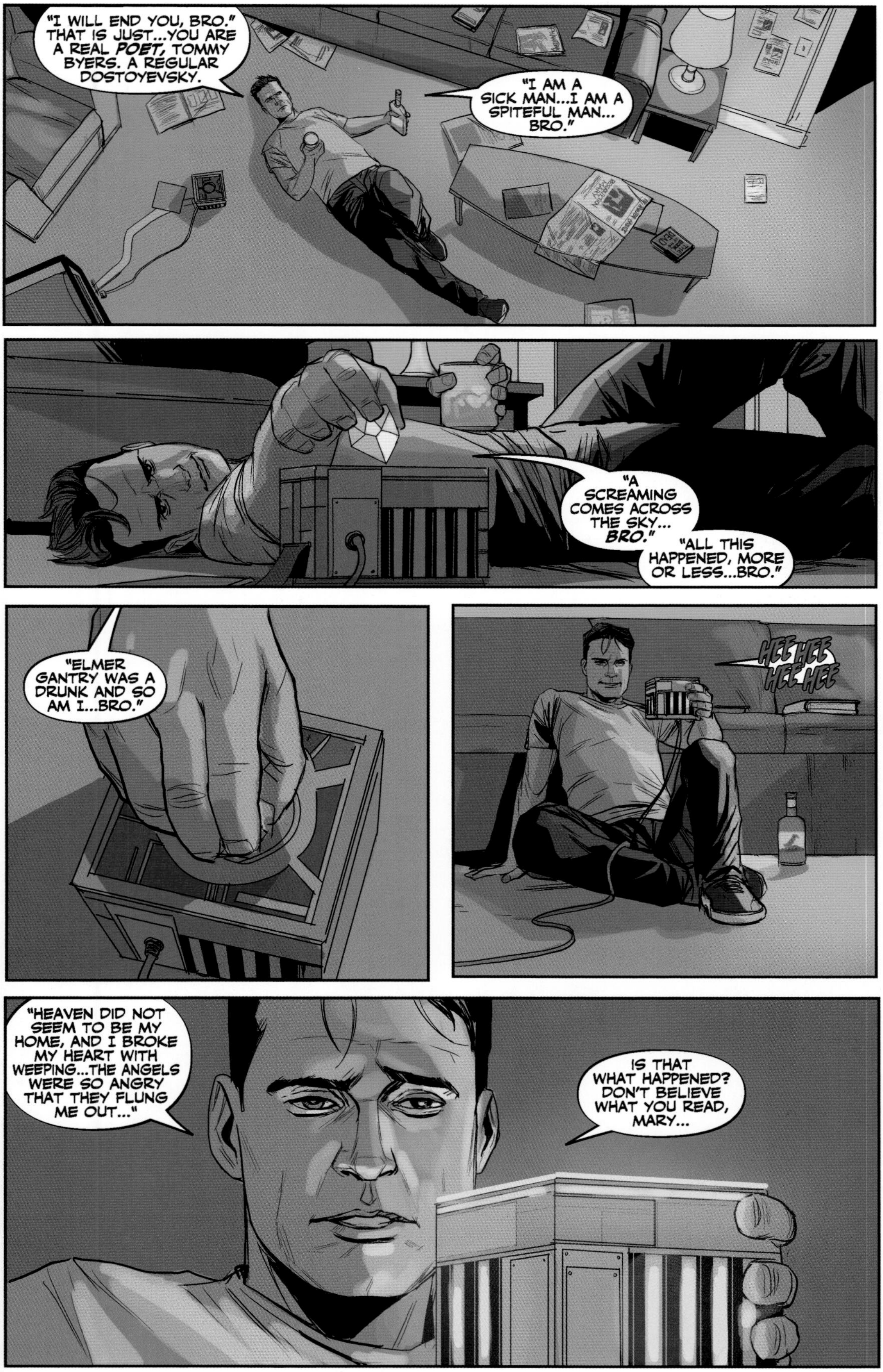
"I WILL END YOU, BRO." THAT IS JUST...YOU ARE A REAL *POET,* TOMMY BYERS. A REGULAR DOSTOYEVSKY.
"I AM A SICK MAN...I AM A SPITEFUL MAN... BRO."
"A SCREAMING COMES ACROSS THE SKY... *BRO.*"
"ALL THIS HAPPENED, MORE OR LESS...BRO."
"ELMER GANTRY WAS A DRUNK AND SO AM I...BRO."
HEE HEE HEE HEE
"HEAVEN DID NOT SEEM TO BE MY HOME, AND I BROKE MY HEART WITH WEEPING...THE ANGELS WERE SO ANGRY THAT THEY FLUNG ME OUT..."
IS THAT WHAT HAPPENED? DON'T BELIEVE WHAT YOU READ, MARY...

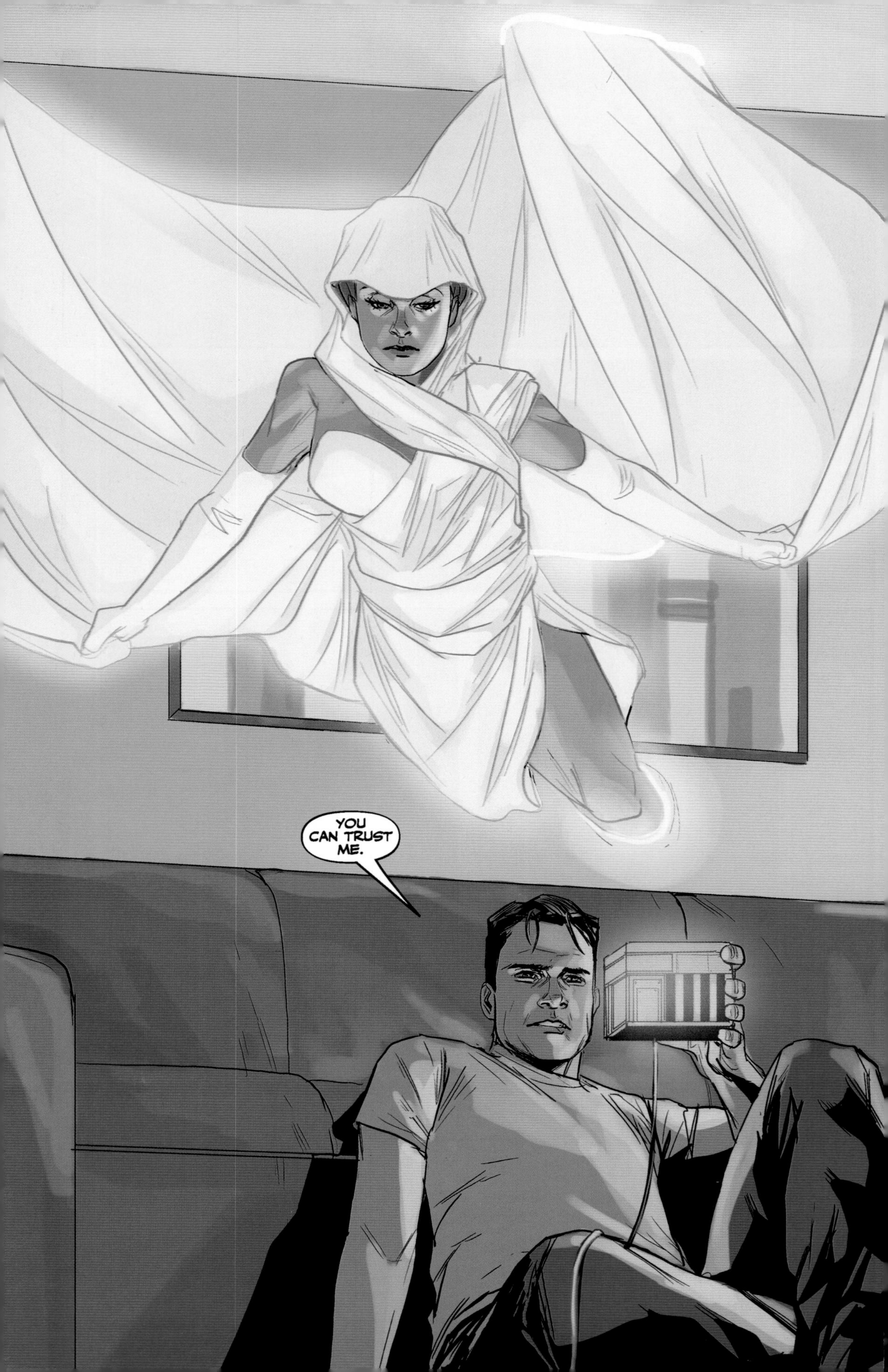
YOU CAN TRUST ME.

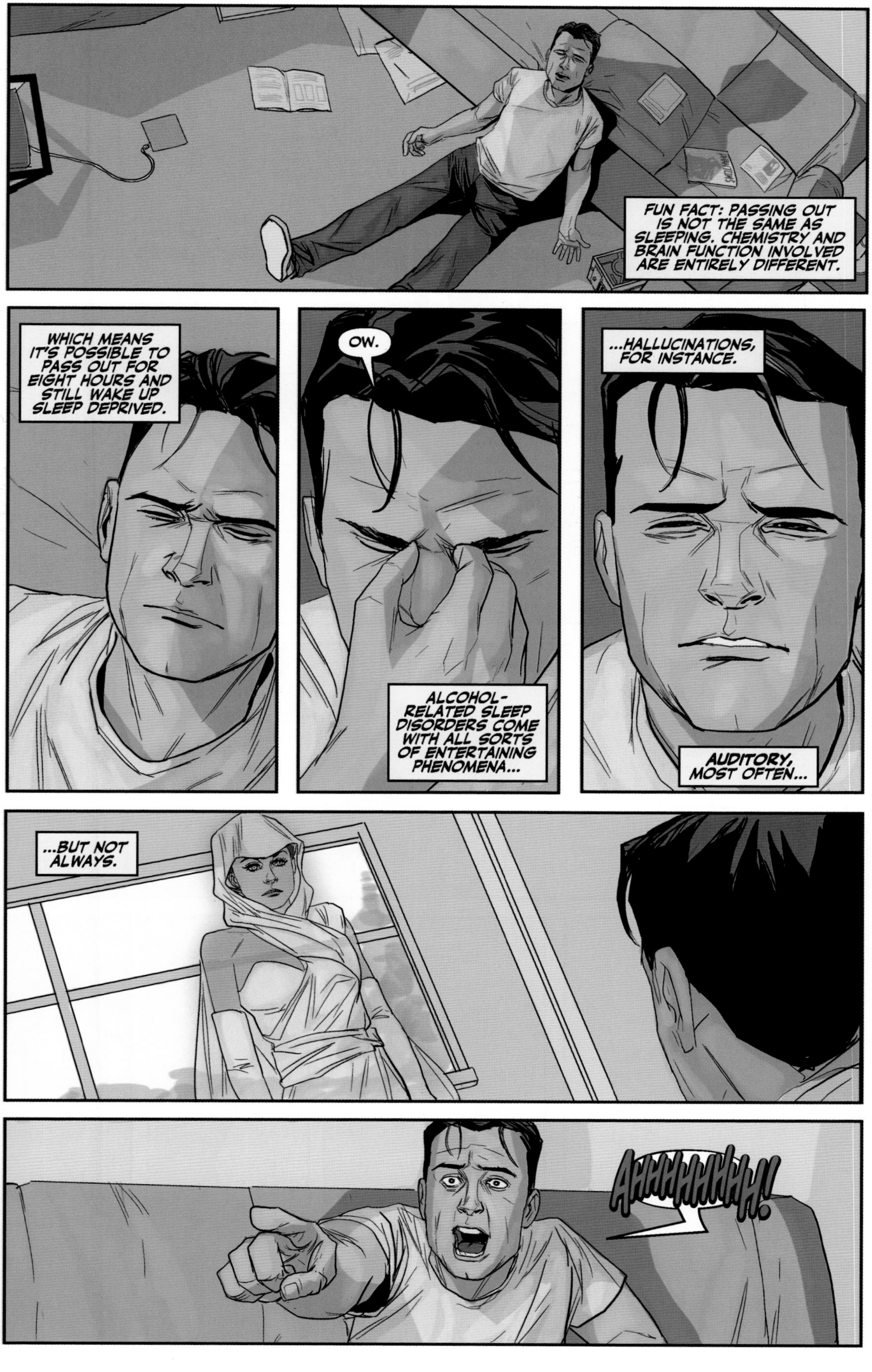

FUN FACT: PASSING OUT IS NOT THE SAME AS SLEEPING. CHEMISTRY AND BRAIN FUNCTION INVOLVED ARE ENTIRELY DIFFERENT.
WHICH MEANS IT'S POSSIBLE TO PASS OUT FOR EIGHT HOURS AND STILL WAKE UP SLEEP DEPRIVED.
OW.
ALCOHOL-RELATED SLEEP DISORDERS COME WITH ALL SORTS OF ENTERTAINING PHENOMENA...
...HALLUCINATIONS, FOR INSTANCE.
AUDITORY, MOST OFTEN...
...BUT NOT ALWAYS.
AHHHHHHHH!

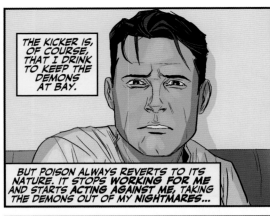

THE KICKER IS, OF COURSE, THAT I DRINK TO KEEP THE DEMONS AT BAY.

BUT POISON ALWAYS REVERTS TO ITS NATURE. IT STOPS *WORKING* FOR ME AND STARTS ACTING *AGAINST* ME, TAKING THE DEMONS OUT OF MY NIGHTMARES...

...AND DEPOSITING THEM IN MY *LIVING ROOM.*

A SILENT SIREN. PROVING ONCE AGAIN THAT THE UNIVERSE HAS A CRUEL SENSE OF HUMOR.

I KNEW I WAS DOOMED EVEN BEFORE THIS. I KNEW IT WHEN I FIRST SAW HER.

HELL, PROBABLY EVEN BEFORE THAT.

I KNEW I WAS DOOMED.

EVERYTHING ELSE WAS A MYSTERY.

ARE YOU THE BOOZE?

OR ARE YOU SOMETHING ELSE ENTIRELY?

KAKK--

THRADOD

DT'S DON'T THROW YOU AGAINST THE WINDOW.

AND AS FAR AS I KNOW...

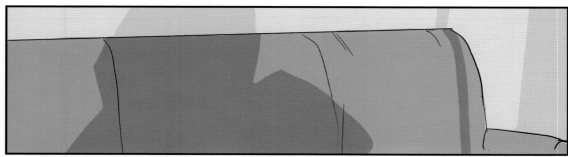

DREAMS DON'T CAST SHADOWS.

I-I MIGHT HAVE AN IDEA HERE... MAYBE...

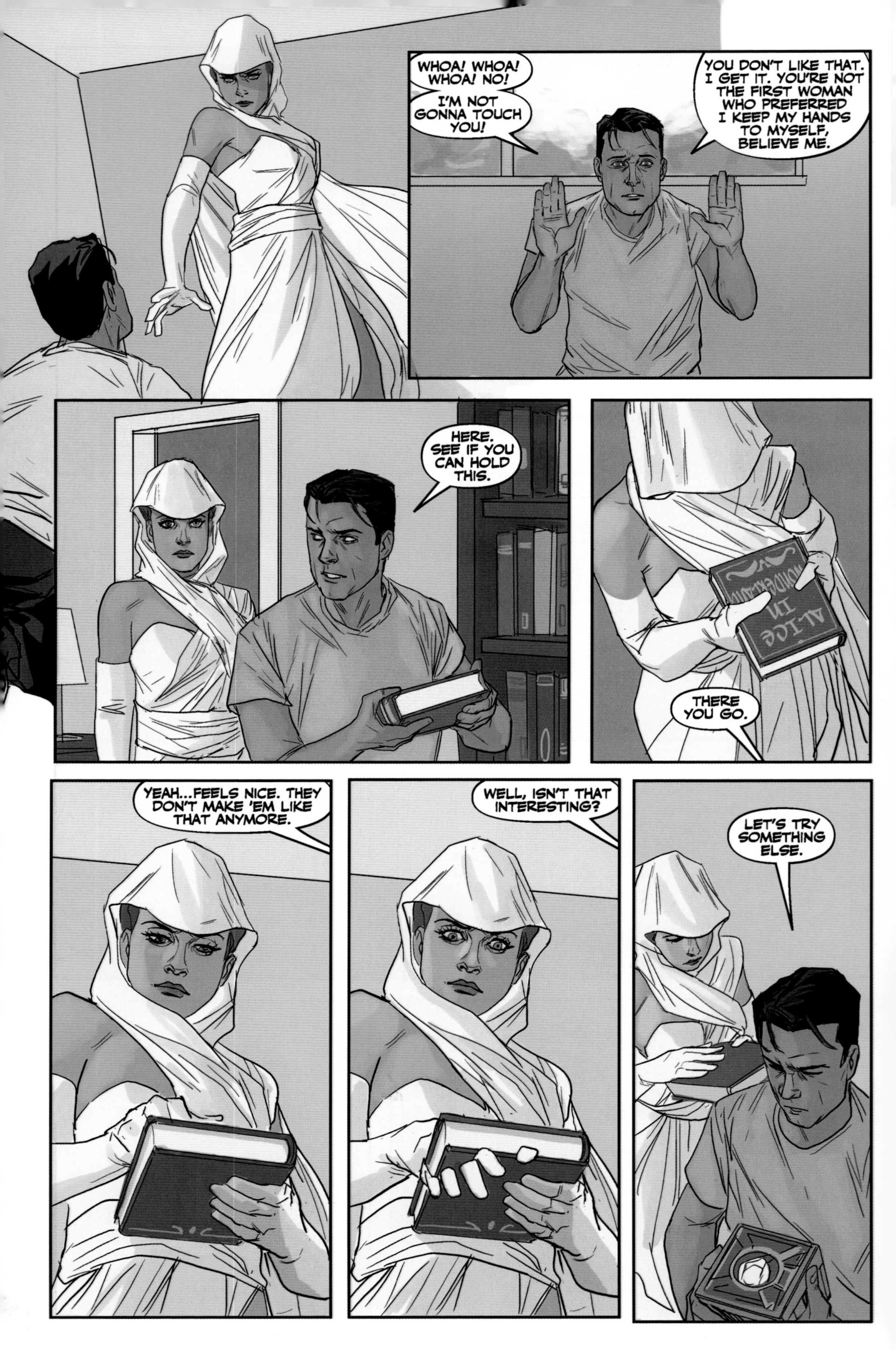
WHOA! WHOA! WHOA! NO!
I'M NOT GONNA TOUCH YOU!
YOU DON'T LIKE THAT. I GET IT. YOU'RE NOT THE FIRST WOMAN WHO PREFERRED I KEEP MY HANDS TO MYSELF, BELIEVE ME.
HERE. SEE IF YOU CAN HOLD THIS.
ALICE IN WONDERLAND
THERE YOU GO.
YEAH...FEELS NICE. THEY DON'T MAKE 'EM LIKE THAT ANYMORE.
WELL, ISN'T THAT INTERESTING?
LET'S TRY SOMETHING ELSE.

I JUST...I WANT TO TEST A THEORY.

STILL HERE?

OKAY...OKAY, GOOD.

I *THINK* THIS BOX IS SOME KIND OF DOOR... AND MAYBE THIS THING WORKS LIKE A KEY. NOW THAT YOU'RE HERE...

PROBABLY A GOOD IDEA TO CLOSE THE DOOR.

IT'S ONE THEORY, ANYWAY. THEORY TWO IS THAT I'VE LOST MY MIND ENTIRELY.

KRAK

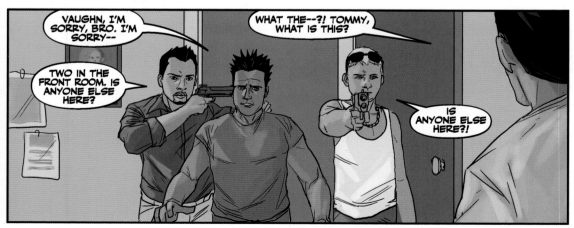

VAUGHN, I'M SORRY, BRO. I'M SORRY--

TWO IN THE FRONT ROOM. IS ANYONE ELSE HERE?

WHAT THE--?! TOMMY, WHAT IS THIS?

IS ANYONE ELSE HERE?!

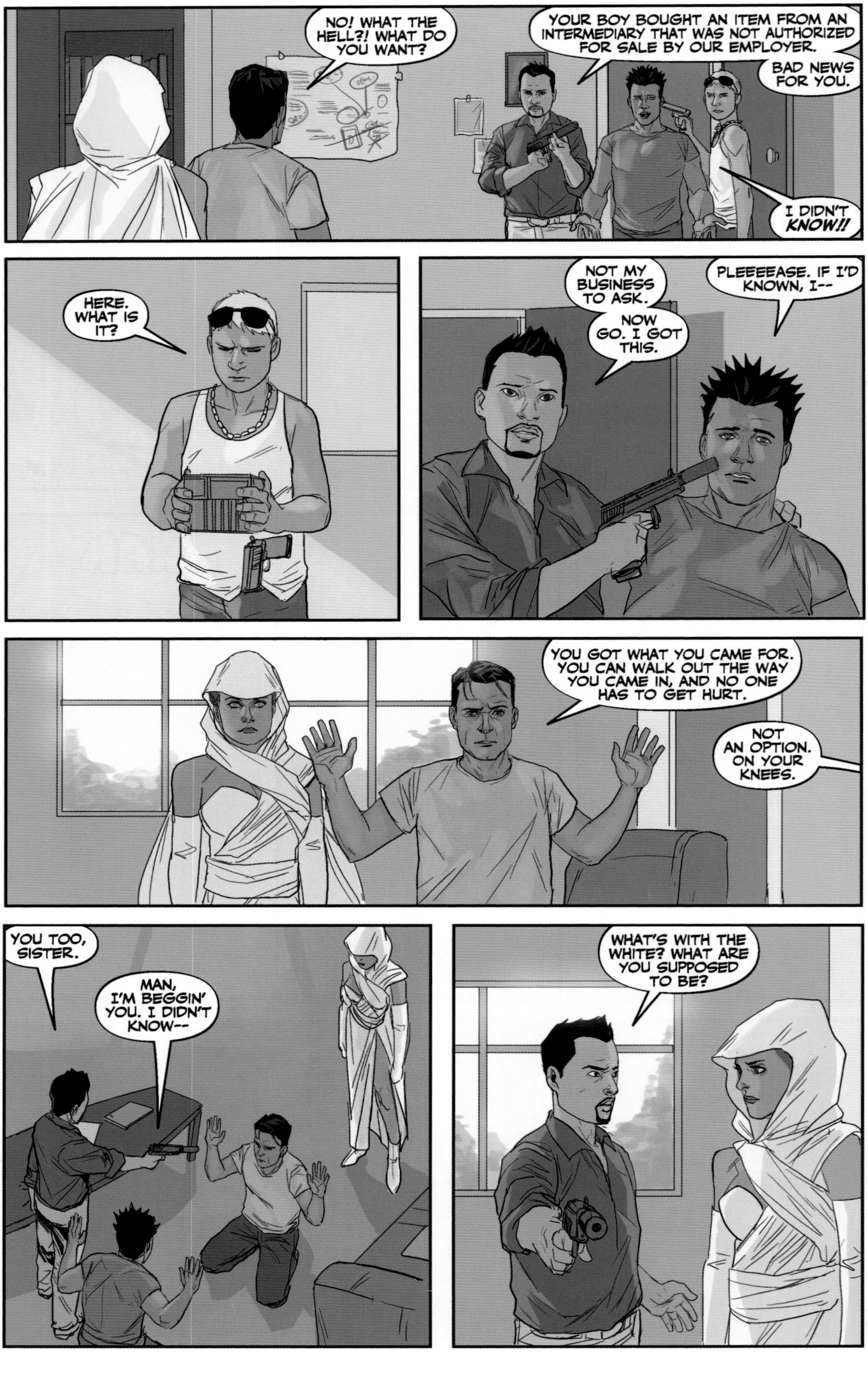
NO! WHAT THE HELL?! WHAT DO YOU WANT?
YOUR BOY BOUGHT AN ITEM FROM AN INTERMEDIARY THAT WAS NOT AUTHORIZED FOR SALE BY OUR EMPLOYER.
BAD NEWS FOR YOU.
I DIDN'T KNOW!!
HERE. WHAT IS IT?
NOT MY BUSINESS TO ASK.
NOW GO. I GOT THIS.
PLEEEEASE. IF I'D KNOWN, I--
YOU GOT WHAT YOU CAME FOR. YOU CAN WALK OUT THE WAY YOU CAME IN, AND NO ONE HAS TO GET HURT.
NOT AN OPTION. ON YOUR KNEES.
YOU TOO, SISTER.
MAN, I'M BEGGIN' YOU. I DIDN'T KNOW--
WHAT'S WITH THE WHITE? WHAT ARE YOU SUPPOSED TO BE?

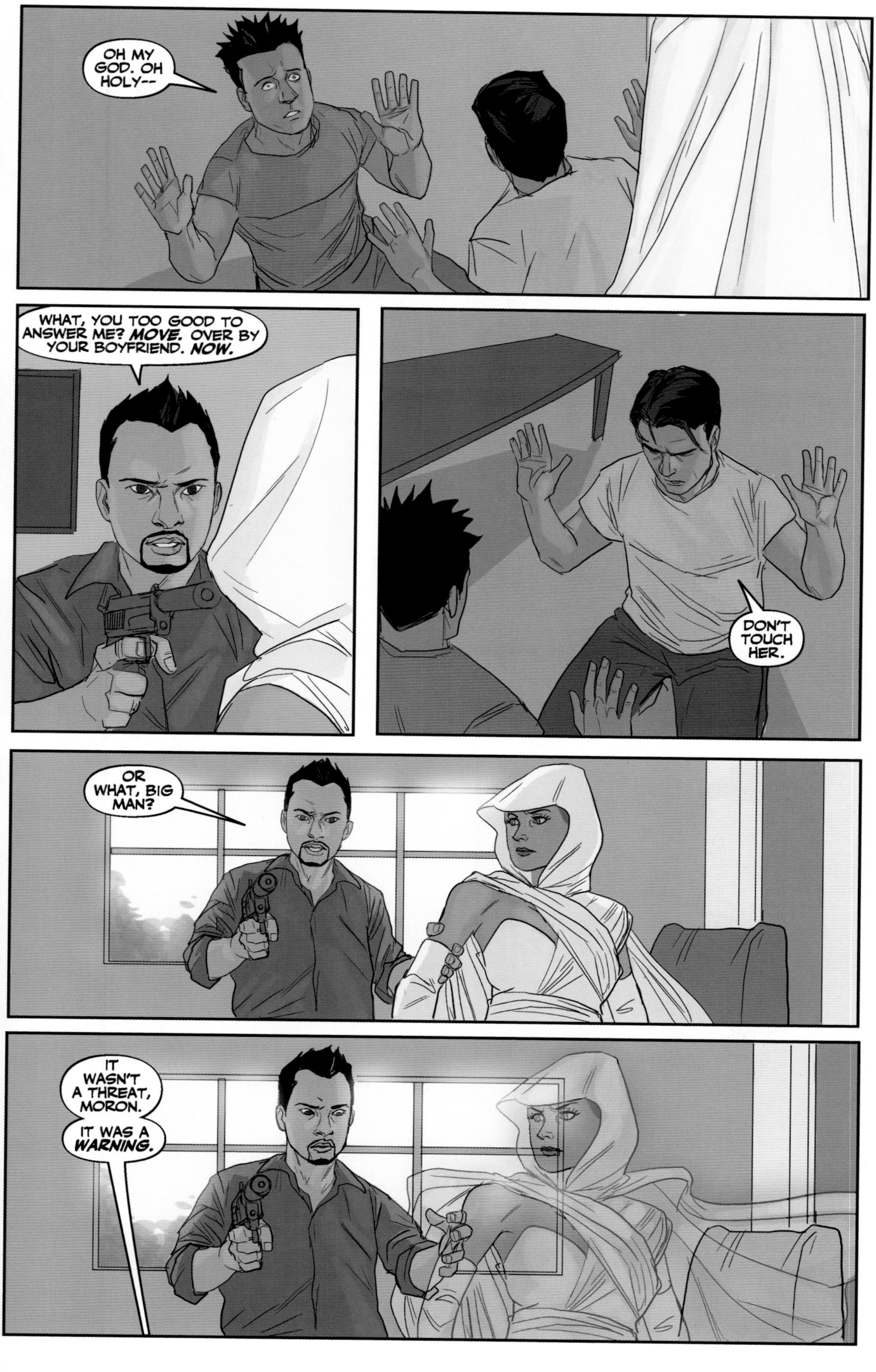
OH MY GOD. OH HOLY--
WHAT, YOU TOO GOOD TO ANSWER ME? *MOVE.* OVER BY YOUR BOYFRIEND. *NOW.*
DON'T TOUCH HER.
OR WHAT, BIG MAN?
IT WASN'T A THREAT, MORON.
IT WAS A *WARNING.*

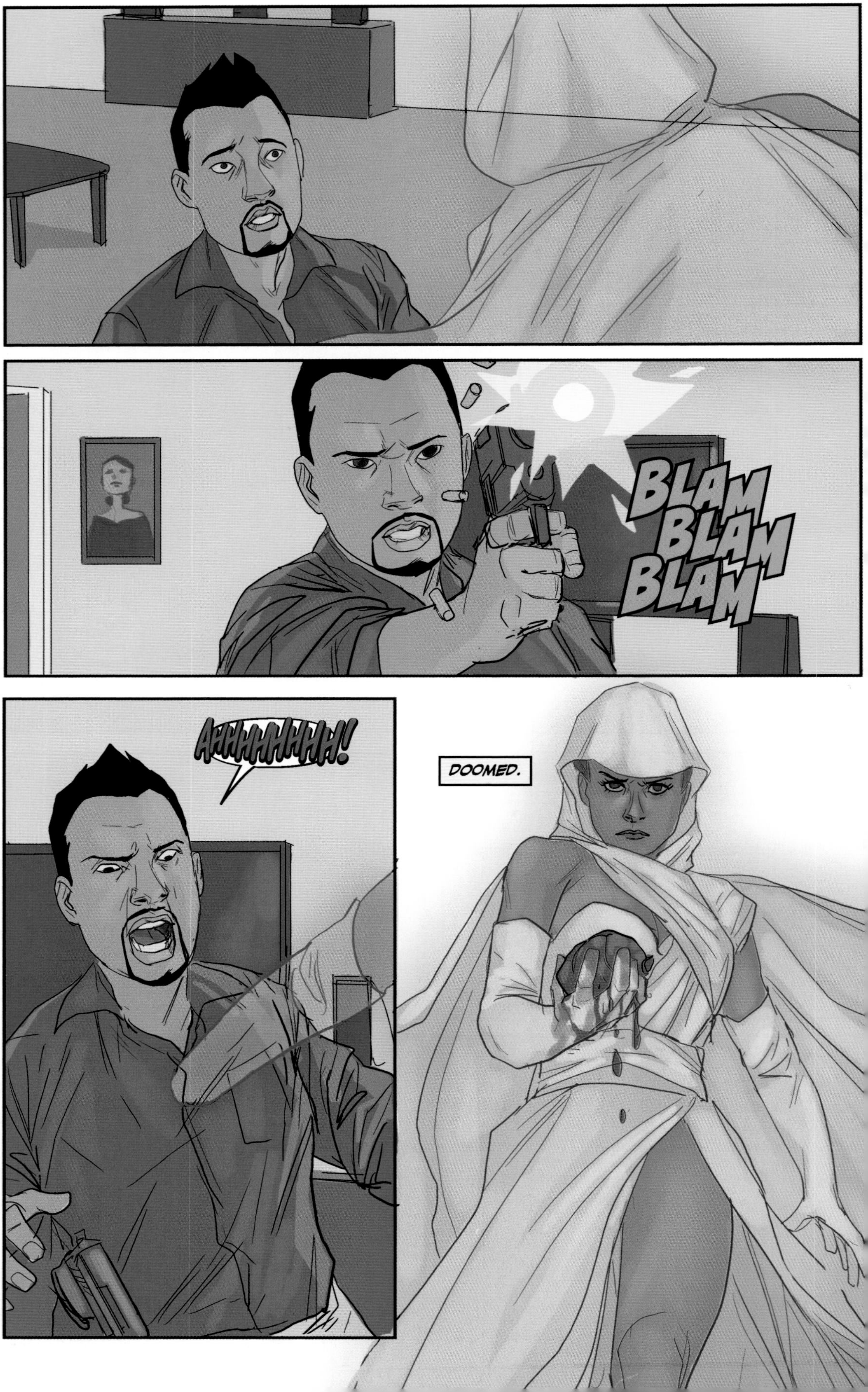
BLAM BLAM BLAM
AHHHHHHHH!
DOOMED.

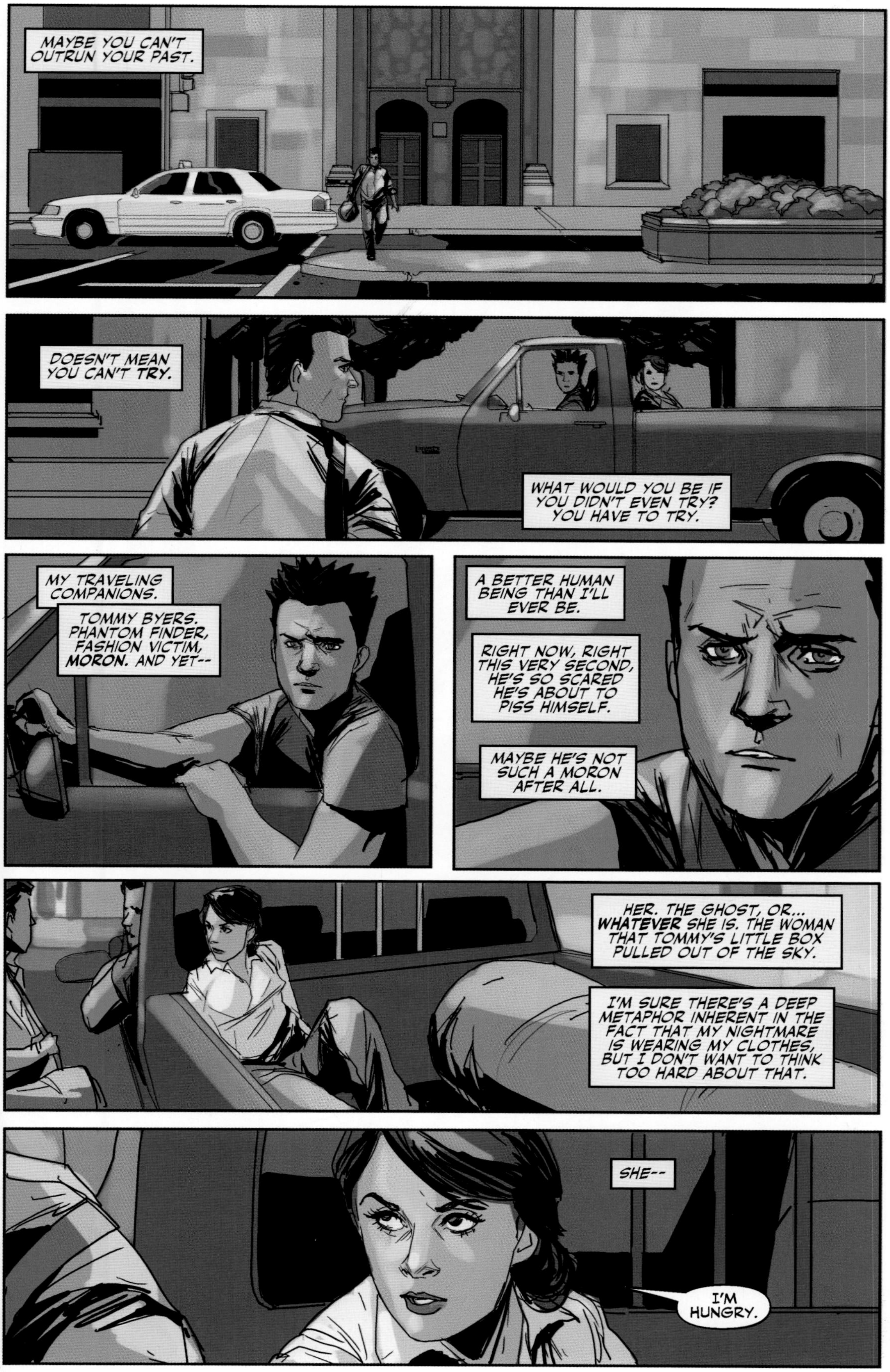
MAYBE YOU CAN'T OUTRUN YOUR PAST.
DOESN'T MEAN YOU CAN'T TRY.
WHAT WOULD YOU BE IF YOU DIDN'T EVEN TRY? YOU HAVE TO TRY.
MY TRAVELING COMPANIONS.
TOMMY BYERS. PHANTOM FINDER, FASHION VICTIM, MORON. AND YET--
A BETTER HUMAN BEING THAN I'LL EVER BE.
RIGHT NOW, RIGHT THIS VERY SECOND, HE'S SO SCARED HE'S ABOUT TO PISS HIMSELF.
MAYBE HE'S NOT SUCH A MORON AFTER ALL.
HER. THE GHOST, OR... WHATEVER SHE IS. THE WOMAN THAT TOMMY'S LITTLE BOX PULLED OUT OF THE SKY.
I'M SURE THERE'S A DEEP METAPHOR INHERENT IN THE FACT THAT MY NIGHTMARE IS WEARING MY CLOTHES, BUT I DON'T WANT TO THINK TOO HARD ABOUT THAT.
SHE--
I'M HUNGRY.

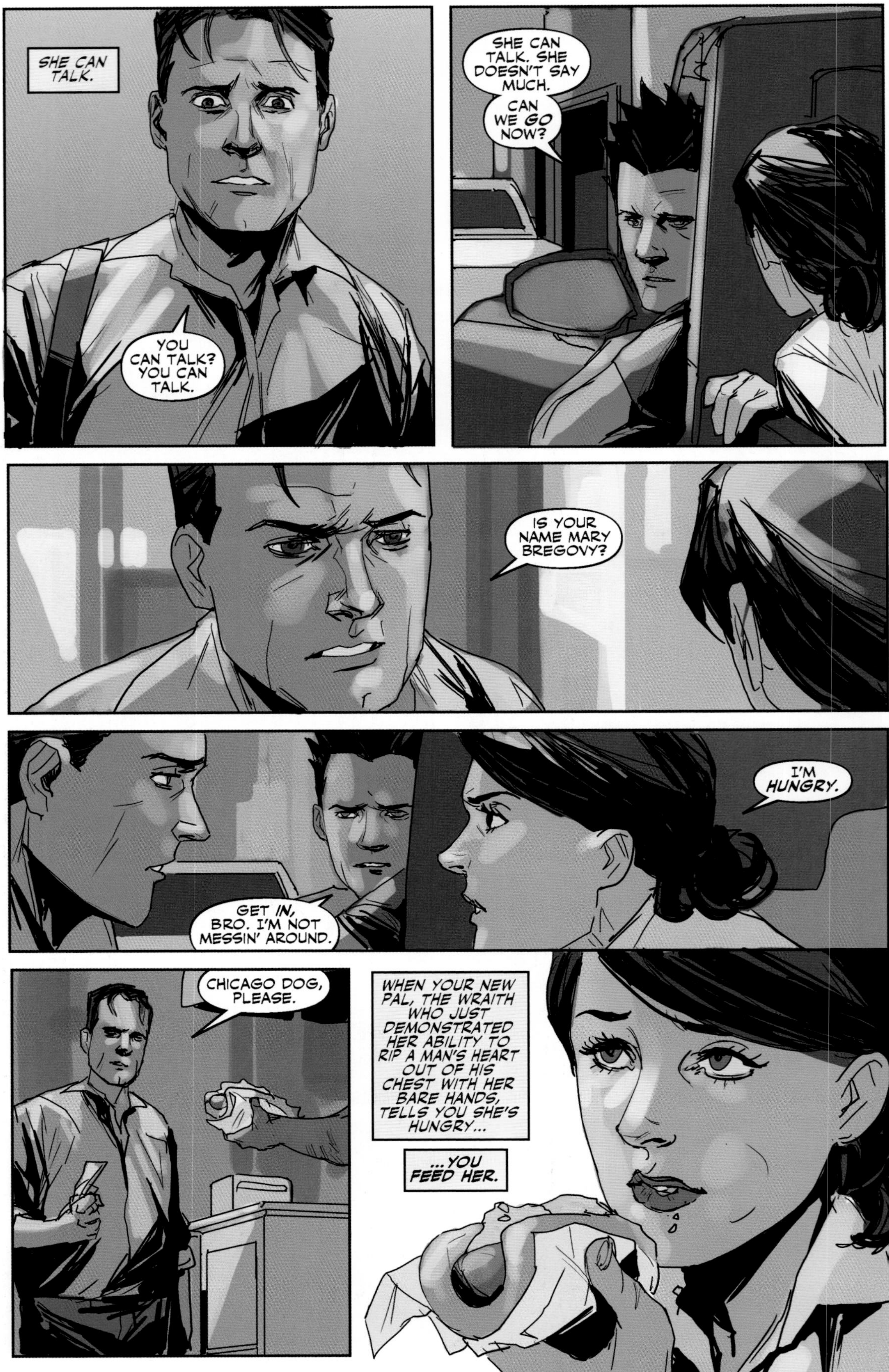
SHE CAN TALK.
YOU CAN TALK? YOU CAN TALK.
SHE CAN TALK. SHE DOESN'T SAY MUCH.
CAN WE GO NOW?
IS YOUR NAME MARY BREGOVY?
I'M HUNGRY.
GET IN, BRO. I'M NOT MESSIN' AROUND.
CHICAGO DOG, PLEASE.
WHEN YOUR NEW PAL, THE WRAITH WHO JUST DEMONSTRATED HER ABILITY TO RIP A MAN'S HEART OUT OF HIS CHEST WITH HER BARE HANDS, TELLS YOU SHE'S HUNGRY...
...YOU FEED HER.

SHE'S NOT FEELING CHATTY. LET'S JUST GO.

REALLY? I WAS HOPING WE'D HANG OUT DOUBLE-PARKED IN FRONT OF TRIBUNE TOWER WITH THAT *THING* IN THE BACK UNTIL A COP CAME BY AND STARTED ASKING QUESTIONS.

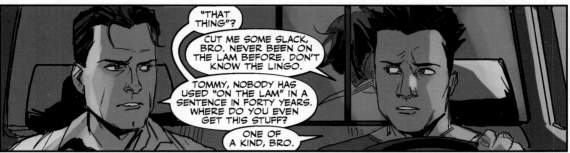

"THAT THING"?

CUT ME SOME SLACK, BRO. NEVER BEEN ON THE LAM BEFORE. DON'T KNOW THE LINGO.

TOMMY, NOBODY HAS USED "ON THE LAM" IN A SENTENCE IN FORTY YEARS. WHERE DO YOU EVEN GET THIS STUFF?

ONE OF A KIND, BRO.

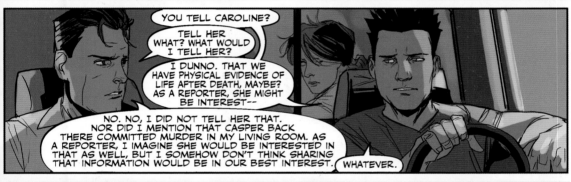

YOU TELL CAROLINE?

TELL HER WHAT? WHAT WOULD I TELL HER?

I DUNNO. THAT WE HAVE PHYSICAL EVIDENCE OF LIFE AFTER DEATH, MAYBE? AS A REPORTER, SHE MIGHT BE INTEREST--

NO. NO, I DID NOT TELL HER THAT. NOR DID I MENTION THAT CASPER BACK THERE COMMITTED MURDER IN MY LIVING ROOM. AS A REPORTER, I IMAGINE SHE WOULD BE INTERESTED IN THAT AS WELL, BUT I SOMEHOW DON'T THINK SHARING THAT INFORMATION WOULD BE IN OUR BEST INTEREST.

WHATEVER.

...

SHE LOOK GOOD? CAROLINE?

WHAT? I WAS JUST ASKING.

"WHAT ARE YOU DOING HERE? YOU CAN'T JUST SHOW UP, VAUGHN. I COULD HAVE YOU ARRESTED."

"I NEED A FAVOR."

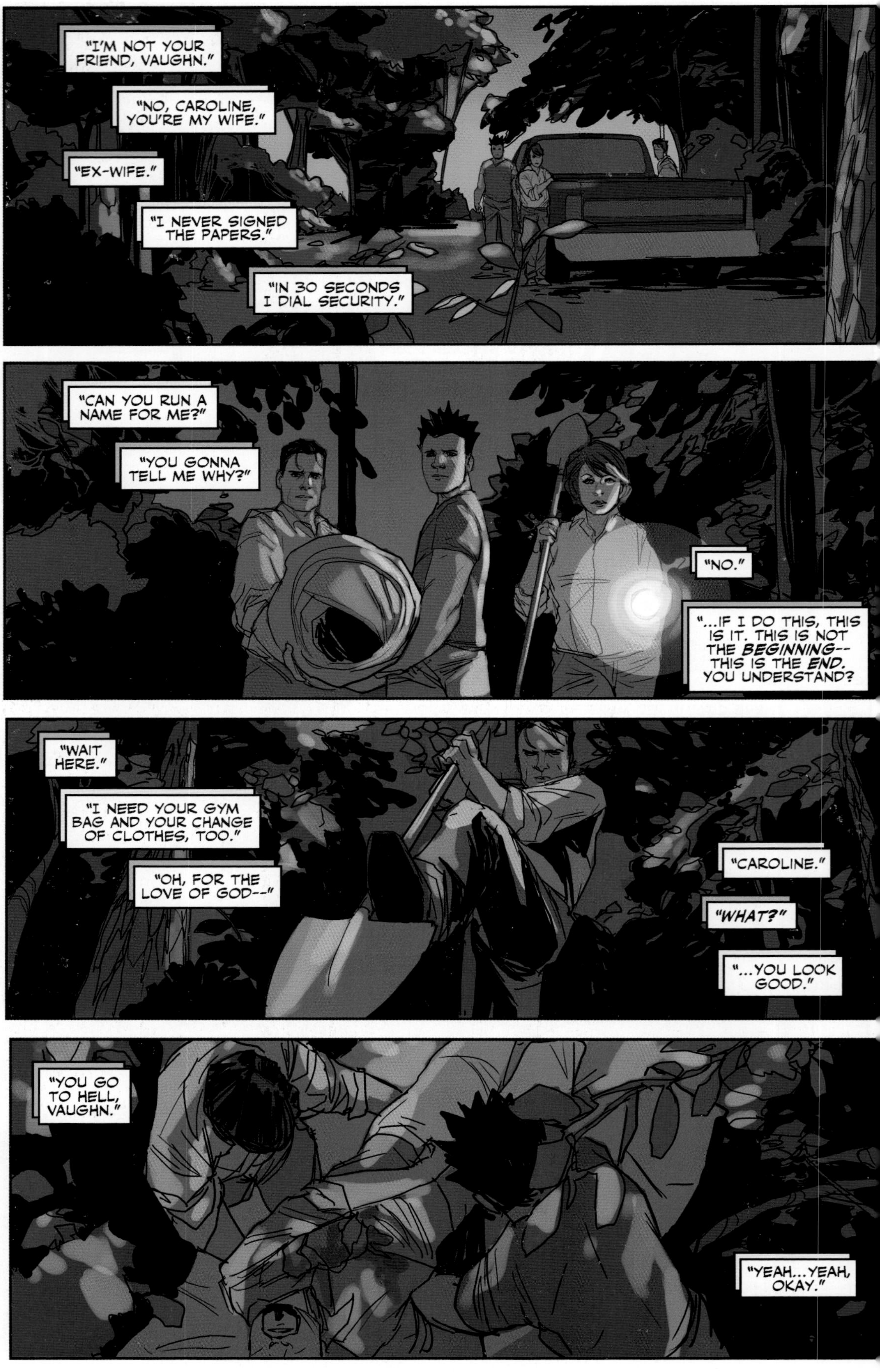
"I'M NOT YOUR FRIEND, VAUGHN."
"NO, CAROLINE, YOU'RE MY WIFE."
"EX-WIFE."
"I NEVER SIGNED THE PAPERS."
"IN 30 SECONDS I DIAL SECURITY."
"CAN YOU RUN A NAME FOR ME?"
"YOU GONNA TELL ME WHY?"
"NO."
"...IF I DO THIS, THIS IS IT. THIS IS NOT THE *BEGINNING*-- THIS IS THE *END.* YOU UNDERSTAND?
"WAIT HERE."
"I NEED YOUR GYM BAG AND YOUR CHANGE OF CLOTHES, TOO."
"OH, FOR THE LOVE OF GOD--"
"CAROLINE."
"WHAT?"
"...YOU LOOK GOOD."
"YOU GO TO HELL, VAUGHN."
"YEAH...YEAH, OKAY."

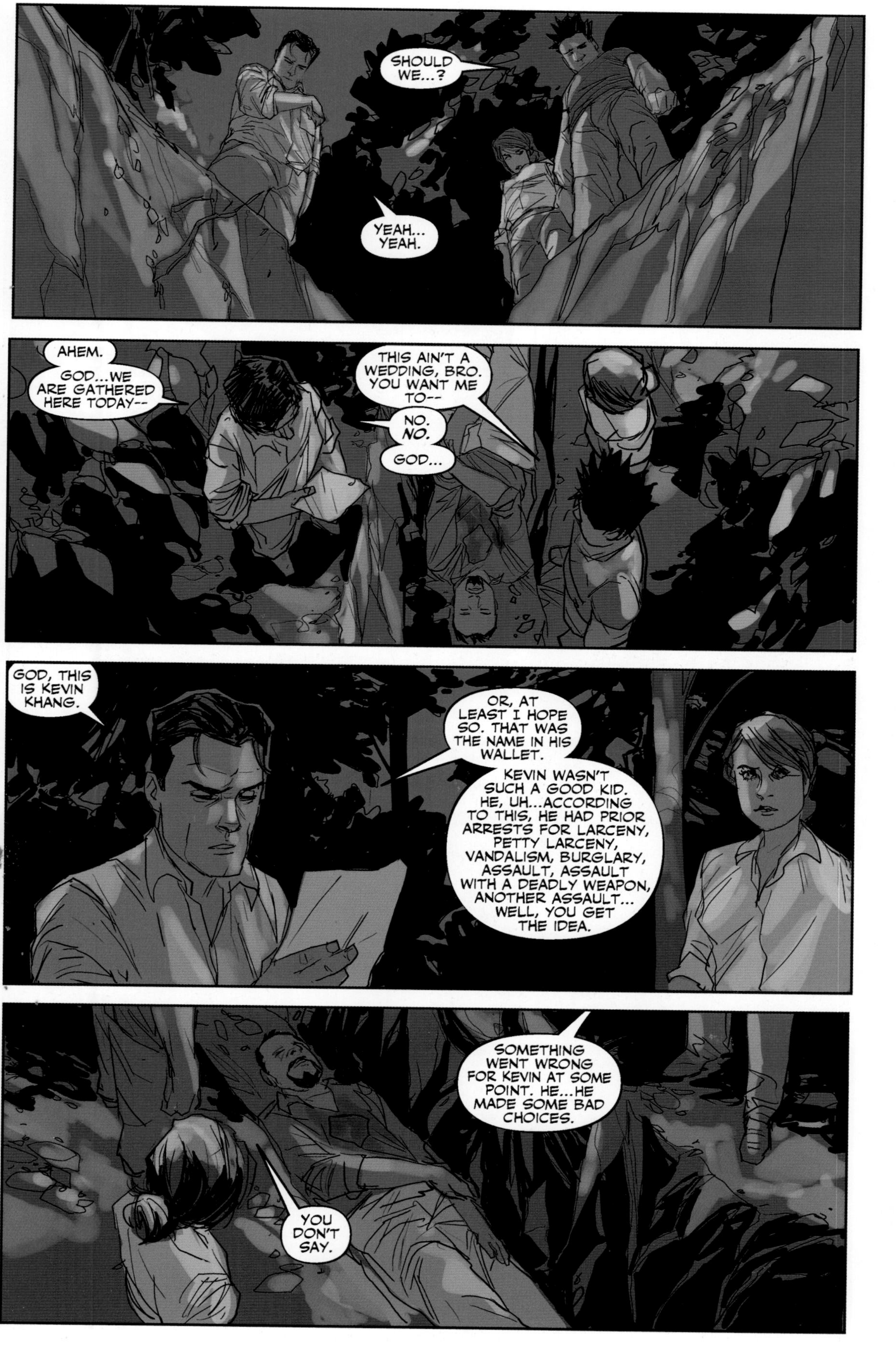
SHOULD WE...?
YEAH... YEAH.
AHEM.
GOD...WE ARE GATHERED HERE TODAY--
THIS AIN'T A WEDDING, BRO. YOU WANT ME TO--
NO. *NO.*
GOD...
GOD, THIS IS KEVIN KHANG.
OR, AT LEAST I HOPE SO. THAT WAS THE NAME IN HIS WALLET.
KEVIN WASN'T SUCH A GOOD KID. HE, UH...ACCORDING TO THIS, HE HAD PRIOR ARRESTS FOR LARCENY, PETTY LARCENY, VANDALISM, BURGLARY, ASSAULT, ASSAULT WITH A DEADLY WEAPON, ANOTHER ASSAULT... WELL, YOU GET THE IDEA.
SOMETHING WENT WRONG FOR KEVIN AT SOME POINT. HE...HE MADE SOME BAD CHOICES.
YOU DON'T SAY.

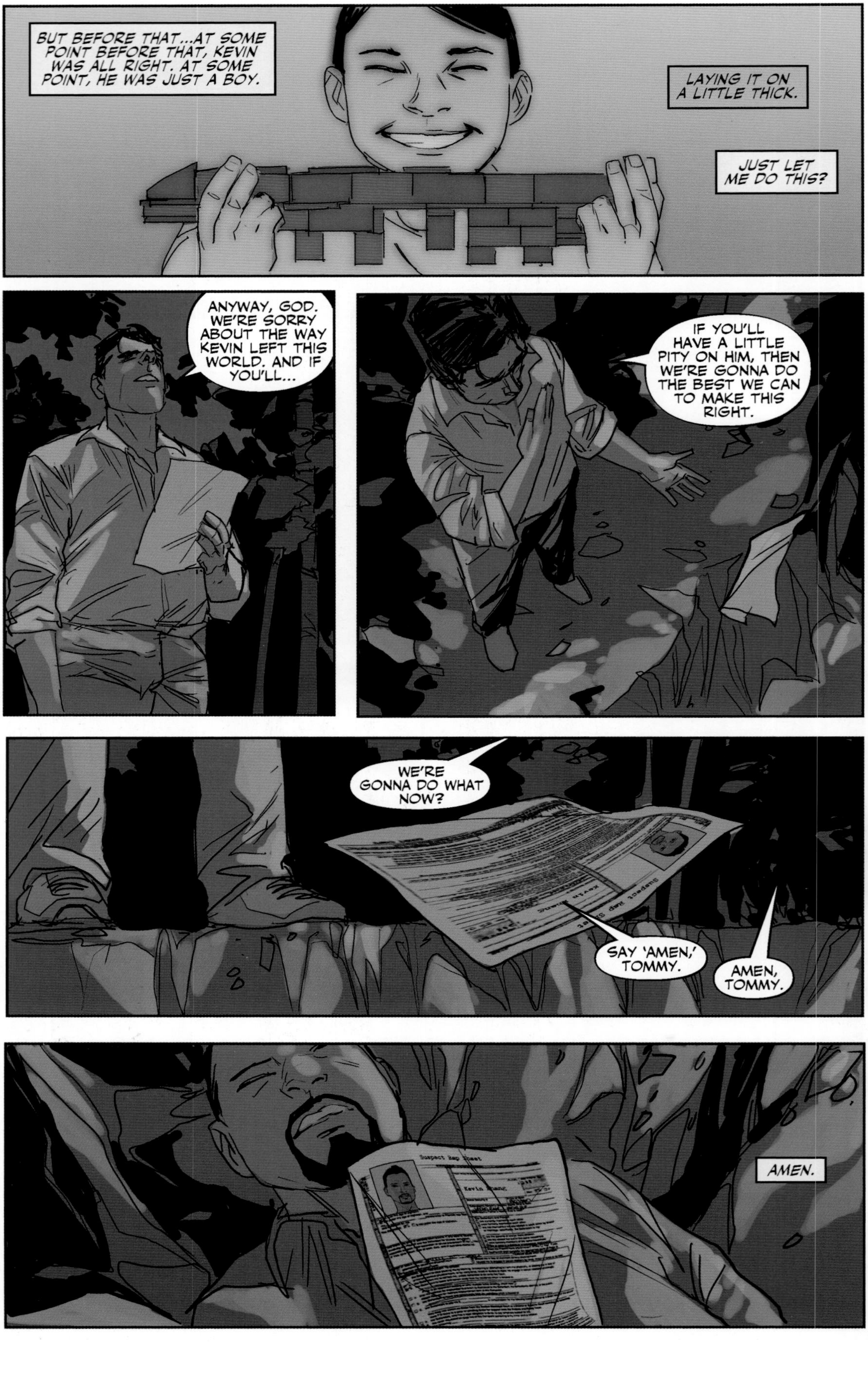
BUT BEFORE THAT...AT SOME POINT BEFORE THAT, KEVIN WAS ALL RIGHT. AT SOME POINT, HE WAS JUST A BOY.
LAYING IT ON A LITTLE THICK.
JUST LET ME DO THIS?
ANYWAY, GOD. WE'RE SORRY ABOUT THE WAY KEVIN LEFT THIS WORLD. AND IF YOU'LL...
IF YOU'LL HAVE A LITTLE PITY ON HIM, THEN WE'RE GONNA DO THE BEST WE CAN TO MAKE THIS RIGHT.
WE'RE GONNA DO WHAT NOW?
SAY 'AMEN,' TOMMY.
AMEN, TOMMY.
Suspect Rap Sheet
AMEN.

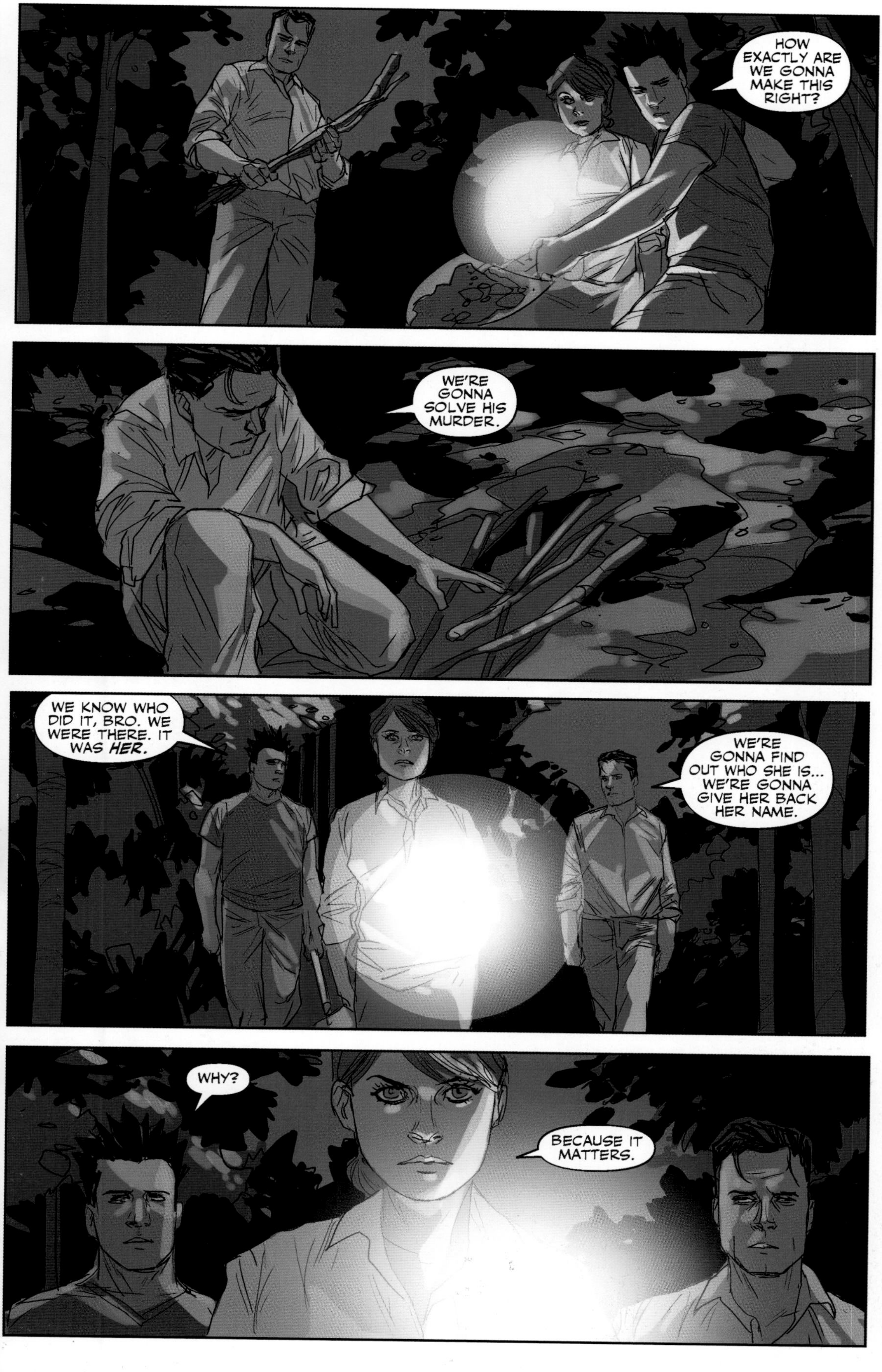
HOW EXACTLY ARE WE GONNA MAKE THIS RIGHT?
WE'RE GONNA SOLVE HIS MURDER.
WE KNOW WHO DID IT, BRO. WE WERE THERE. IT WAS *HER*.
WE'RE GONNA FIND OUT WHO SHE IS... WE'RE GONNA GIVE HER BACK HER NAME.
WHY?
BECAUSE IT MATTERS.

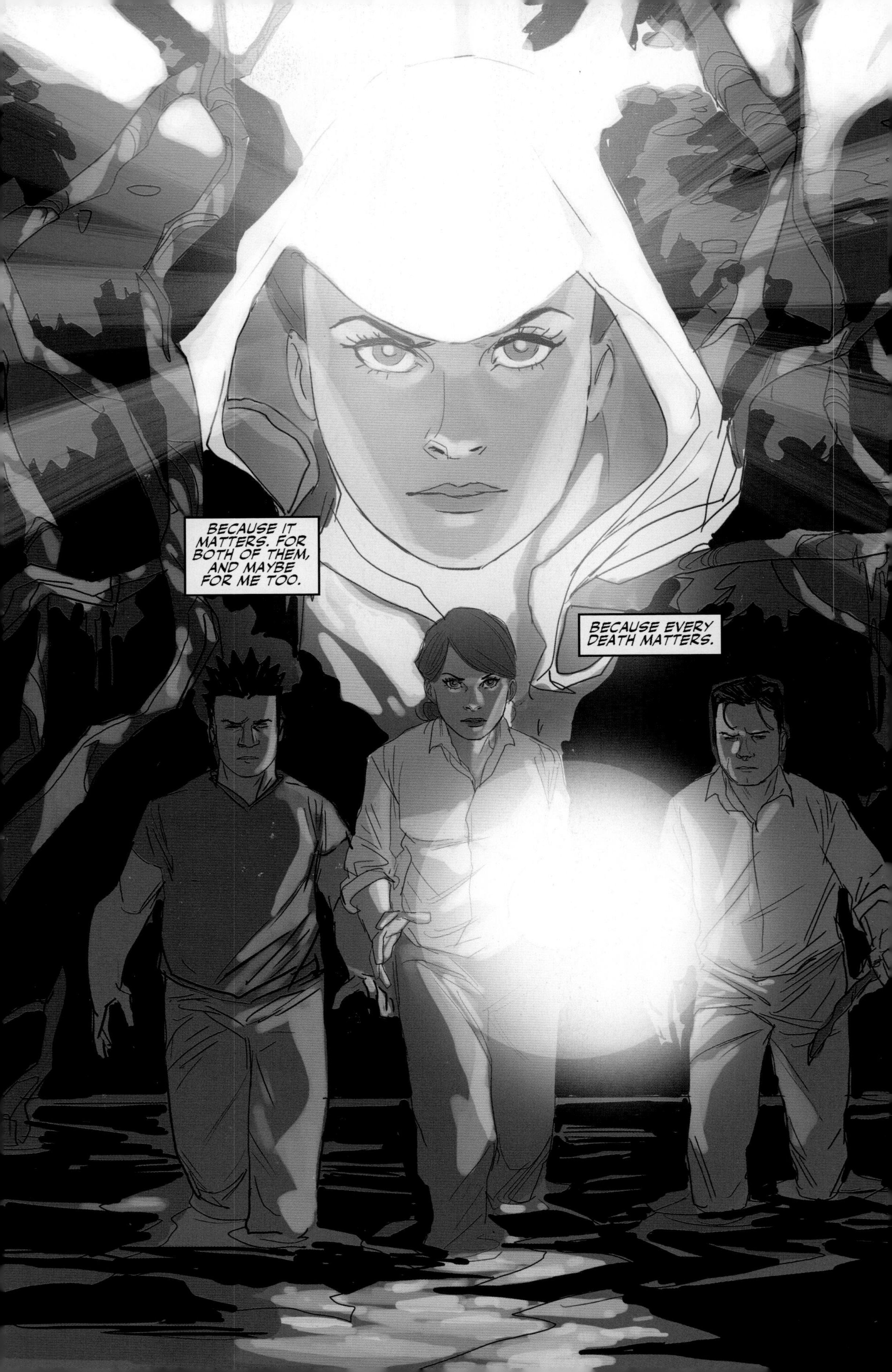
BECAUSE IT MATTERS. FOR BOTH OF THEM, AND MAYBE FOR ME TOO.
BECAUSE EVERY DEATH MATTERS.

CHAPTER 1

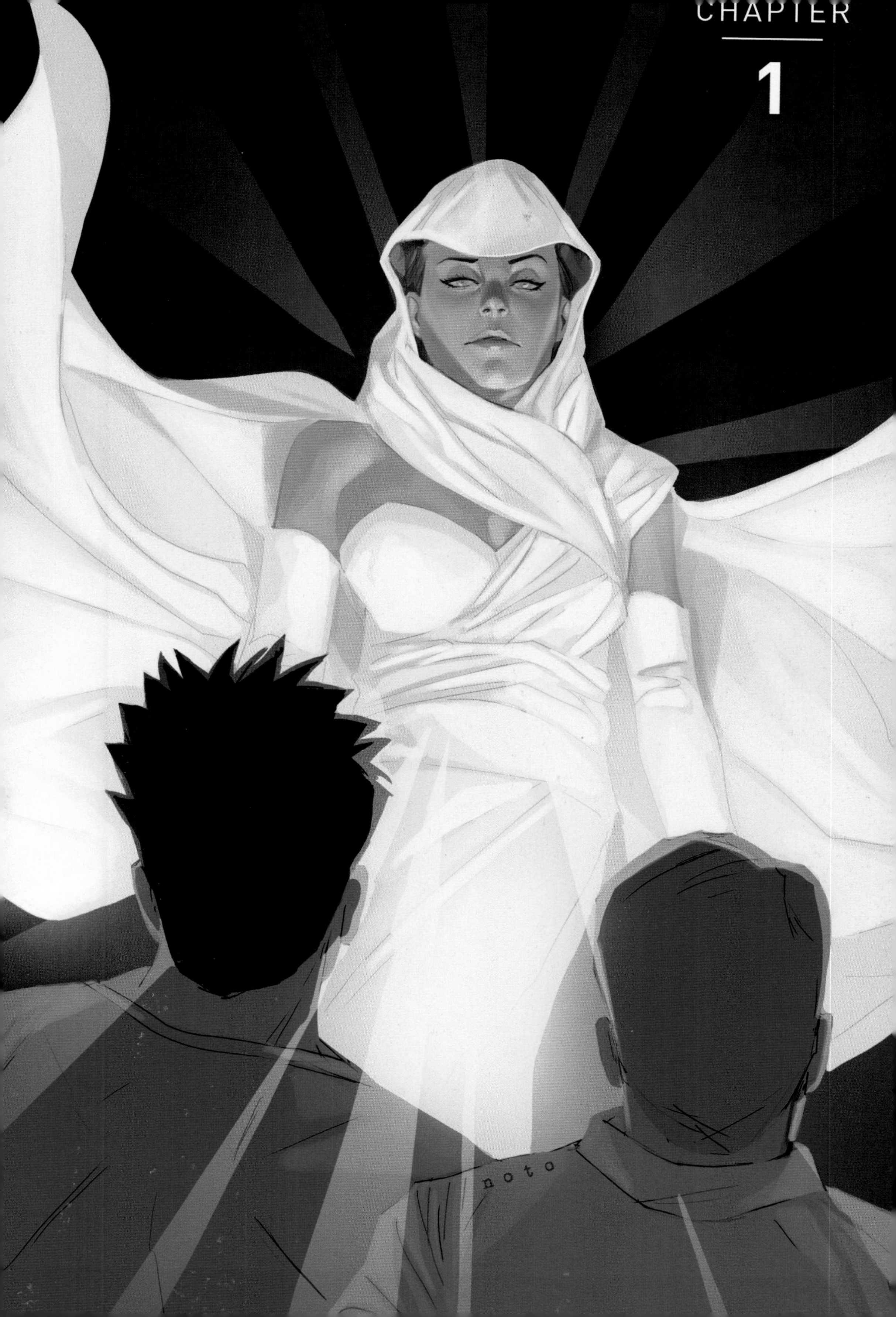
noto

"ATHENA WAS THE GODDESS OF WISDOM AND WAR.
I ALREADY KNOW HER FURY . . . AND HER PAIN."

THE BIRTH OF ATHENA.
I KNOW THIS STORY.

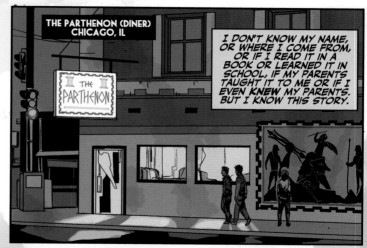

THE PARTHENON (DINER)
CHICAGO, IL

I DON'T KNOW MY NAME,
OR WHERE I COME FROM,
OR IF I READ IT IN A
BOOK OR LEARNED IT IN
SCHOOL, IF MY PARENTS
TAUGHT IT TO ME OR IF I
EVEN KNEW MY PARENTS.
BUT I KNOW THIS STORY.

NOT LONG AFTER
CONSUMING--LITERALLY
CONSUMING--THE
TITANESS METIS, ZEUS'S
HEAD BEGAN TO ACHE.

THE PAIN WAS
SO INTENSE HE
ASKED HIS SON
THE BLACKSMITH
TO CLEAVE A
METAL AXE INTO
HIS SKULL.

OUT OF THAT WOUND
SPRANG--IT'S ALWAYS
"SPRANG"--ATHENA, THE
GODDESS OF WISDOM AND
WAR, FULLY GROWN AND
ARMORED FOR BATTLE.

MUCH IS WRITTEN ABOUT
ZEUS'S AGONY, THE GOD
OF GODS, HUMBLED IN
THE THROES OF BIRTH.

WHAT DO THEY
SAY ABOUT
ATHENA'S PAIN?

NOT.

ONE.

WORD.

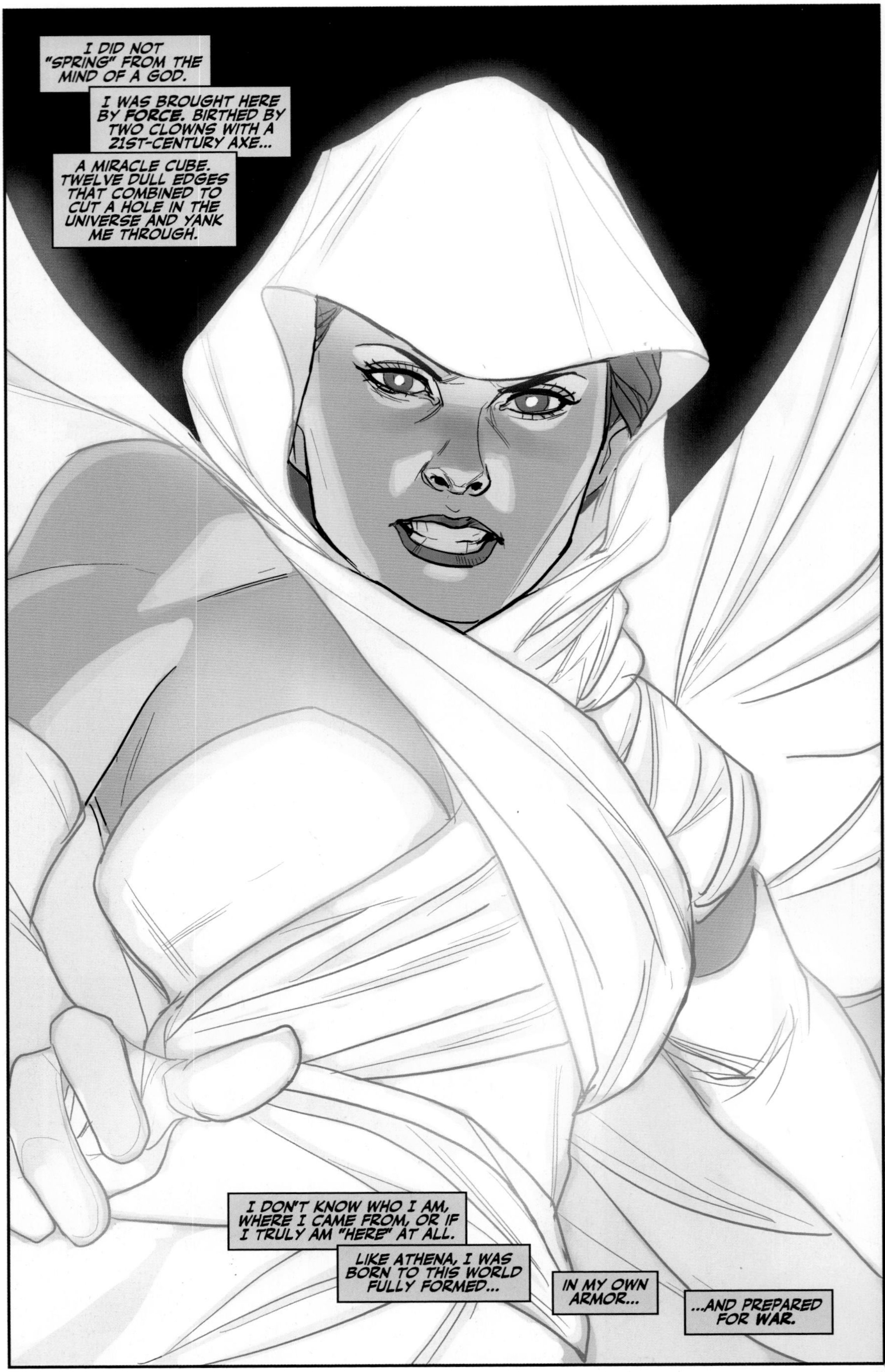
I DID NOT "SPRING" FROM THE MIND OF A GOD.
I WAS BROUGHT HERE BY FORCE. BIRTHED BY TWO CLOWNS WITH A 21ST-CENTURY AXE...
A MIRACLE CUBE. TWELVE DULL EDGES THAT COMBINED TO CUT A HOLE IN THE UNIVERSE AND YANK ME THROUGH.
I DON'T KNOW WHO I AM, WHERE I CAME FROM, OR IF I TRULY AM "HERE" AT ALL.
LIKE ATHENA, I WAS BORN TO THIS WORLD FULLY FORMED...
IN MY OWN ARMOR...
...AND PREPARED FOR WAR.

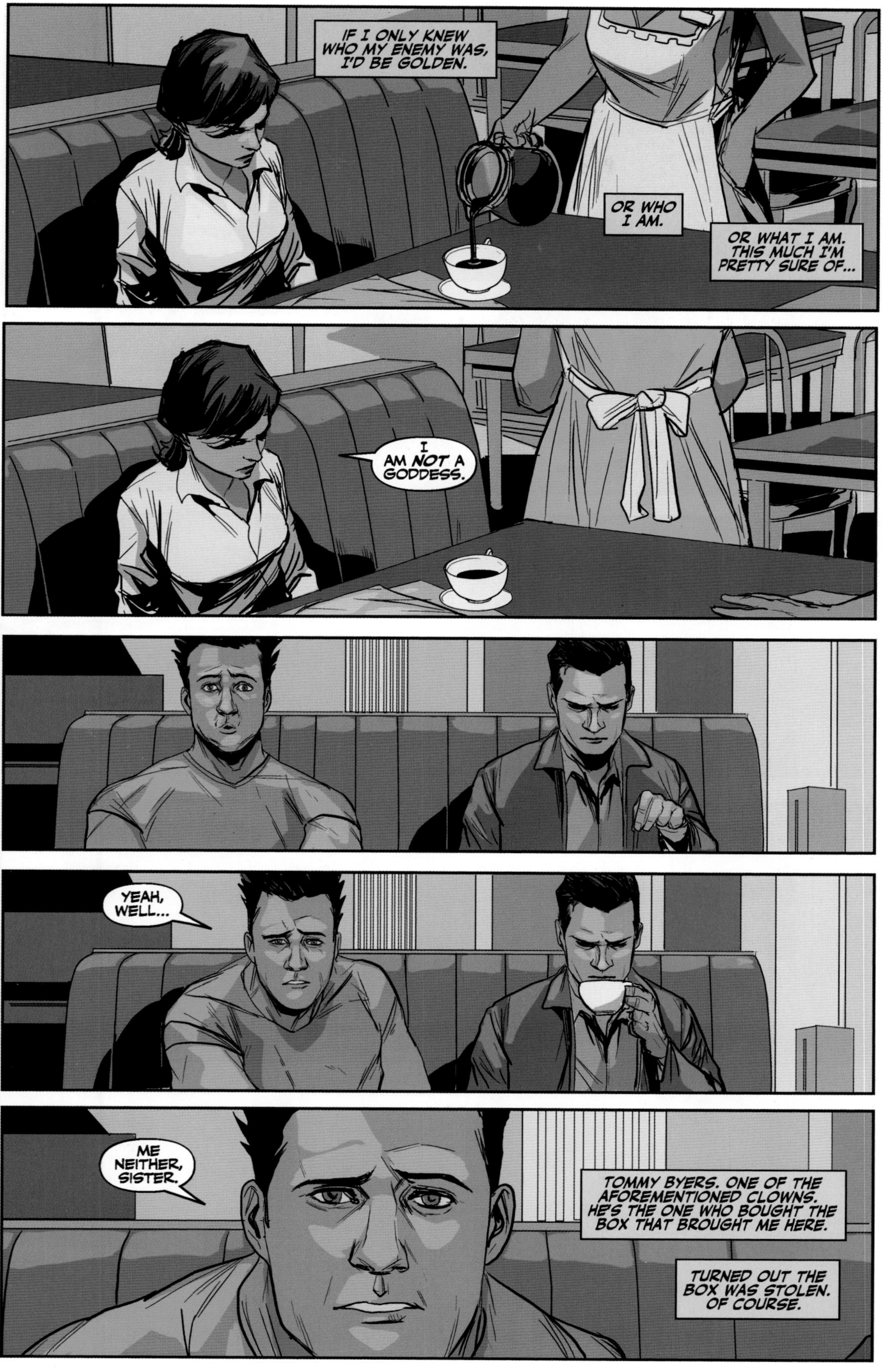
IF I ONLY KNEW WHO MY ENEMY WAS, I'D BE GOLDEN.
OR WHO I AM.
OR WHAT I AM. THIS MUCH I'M PRETTY SURE OF...
I AM NOT A GODDESS.
YEAH, WELL...
ME NEITHER, SISTER.
TOMMY BYERS. ONE OF THE AFOREMENTIONED CLOWNS. HE'S THE ONE WHO BOUGHT THE BOX THAT BROUGHT ME HERE.
TURNED OUT THE BOX WAS STOLEN. OF COURSE.

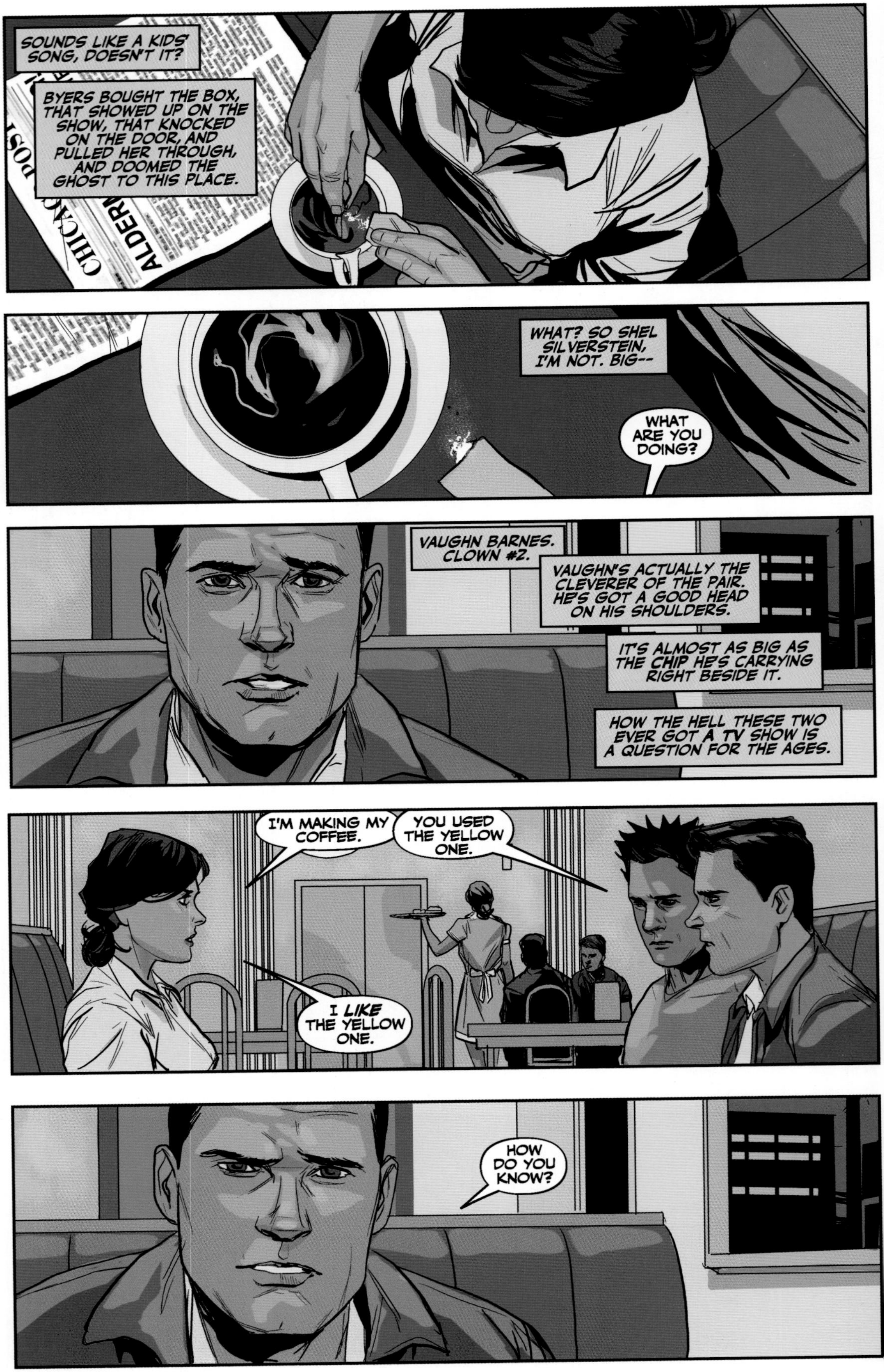
SOUNDS LIKE A KIDS' SONG, DOESN'T IT?
BYERS BOUGHT THE BOX, THAT SHOWED UP ON THE SHOW, THAT KNOCKED ON THE DOOR, AND PULLED HER THROUGH, AND DOOMED THE GHOST TO THIS PLACE.
WHAT? SO SHEL SILVERSTEIN, I'M NOT. BIG--
WHAT ARE YOU DOING?
VAUGHN BARNES. CLOWN #2.
VAUGHN'S ACTUALLY THE CLEVERER OF THE PAIR. HE'S GOT A GOOD HEAD ON HIS SHOULDERS.
IT'S ALMOST AS BIG AS THE CHIP HE'S CARRYING RIGHT BESIDE IT.
HOW THE HELL THESE TWO EVER GOT A TV SHOW IS A QUESTION FOR THE AGES.
I'M MAKING MY COFFEE.
YOU USED THE YELLOW ONE.
I LIKE THE YELLOW ONE.
HOW DO YOU KNOW?

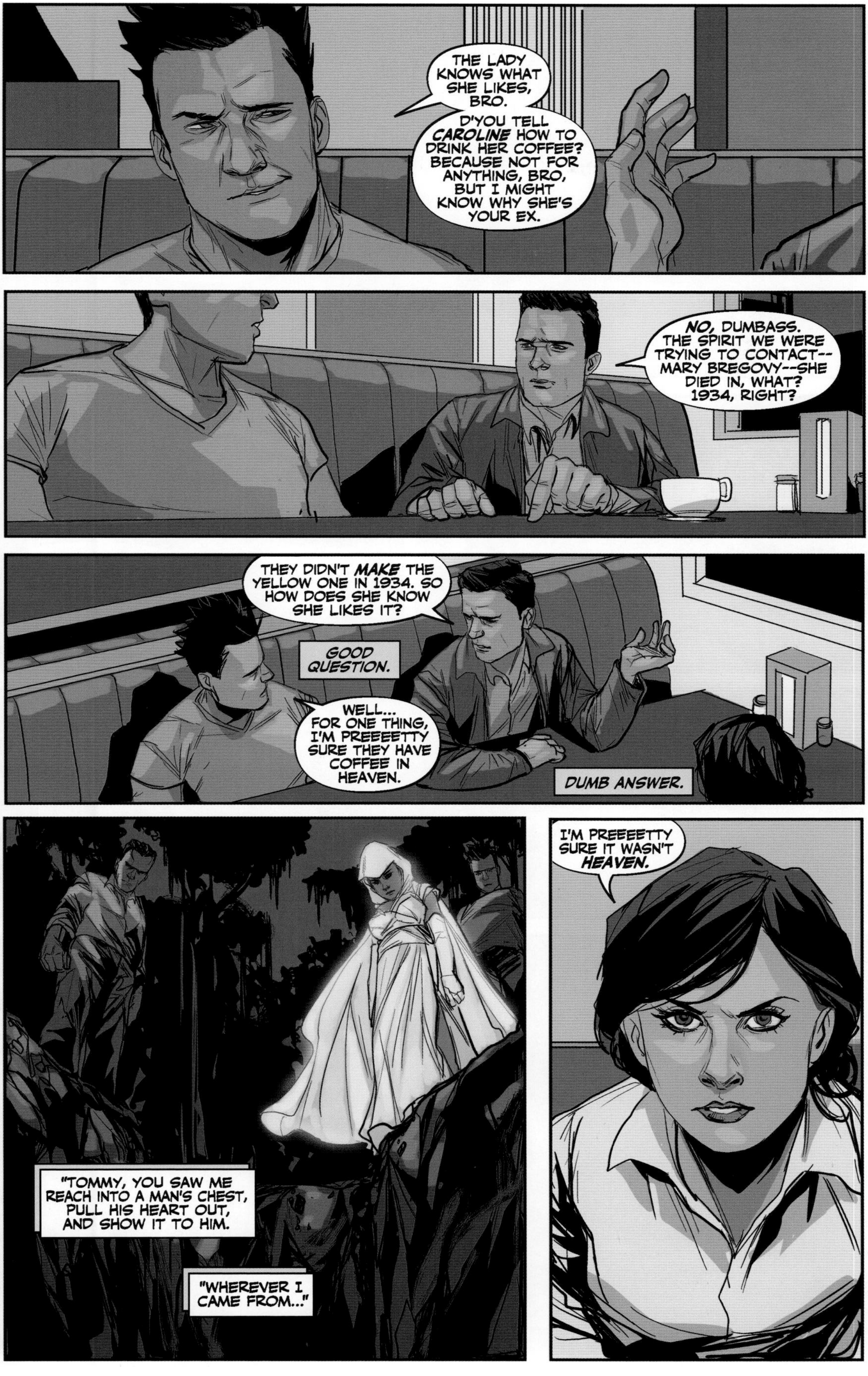
THE LADY KNOWS WHAT SHE LIKES, BRO.
D'YOU TELL CAROLINE HOW TO DRINK HER COFFEE? BECAUSE NOT FOR ANYTHING, BRO, BUT I MIGHT KNOW WHY SHE'S YOUR EX.
NO, DUMBASS. THE SPIRIT WE WERE TRYING TO CONTACT--MARY BREGOVY--SHE DIED IN, WHAT? 1934, RIGHT?
THEY DIDN'T MAKE THE YELLOW ONE IN 1934. SO HOW DOES SHE KNOW SHE LIKES IT?
GOOD QUESTION.
WELL... FOR ONE THING, I'M PREEEETTY SURE THEY HAVE COFFEE IN HEAVEN.
DUMB ANSWER.
"TOMMY, YOU SAW ME REACH INTO A MAN'S CHEST, PULL HIS HEART OUT, AND SHOW IT TO HIM.
"WHEREVER I CAME FROM..."
I'M PREEEETTY SURE IT WASN'T HEAVEN.

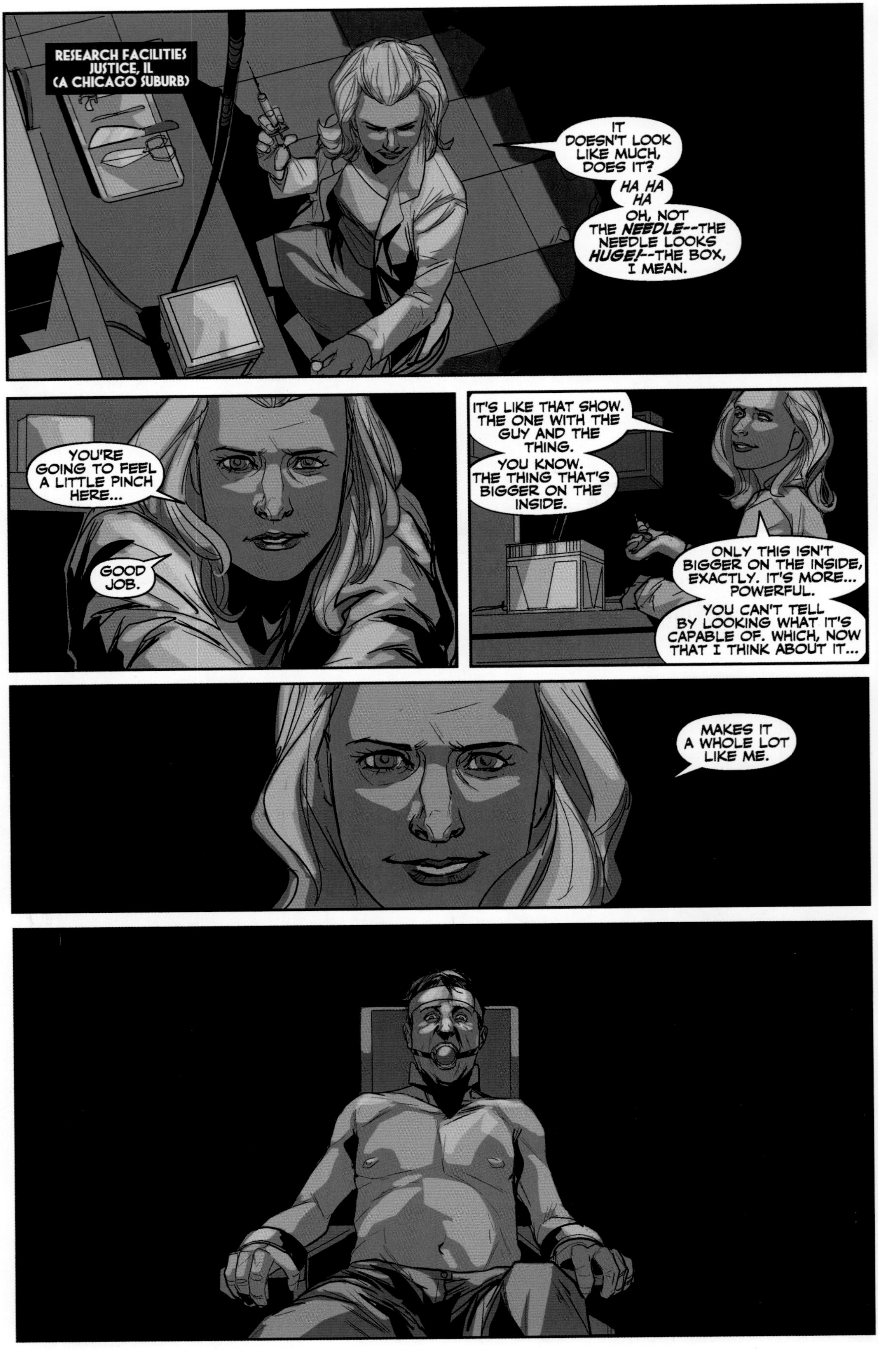
RESEARCH FACILITIES
JUSTICE, IL
(A CHICAGO SUBURB)
IT DOESN'T LOOK LIKE MUCH, DOES IT?
HA HA HA
OH, NOT THE NEEDLE--THE NEEDLE LOOKS HUGE!--THE BOX, I MEAN.
YOU'RE GOING TO FEEL A LITTLE PINCH HERE...
GOOD JOB.
IT'S LIKE THAT SHOW. THE ONE WITH THE GUY AND THE THING.
YOU KNOW. THE THING THAT'S BIGGER ON THE INSIDE.
ONLY THIS ISN'T BIGGER ON THE INSIDE, EXACTLY. IT'S MORE... POWERFUL.
YOU CAN'T TELL BY LOOKING WHAT IT'S CAPABLE OF. WHICH, NOW THAT I THINK ABOUT IT...
MAKES IT A WHOLE LOT LIKE ME.

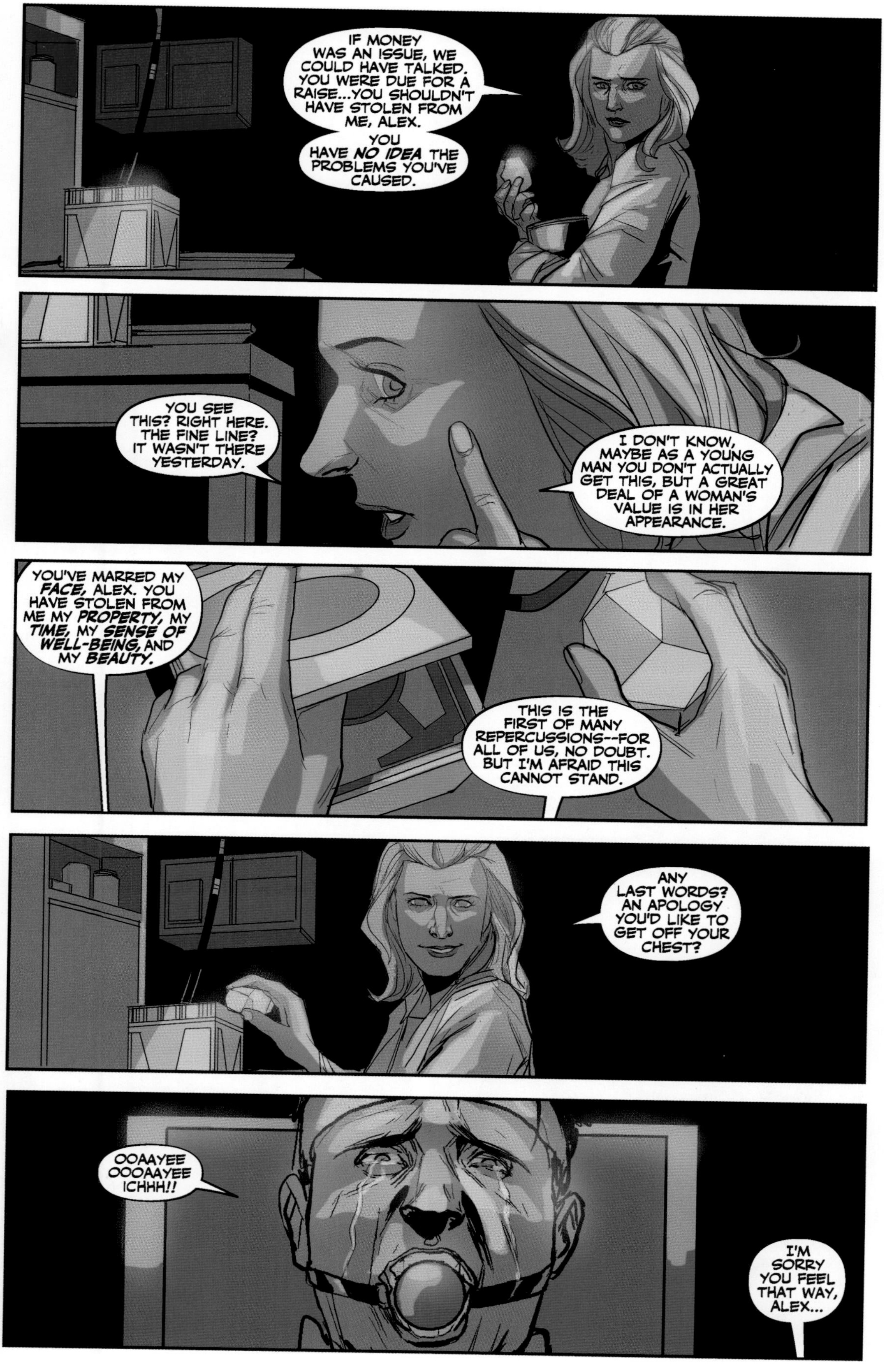
IF MONEY WAS AN ISSUE, WE COULD HAVE TALKED. YOU WERE DUE FOR A RAISE...YOU SHOULDN'T HAVE STOLEN FROM ME, ALEX.
YOU HAVE *NO IDEA* THE PROBLEMS YOU'VE CAUSED.
YOU SEE THIS? RIGHT HERE. THE FINE LINE? IT WASN'T THERE YESTERDAY.
I DON'T KNOW, MAYBE AS A YOUNG MAN YOU DON'T ACTUALLY GET THIS, BUT A GREAT DEAL OF A WOMAN'S VALUE IS IN HER APPEARANCE.
YOU'VE MARRED MY *FACE,* ALEX. YOU HAVE STOLEN FROM ME MY *PROPERTY,* MY *TIME,* MY *SENSE OF WELL-BEING,* AND MY *BEAUTY.*
THIS IS THE FIRST OF MANY REPERCUSSIONS--FOR ALL OF US, NO DOUBT. BUT I'M AFRAID THIS CANNOT STAND.
ANY LAST WORDS? AN APOLOGY YOU'D LIKE TO GET OFF YOUR CHEST?
OOAAYEE OOOAAYEE ICHHH!!
I'M SORRY YOU FEEL THAT WAY, ALEX...

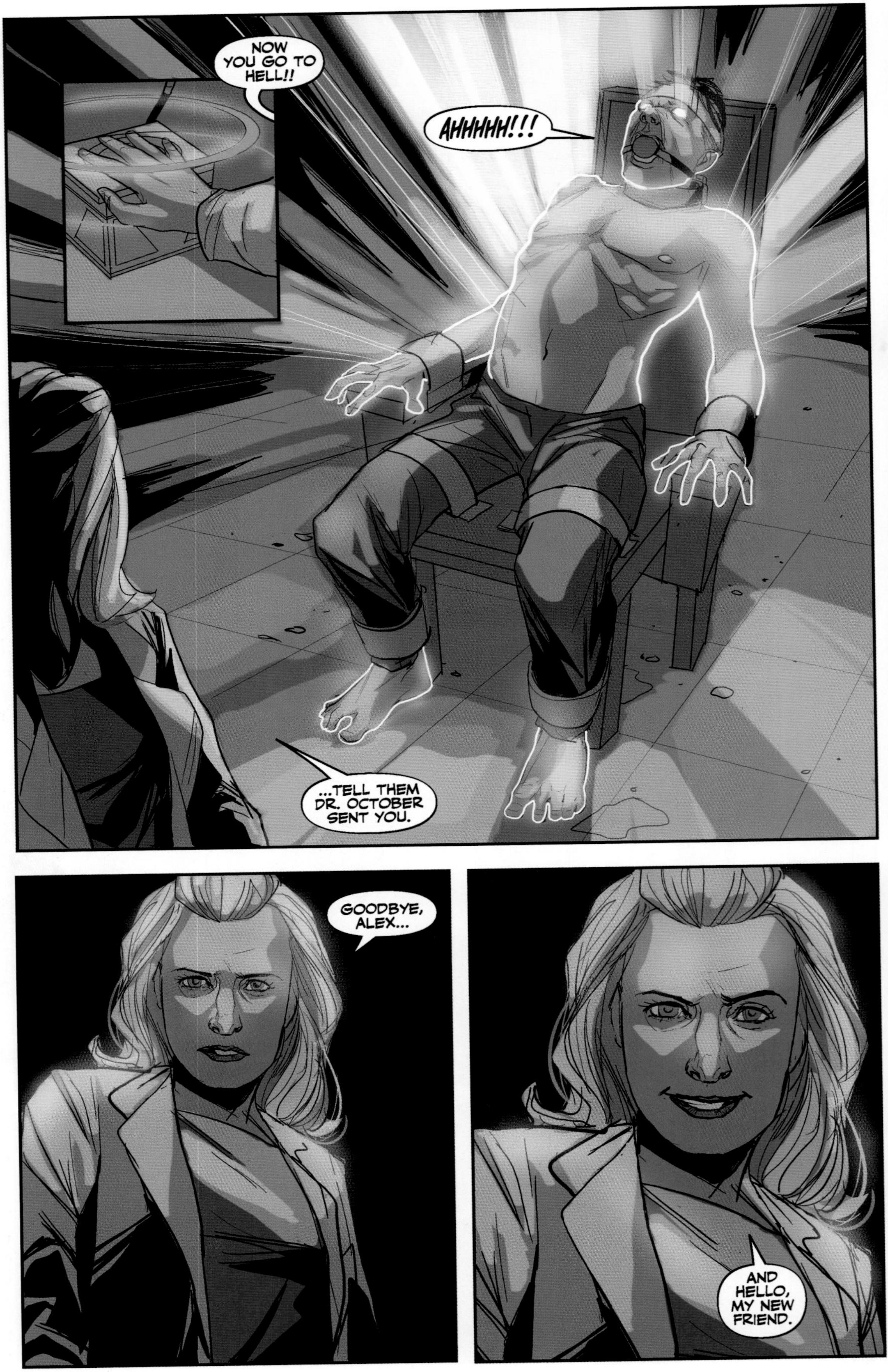
NOW YOU GO TO HELL!!
AHHHHH!!!
...TELL THEM DR. OCTOBER SENT YOU.
GOODBYE, ALEX...
AND HELLO, MY NEW FRIEND.

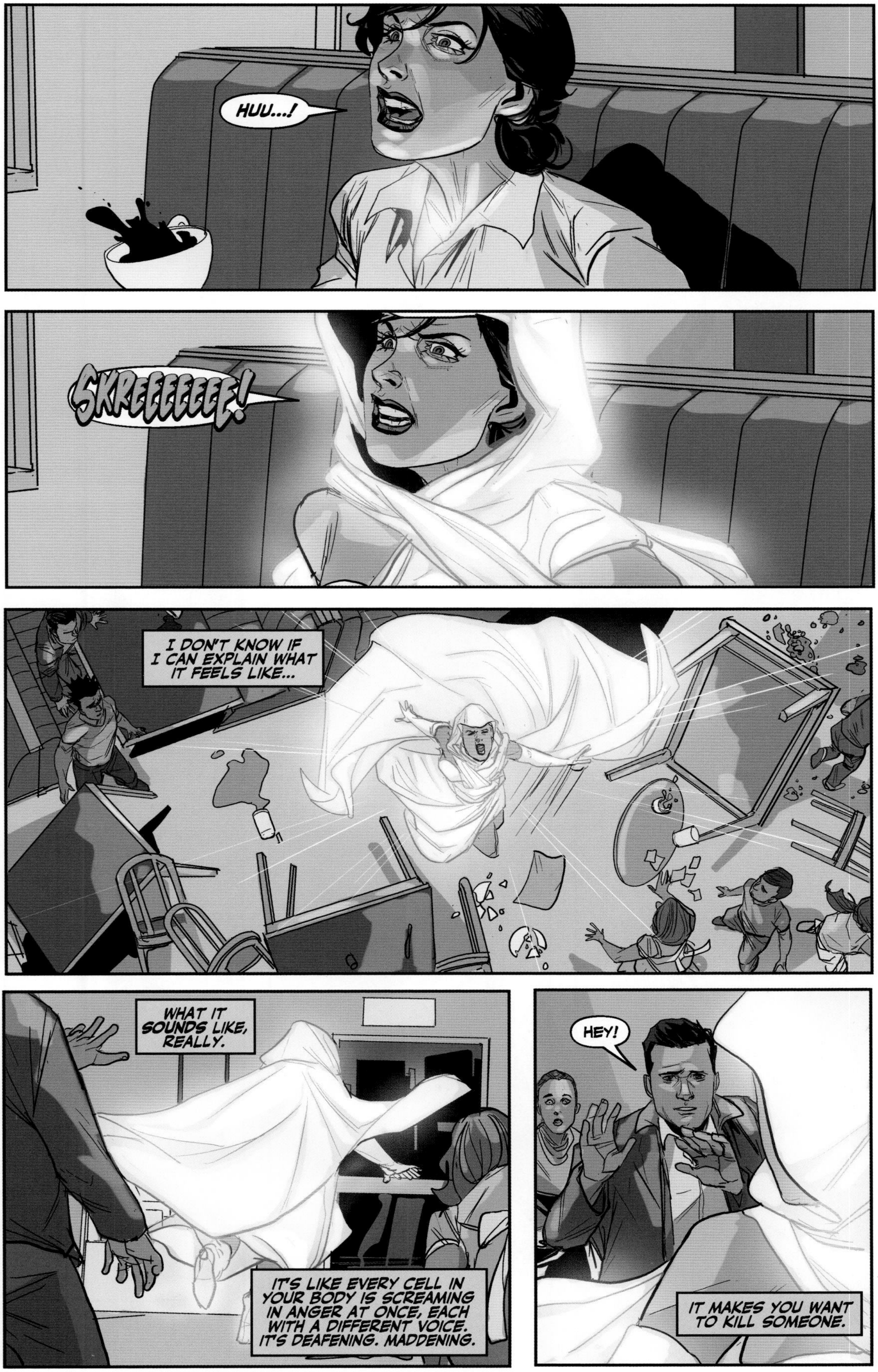
HUU...!
SKREEEEEEEF!
I DON'T KNOW IF I CAN EXPLAIN WHAT IT FEELS LIKE...
WHAT IT SOUNDS LIKE, REALLY.
IT'S LIKE EVERY CELL IN YOUR BODY IS SCREAMING IN ANGER AT ONCE, EACH WITH A DIFFERENT VOICE. IT'S DEAFENING. MADDENING.
HEY!
IT MAKES YOU WANT TO KILL SOMEONE.

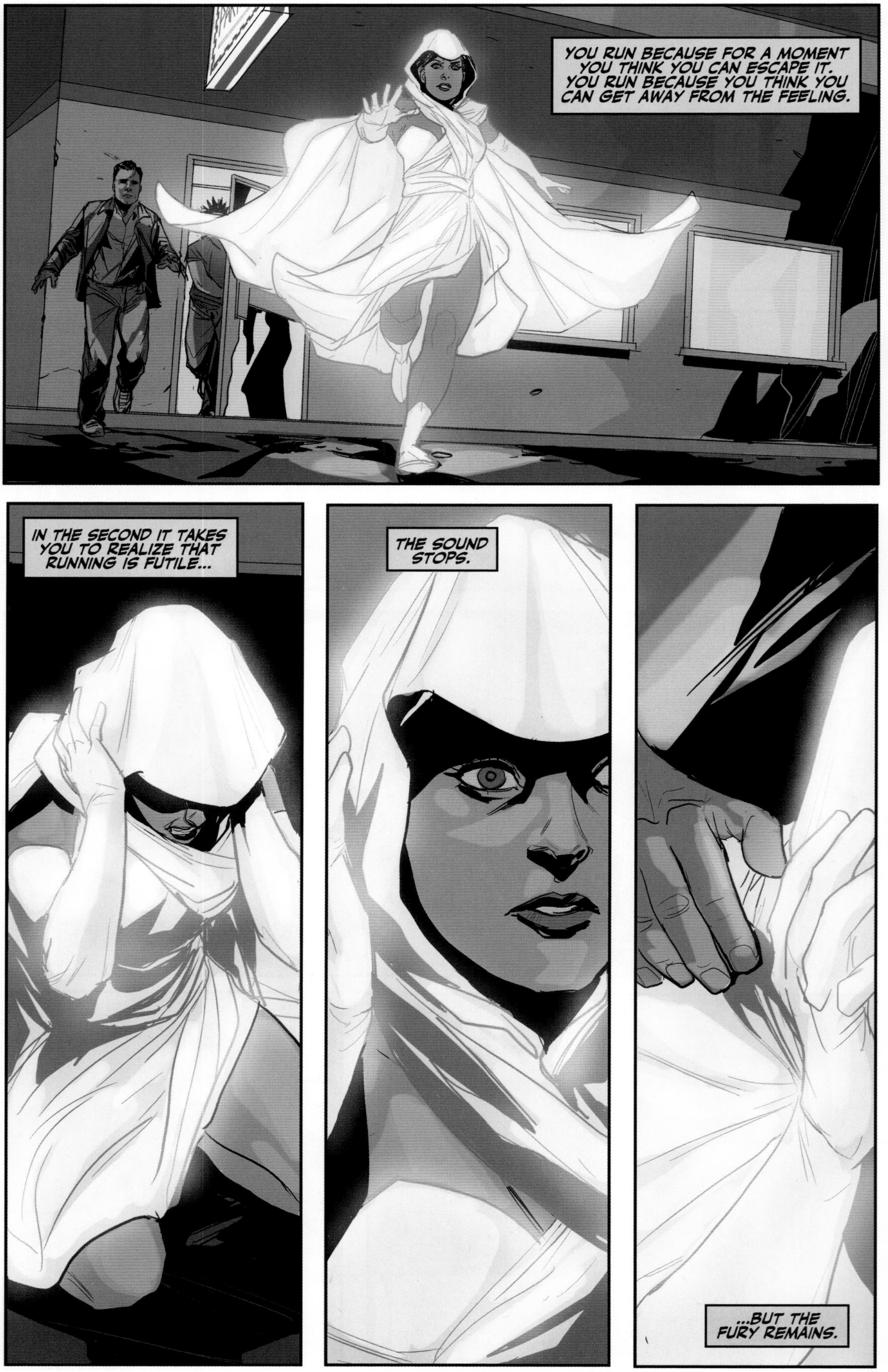
YOU RUN BECAUSE FOR A MOMENT YOU THINK YOU CAN ESCAPE IT. YOU RUN BECAUSE YOU THINK YOU CAN GET AWAY FROM THE FEELING.
IN THE SECOND IT TAKES YOU TO REALIZE THAT RUNNING IS FUTILE...
THE SOUND STOPS.
...BUT THE FURY REMAINS.

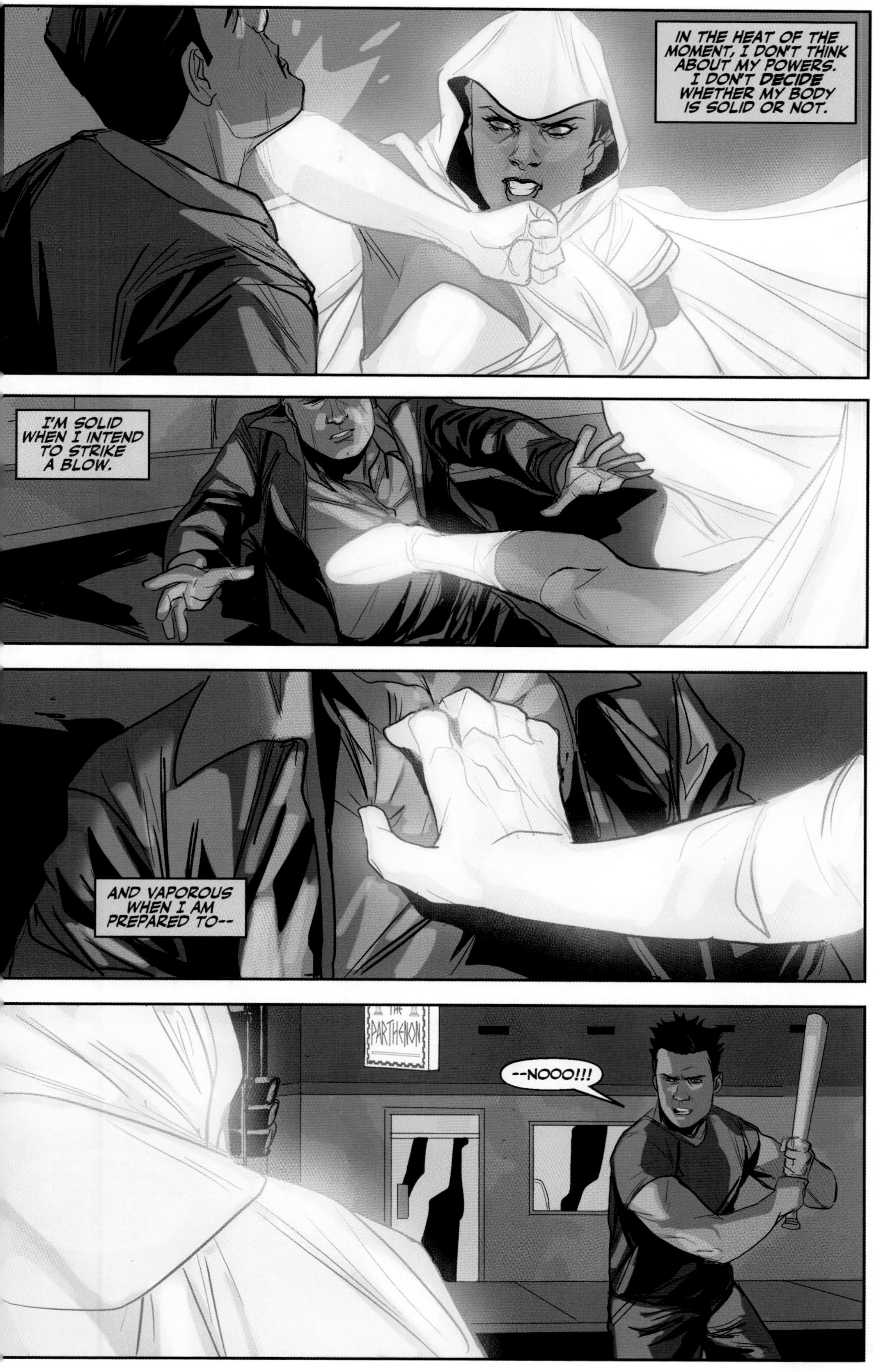
IN THE HEAT OF THE MOMENT, I DON'T THINK ABOUT MY POWERS. I DON'T DECIDE WHETHER MY BODY IS SOLID OR NOT.
I'M SOLID WHEN I INTEND TO STRIKE A BLOW.
AND VAPOROUS WHEN I AM PREPARED TO--
THE PARTHENON
--NOOO!!!

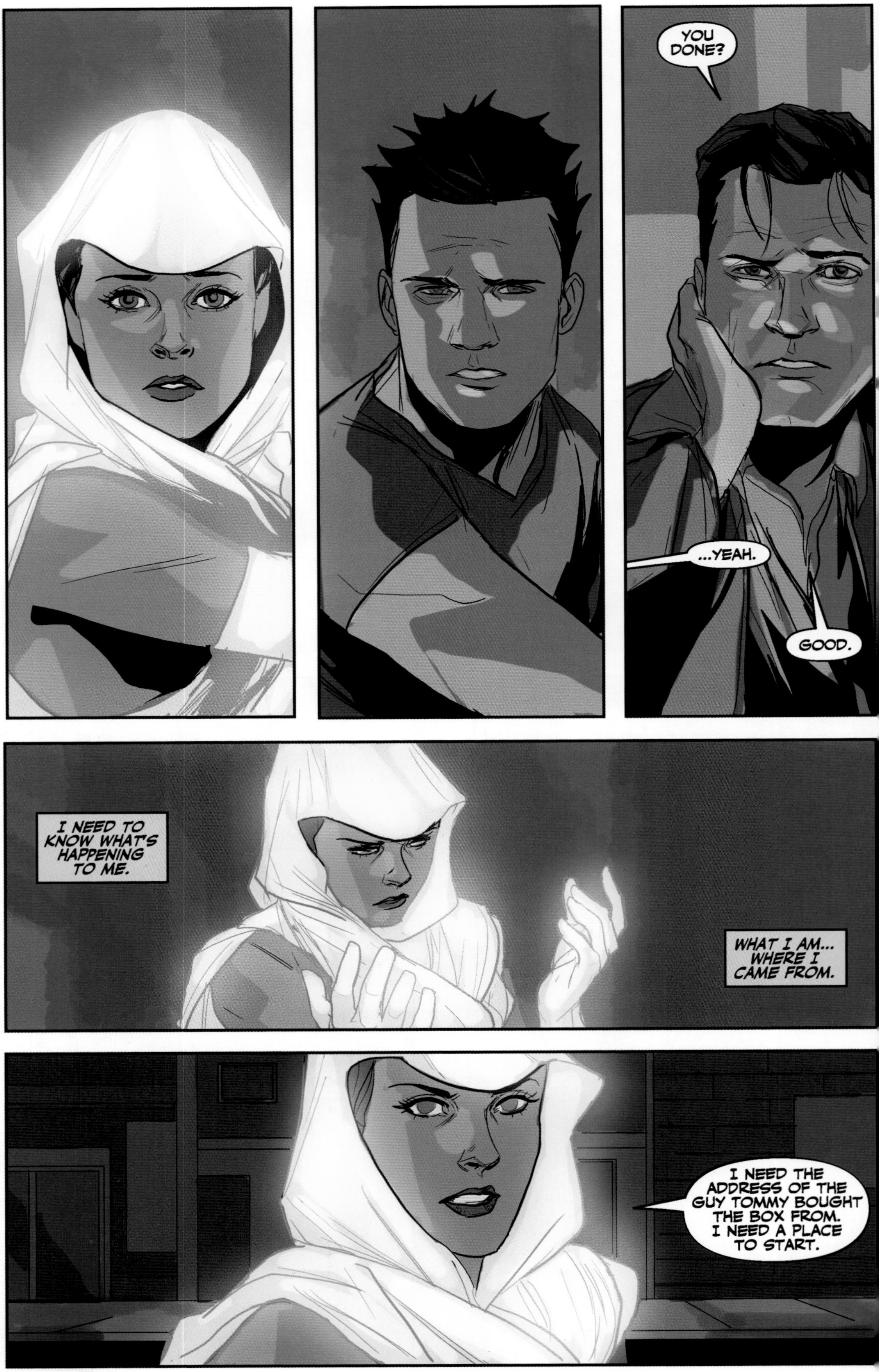
YOU DONE?
...YEAH.
GOOD.
I NEED TO KNOW WHAT'S HAPPENING TO ME.
WHAT I AM... WHERE I CAME FROM.
I NEED THE ADDRESS OF THE GUY TOMMY BOUGHT THE BOX FROM. I NEED A PLACE TO START.

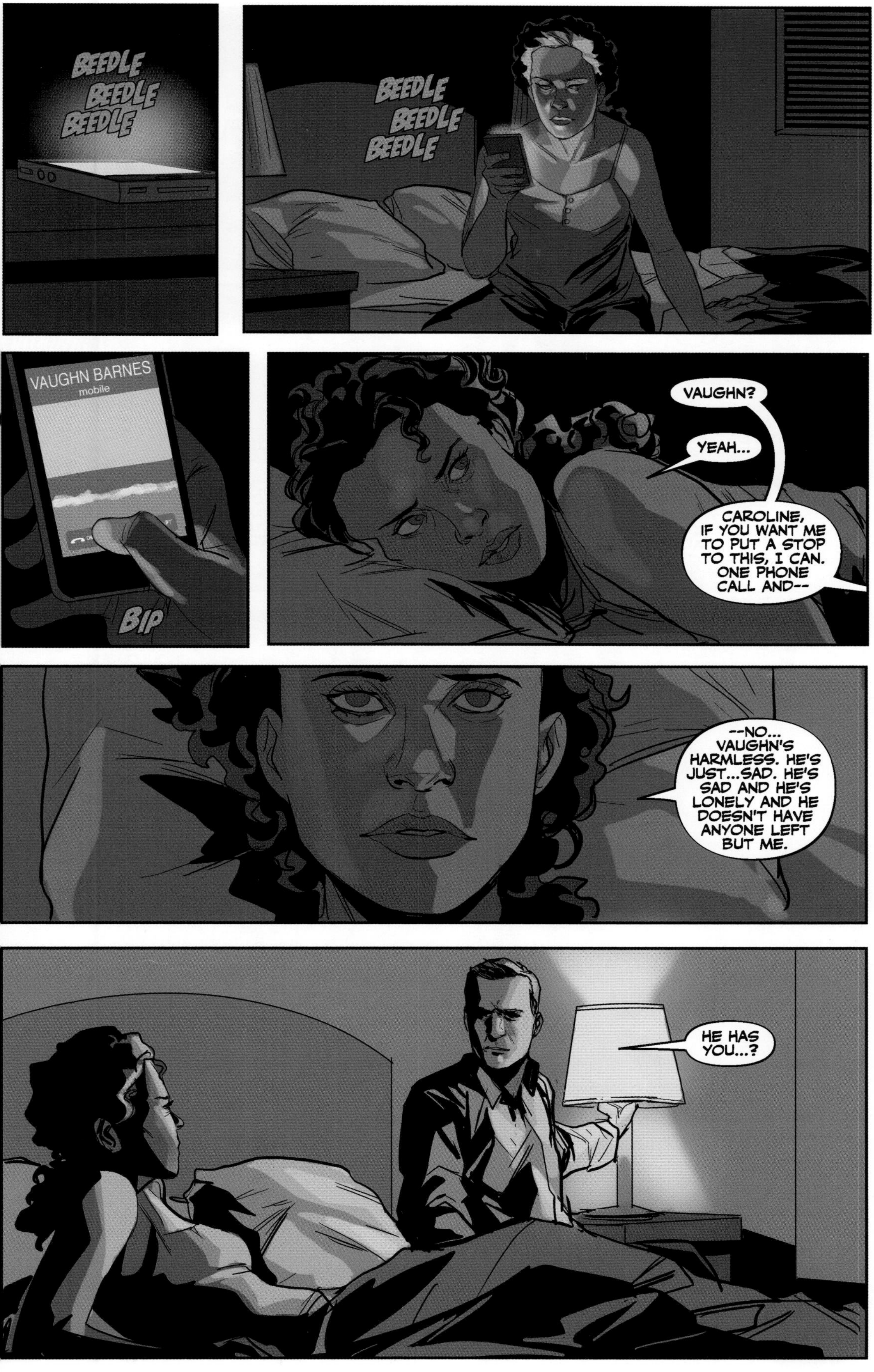
BEEDLE BEEDLE BEEDLE
BEEDLE BEEDLE BEEDLE
VAUGHN BARNES
mobile
BIP
VAUGHN?
YEAH...
CAROLINE, IF YOU WANT ME TO PUT A STOP TO THIS, I CAN. ONE PHONE CALL AND--
--NO... VAUGHN'S HARMLESS. HE'S JUST...SAD. HE'S SAD AND HE'S LONELY AND HE DOESN'T HAVE ANYONE LEFT BUT ME.
HE HAS YOU...?

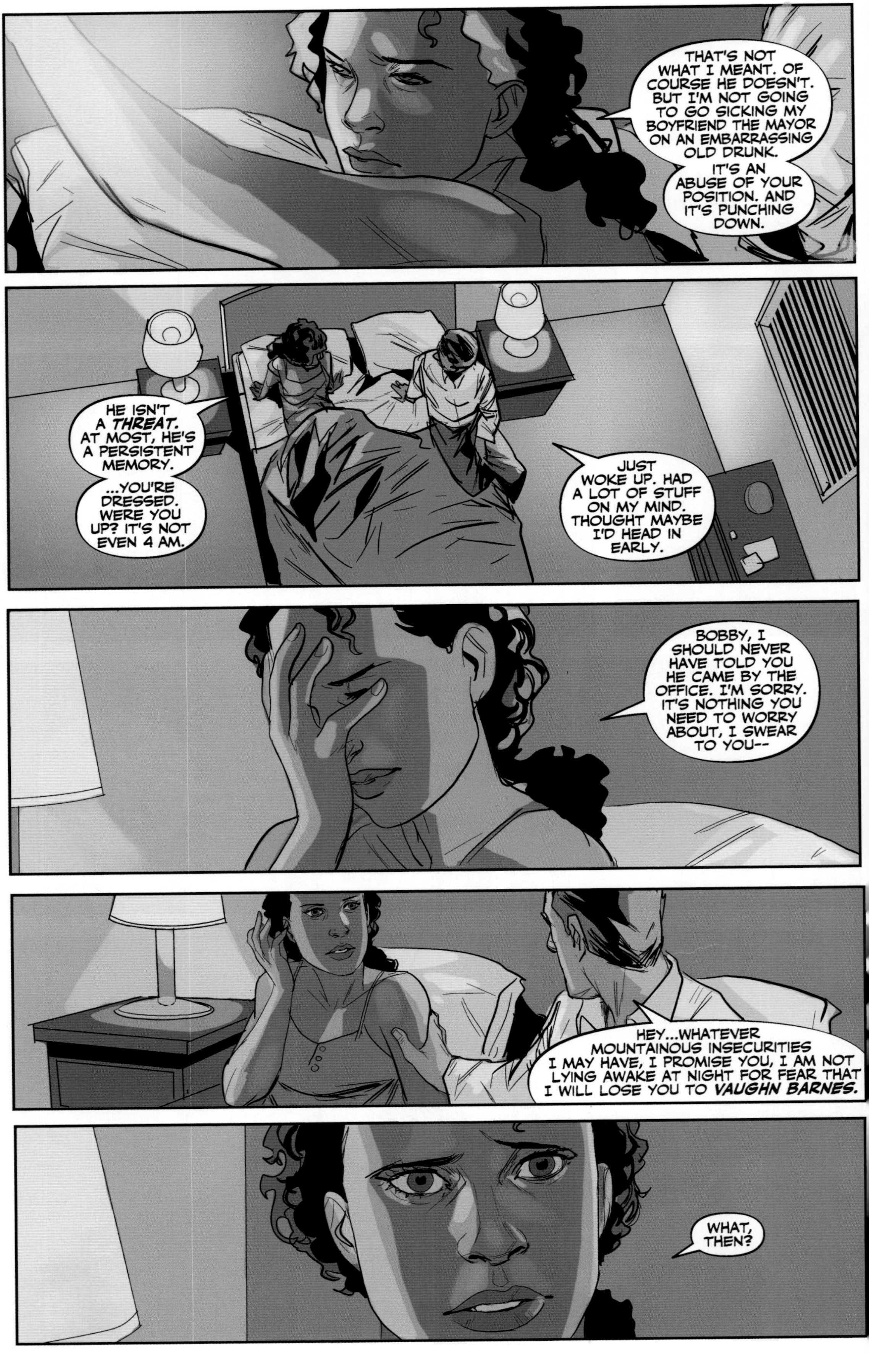
THAT'S NOT WHAT I MEANT. OF COURSE HE DOESN'T. BUT I'M NOT GOING TO GO SICKING MY BOYFRIEND THE MAYOR ON AN EMBARRASSING OLD DRUNK.
IT'S AN ABUSE OF YOUR POSITION. AND IT'S PUNCHING DOWN.
HE ISN'T A *THREAT.* AT MOST, HE'S A PERSISTENT MEMORY.
...YOU'RE DRESSED. WERE YOU UP? IT'S NOT EVEN 4 AM.
JUST WOKE UP. HAD A LOT OF STUFF ON MY MIND. THOUGHT MAYBE I'D HEAD IN EARLY.
BOBBY, I SHOULD NEVER HAVE TOLD YOU HE CAME BY THE OFFICE. I'M SORRY. IT'S NOTHING YOU NEED TO WORRY ABOUT, I SWEAR TO YOU--
HEY...WHATEVER MOUNTAINOUS INSECURITIES I MAY HAVE, I PROMISE YOU, I AM NOT LYING AWAKE AT NIGHT FOR FEAR THAT I WILL LOSE YOU TO *VAUGHN BARNES.*
WHAT, THEN?

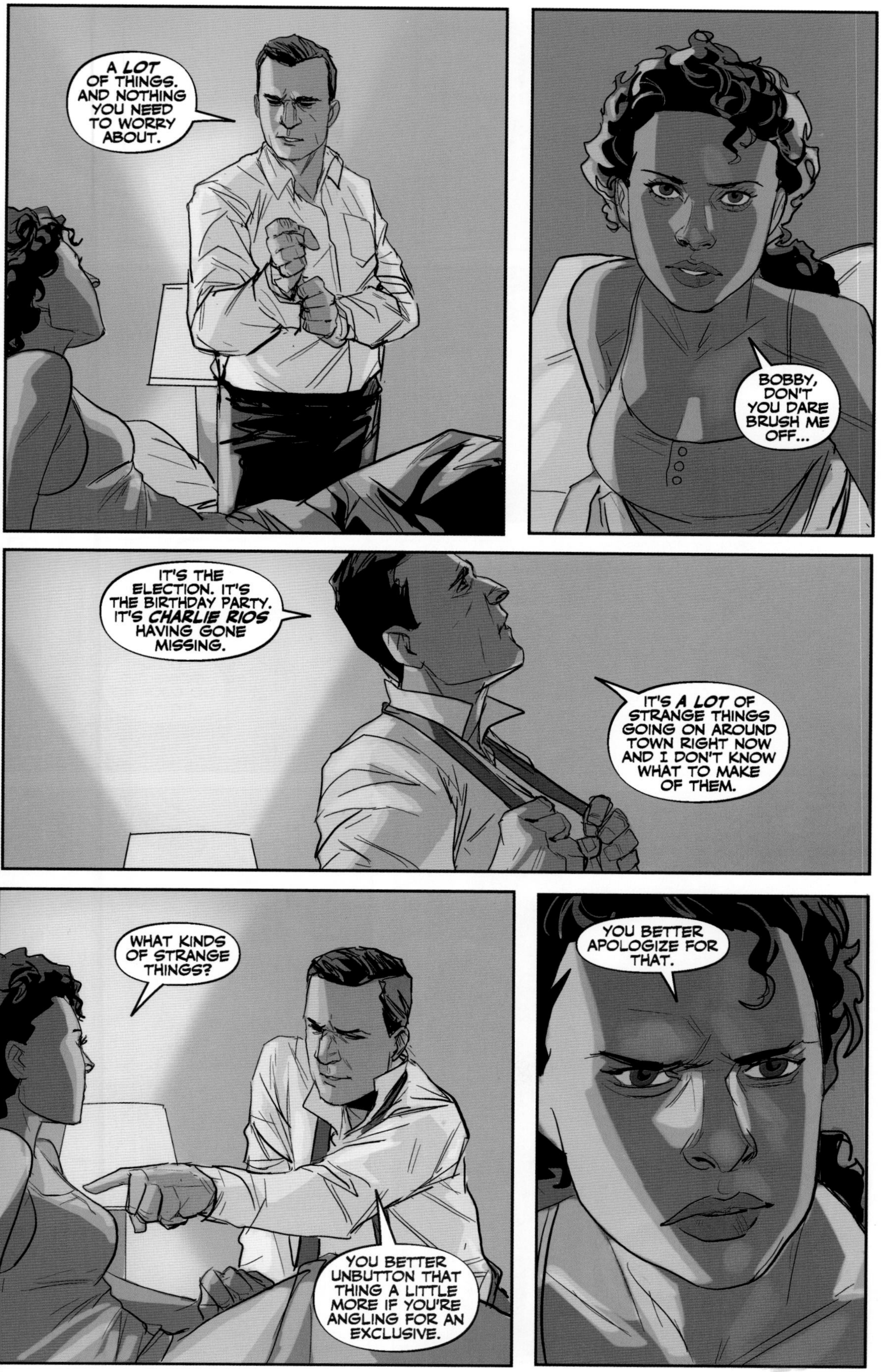
A LOT OF THINGS. AND NOTHING YOU NEED TO WORRY ABOUT.
BOBBY, DON'T YOU DARE BRUSH ME OFF...
IT'S THE ELECTION. IT'S THE BIRTHDAY PARTY. IT'S CHARLIE RIOS HAVING GONE MISSING.
IT'S A LOT OF STRANGE THINGS GOING ON AROUND TOWN RIGHT NOW AND I DON'T KNOW WHAT TO MAKE OF THEM.
WHAT KINDS OF STRANGE THINGS?
YOU BETTER UNBUTTON THAT THING A LITTLE MORE IF YOU'RE ANGLING FOR AN EXCLUSIVE.
YOU BETTER APOLOGIZE FOR THAT.

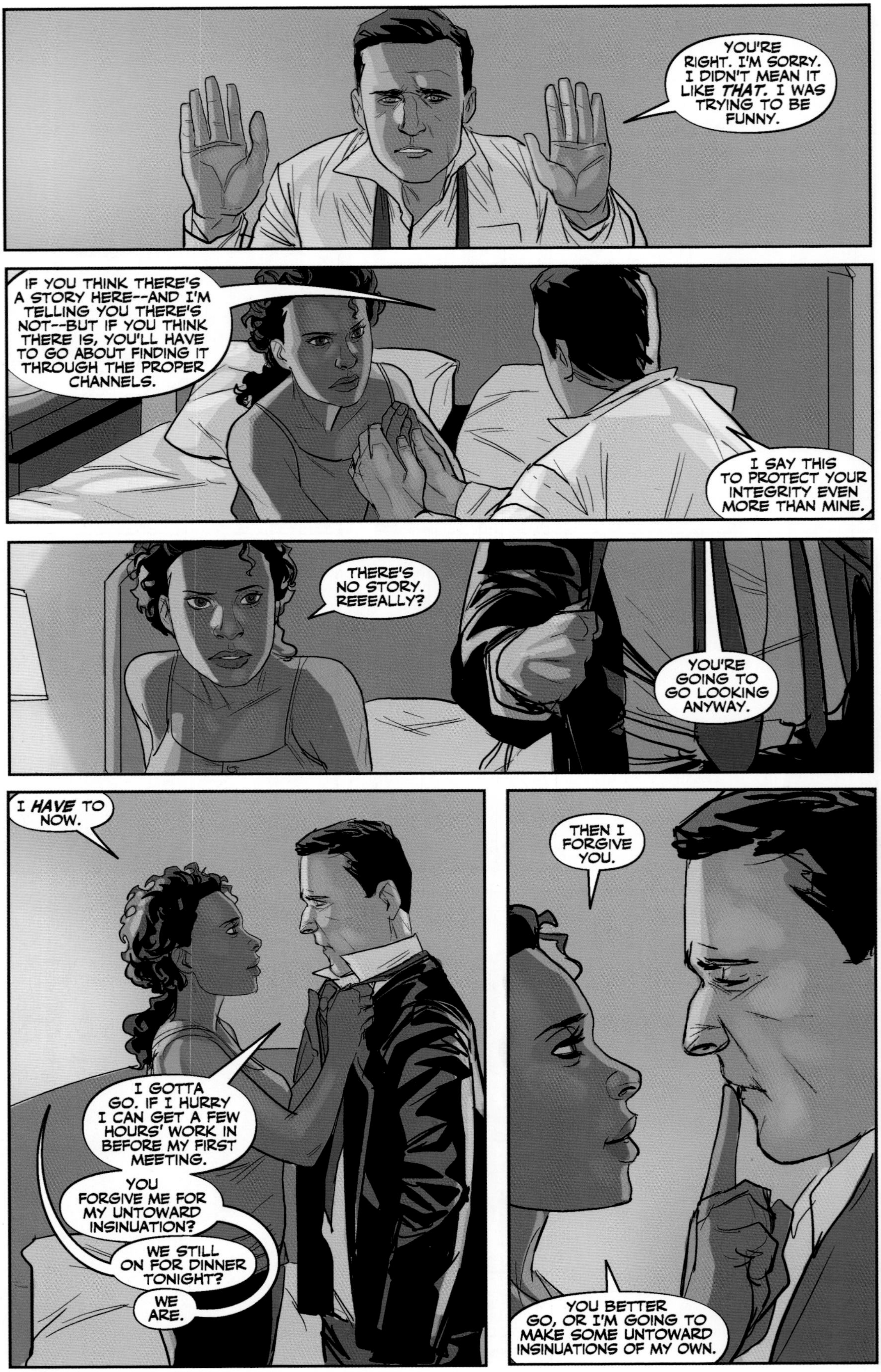
YOU'RE RIGHT. I'M SORRY. I DIDN'T MEAN IT LIKE *THAT.* I WAS TRYING TO BE FUNNY.
IF YOU THINK THERE'S A STORY HERE--AND I'M TELLING YOU THERE'S NOT--BUT IF YOU THINK THERE IS, YOU'LL HAVE TO GO ABOUT FINDING IT THROUGH THE PROPER CHANNELS.
I SAY THIS TO PROTECT YOUR INTEGRITY EVEN MORE THAN MINE.
THERE'S NO STORY. REEEALLY?
YOU'RE GOING TO GO LOOKING ANYWAY.
I *HAVE* TO NOW.
I GOTTA GO. IF I HURRY I CAN GET A FEW HOURS' WORK IN BEFORE MY FIRST MEETING.
YOU FORGIVE ME FOR MY UNTOWARD INSINUATION?
WE STILL ON FOR DINNER TONIGHT?
WE ARE.
THEN I FORGIVE YOU.
YOU BETTER GO, OR I'M GOING TO MAKE SOME UNTOWARD INSINUATIONS OF MY OWN.

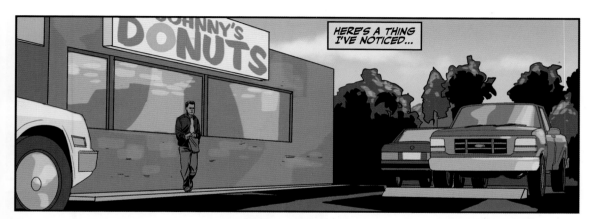

HERE'S A THING I'VE NOTICED...

WHATEVER I AM, I'M HUNGRY. ALL THE TIME.

ALL THE TIME. MAYBE I WAS A NERVOUS EATER IN MY... PAST LIFE.

OR WHATEVER.

YOU'VE GOT A LITTLE THING...

WHIPPED CREAM FROM YOUR WAFFLES MAYBE...? OR THE ICE CREAM? I CAN'T TELL...

YOU'RE RIGHT. IT'S COOL. IT LOOKS GOOD THERE. YOU SHOULD LEAVE IT. IT'S, LIKE...YOUR THING.

GOT IT.

THE CRULLER?

THE LEAD.

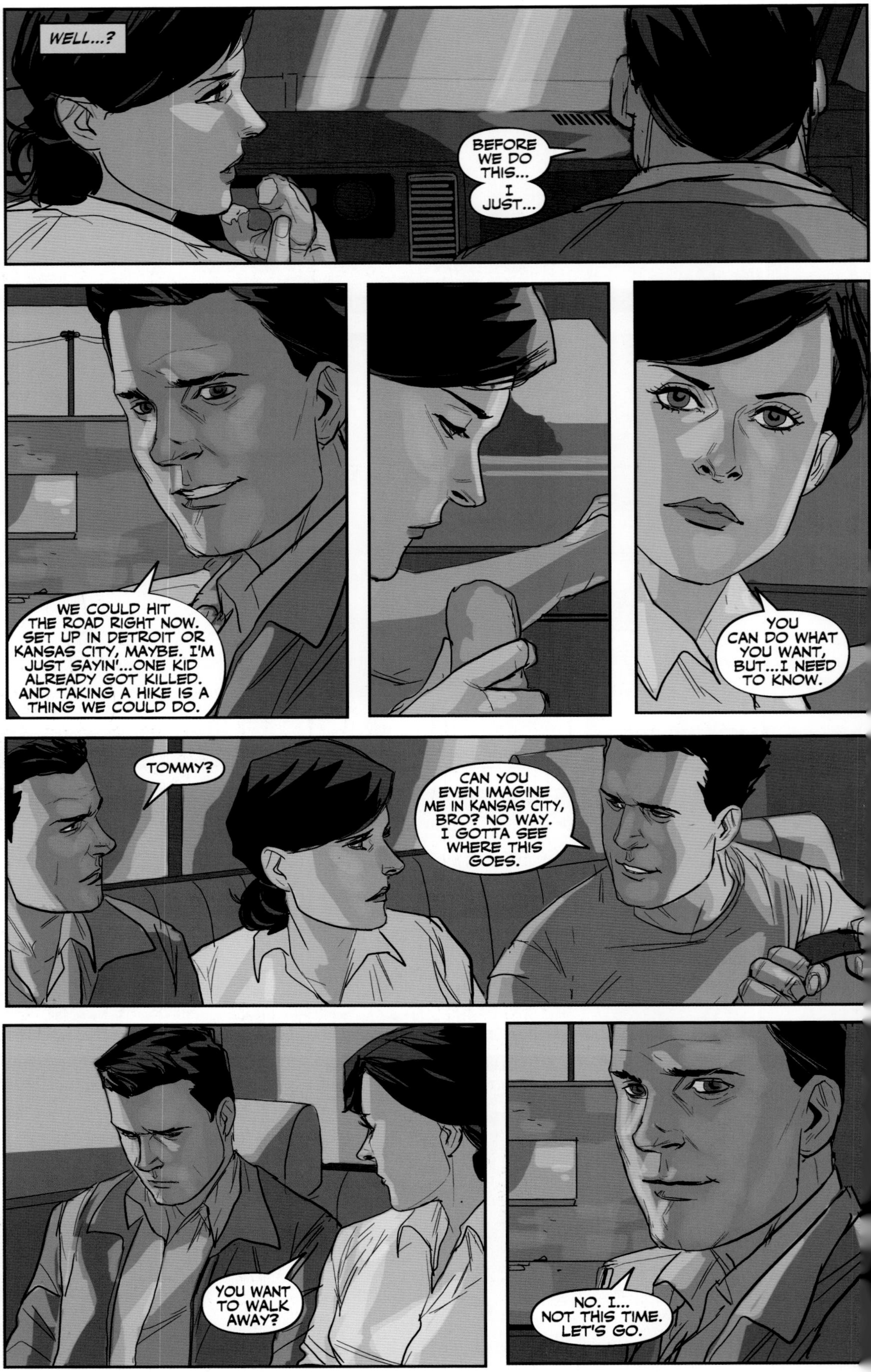
WELL...?
BEFORE WE DO THIS... I JUST...
WE COULD HIT THE ROAD RIGHT NOW. SET UP IN DETROIT OR KANSAS CITY, MAYBE. I'M JUST SAYIN'...ONE KID ALREADY GOT KILLED. AND TAKING A HIKE IS A THING WE COULD DO.
YOU CAN DO WHAT YOU WANT, BUT...I NEED TO KNOW.
TOMMY?
CAN YOU EVEN IMAGINE ME IN KANSAS CITY, BRO? NO WAY. I GOTTA SEE WHERE THIS GOES.
YOU WANT TO WALK AWAY?
NO. I... NOT THIS TIME. LET'S GO.

OKAY, CAROLINE'S GOT WISE AND SHE'S NOT TAKING MY CALLS.

SORRY, BRO.

IT'S OKAY, TOMMY. SHE'S... SHE'S BETTER OFF.

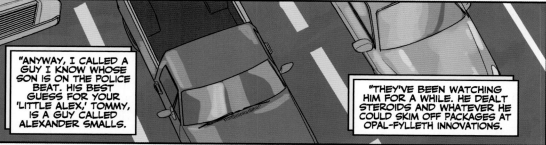

"ANYWAY, I CALLED A GUY I KNOW WHOSE SON IS ON THE POLICE BEAT. HIS BEST GUESS FOR YOUR 'LITTLE ALEX,' TOMMY, IS A GUY CALLED ALEXANDER SMALLS."

"THEY'VE BEEN WATCHING HIM FOR A WHILE. HE DEALT STEROIDS AND WHATEVER HE COULD SKIM OFF PACKAGES AT OPAL-FYLLETH INNOVATIONS."

"DISTRICT ATTORNEY WAS TRYING TO BUILD A CASE AGAINST THE COMPANY, SO THEY LEFT HIM IN PLACE, HOPING THEY COULD TURN HIM LATER.

"MIKEY FIGURES HE MIGHT HAVE MOVED ON TO WHATEVER EQUIPMENT THEY HAD LYING AROUND. PROBABLY HAD NO IDEA WHAT HE WAS SELLING."

"I HAD NO IDEA WHAT I WAS BUYING, THAT'S FOR SURE."

"WHERE'M I GOIN' EXACTLY?"

"OFFICE OF DR.... LINDA OCTOBER..."

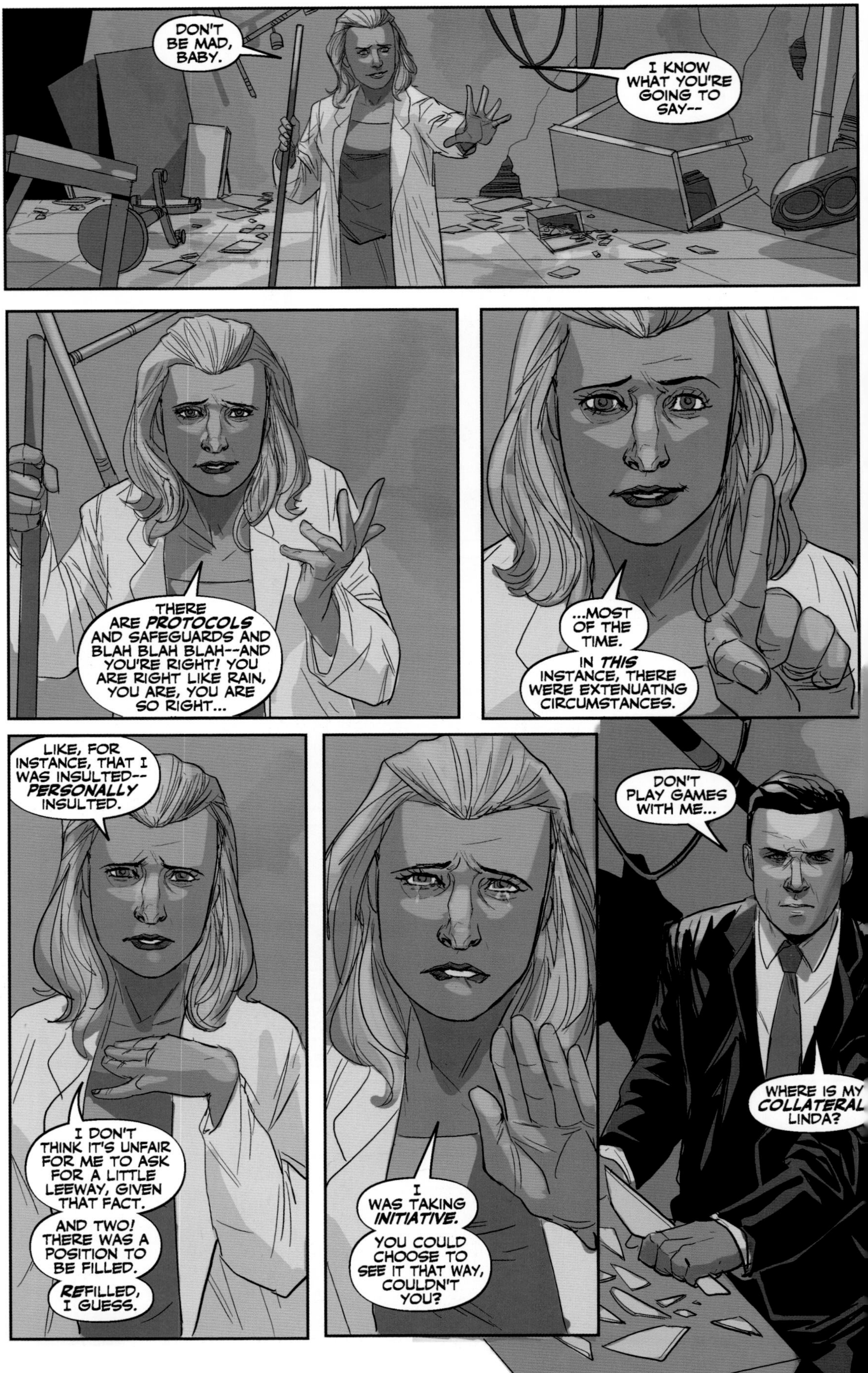
DON'T BE MAD, BABY.
I KNOW WHAT YOU'RE GOING TO SAY--
THERE ARE PROTOCOLS AND SAFEGUARDS AND BLAH BLAH BLAH--AND YOU'RE RIGHT! YOU ARE RIGHT LIKE RAIN, YOU ARE, YOU ARE SO RIGHT...
...MOST OF THE TIME.
IN THIS INSTANCE, THERE WERE EXTENUATING CIRCUMSTANCES.
LIKE, FOR INSTANCE, THAT I WAS INSULTED-- PERSONALLY INSULTED.
I DON'T THINK IT'S UNFAIR FOR ME TO ASK FOR A LITTLE LEEWAY, GIVEN THAT FACT.
AND TWO! THERE WAS A POSITION TO BE FILLED.
REFILLED, I GUESS.
I WAS TAKING INITIATIVE.
YOU COULD CHOOSE TO SEE IT THAT WAY, COULDN'T YOU?
DON'T PLAY GAMES WITH ME...
WHERE IS MY COLLATERAL, LINDA?

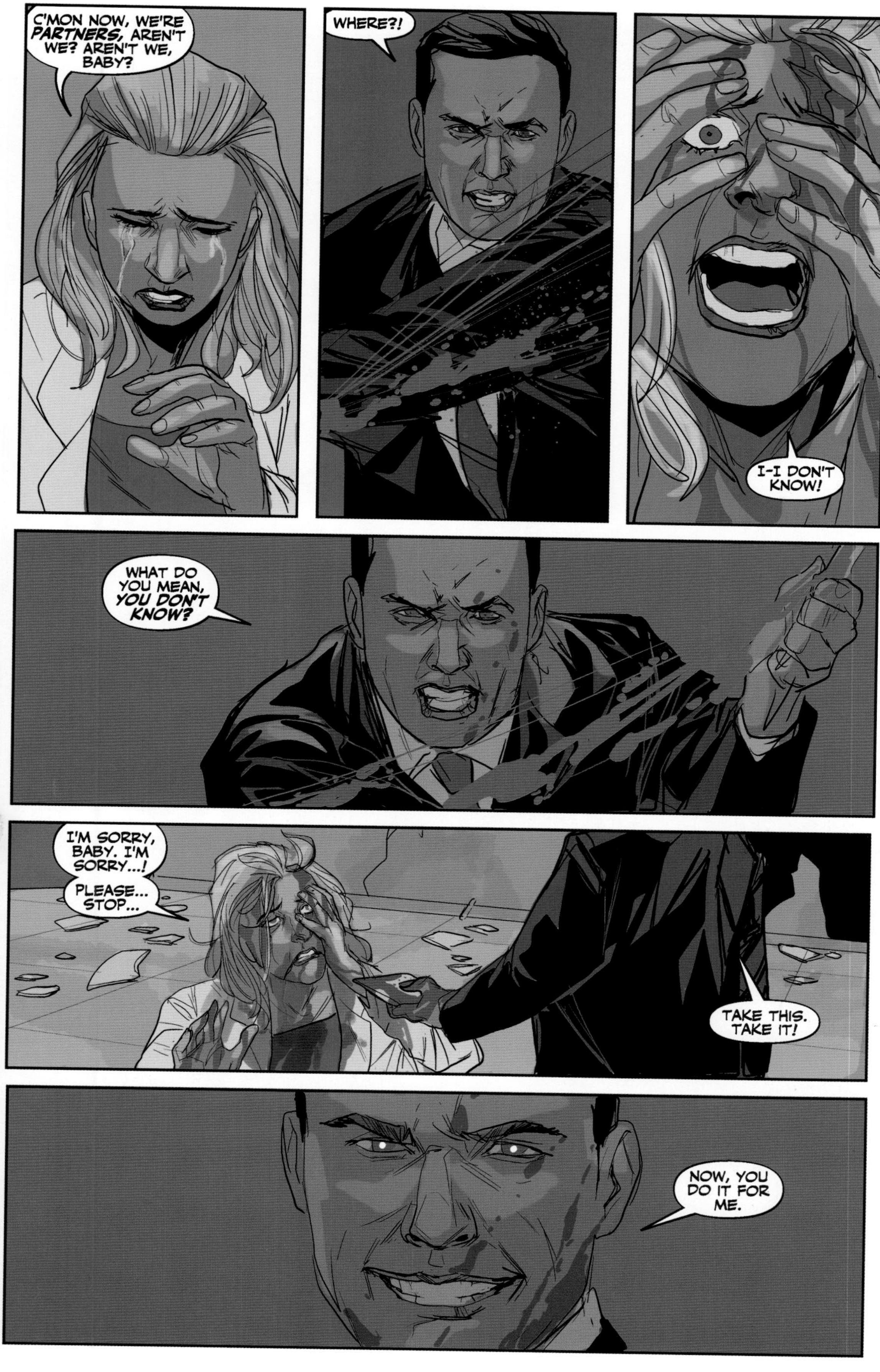
C'MON NOW, WE'RE *PARTNERS,* AREN'T WE? AREN'T WE, BABY?
WHERE?!
I-I DON'T KNOW!
WHAT DO YOU MEAN, *YOU DON'T KNOW?*
I'M SORRY, BABY. I'M SORRY...!
PLEASE... STOP...
TAKE THIS. TAKE IT!
NOW, YOU DO IT FOR ME.

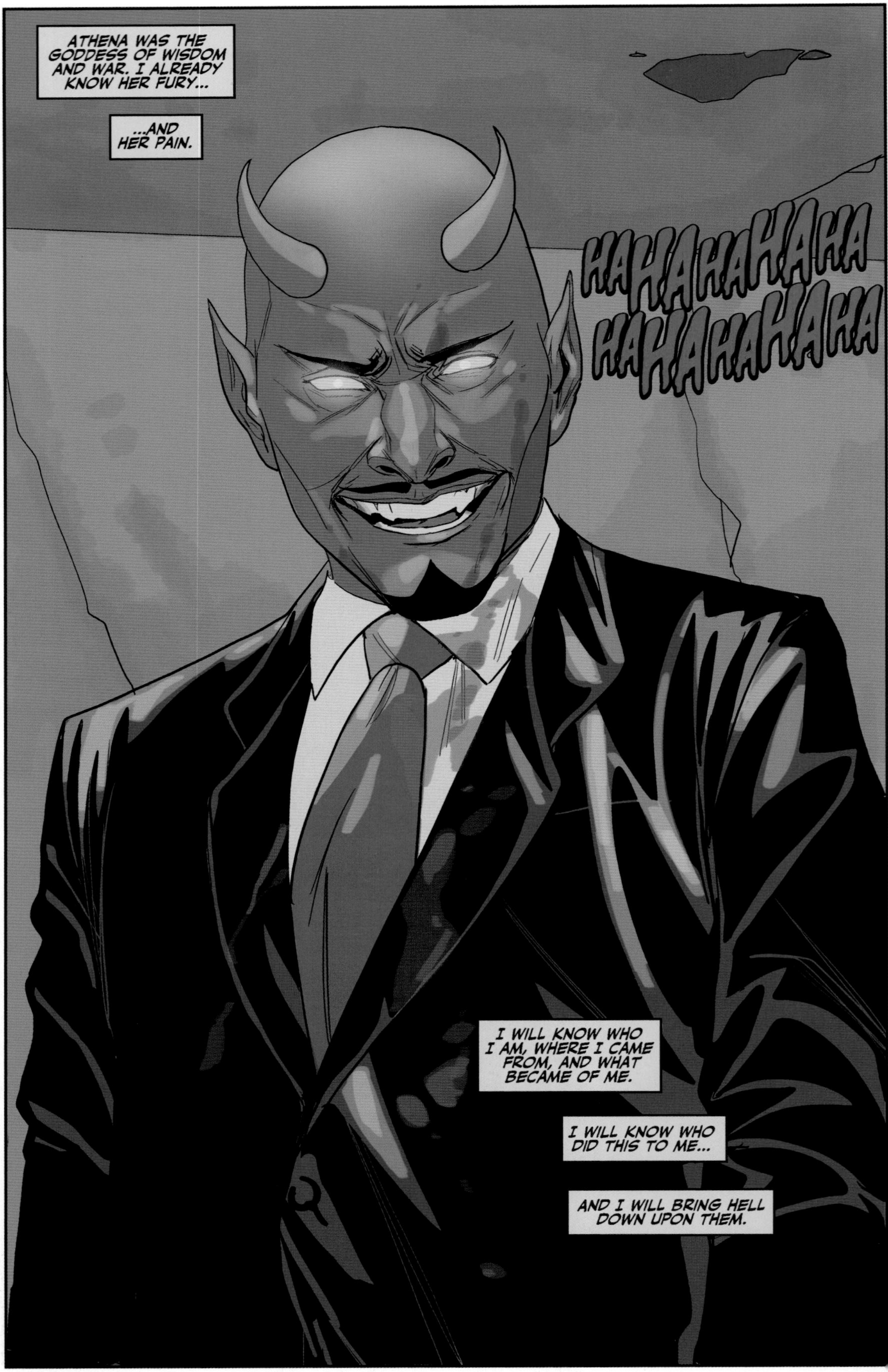
ATHENA WAS THE GODDESS OF WISDOM AND WAR. I ALREADY KNOW HER FURY...
...AND HER PAIN.
HAHAHAHAHAHA
HAHAHAHAHAHA
I WILL KNOW WHO I AM, WHERE I CAME FROM, AND WHAT BECAME OF ME.
I WILL KNOW WHO DID THIS TO ME...
AND I WILL BRING HELL DOWN UPON THEM.

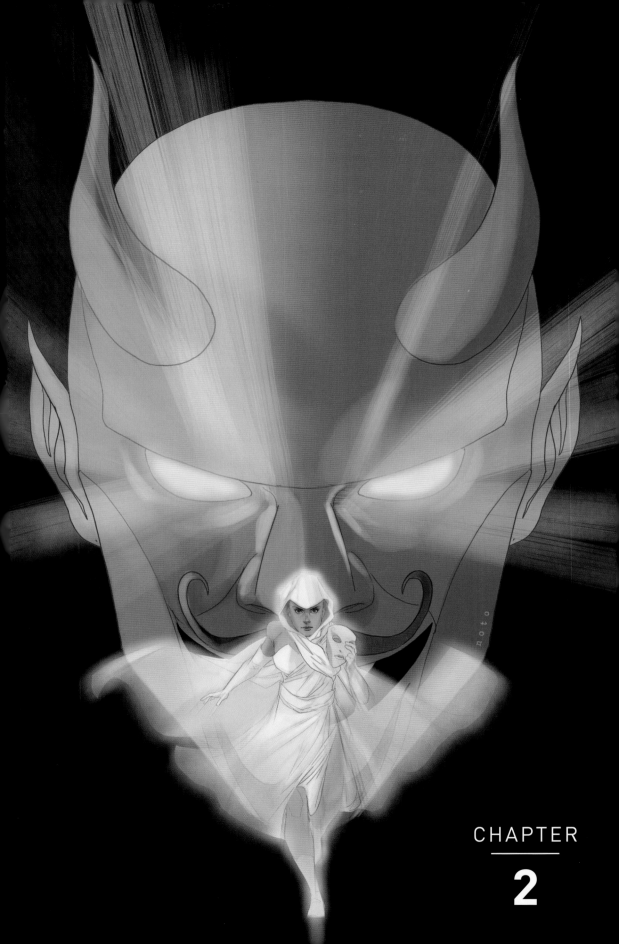

CHAPTER

2

"WE ARE LIKE LIZARD EGGS SNUG INTO A BIRD'S NEST. ONE AT A TIME, EVERY YEAR, ONE MORE. CHICAGO KEEPS US WARM AND SAFE IN HER BOSOM, BLISSFULLY IGNORANT TO THE FACT THAT THESE CHILDREN SHE FOSTERS ARE THE INSTRUMENTS OF HER DEMISE."

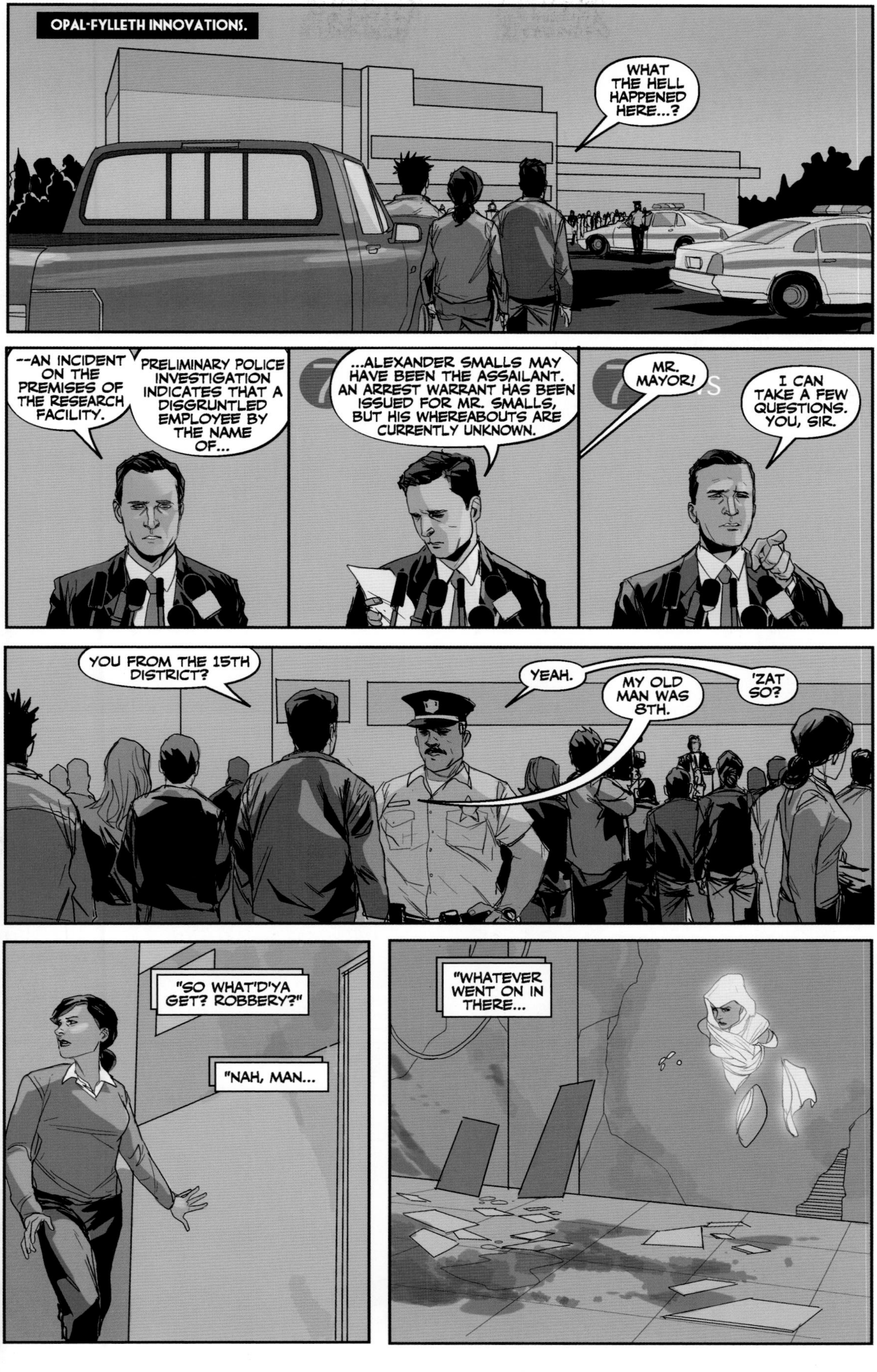
OPAL-FYLLETH INNOVATIONS.
WHAT THE HELL HAPPENED HERE...?
--AN INCIDENT ON THE PREMISES OF THE RESEARCH FACILITY.
PRELIMINARY POLICE INVESTIGATION INDICATES THAT A DISGRUNTLED EMPLOYEE BY THE NAME OF...
...ALEXANDER SMALLS MAY HAVE BEEN THE ASSAILANT. AN ARREST WARRANT HAS BEEN ISSUED FOR MR. SMALLS, BUT HIS WHEREABOUTS ARE CURRENTLY UNKNOWN.
MR. MAYOR!
I CAN TAKE A FEW QUESTIONS. YOU, SIR.
YOU FROM THE 15TH DISTRICT?
YEAH.
MY OLD MAN WAS 8TH.
'ZAT SO?
"SO WHAT'D'YA GET? ROBBERY?"
"NAH, MAN...
"WHATEVER WENT ON IN THERE...

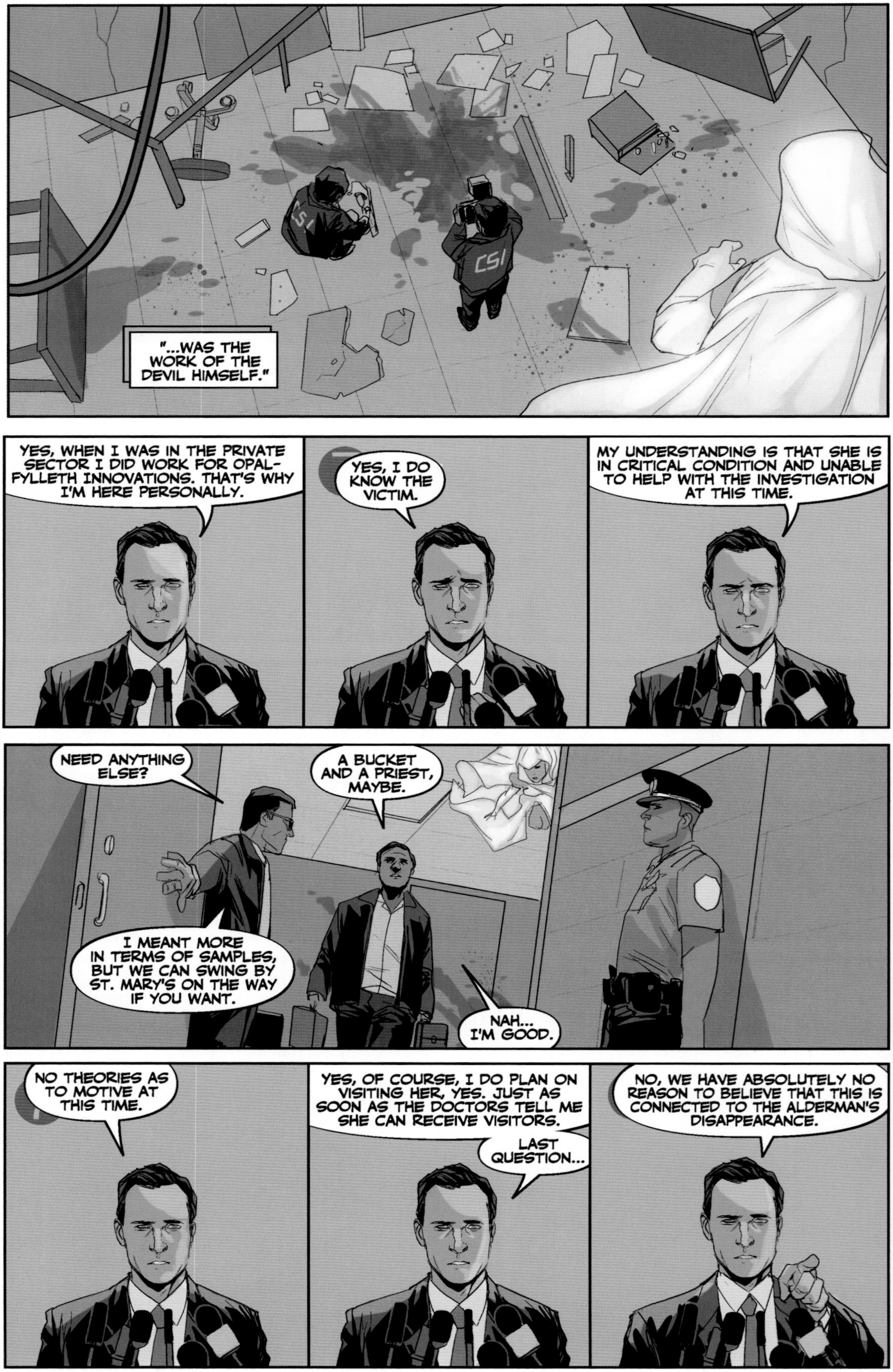
"...WAS THE WORK OF THE DEVIL HIMSELF."
YES, WHEN I WAS IN THE PRIVATE SECTOR I DID WORK FOR OPAL-FYLLETH INNOVATIONS. THAT'S WHY I'M HERE PERSONALLY.
YES, I DO KNOW THE VICTIM.
MY UNDERSTANDING IS THAT SHE IS IN CRITICAL CONDITION AND UNABLE TO HELP WITH THE INVESTIGATION AT THIS TIME.
NEED ANYTHING ELSE?
A BUCKET AND A PRIEST, MAYBE.
I MEANT MORE IN TERMS OF SAMPLES, BUT WE CAN SWING BY ST. MARY'S ON THE WAY IF YOU WANT.
NAH... I'M GOOD.
NO THEORIES AS TO MOTIVE AT THIS TIME.
YES, OF COURSE, I DO PLAN ON VISITING HER, YES. JUST AS SOON AS THE DOCTORS TELL ME SHE CAN RECEIVE VISITORS.
LAST QUESTION...
NO, WE HAVE ABSOLUTELY NO REASON TO BELIEVE THAT THIS IS CONNECTED TO THE ALDERMAN'S DISAPPEARANCE.

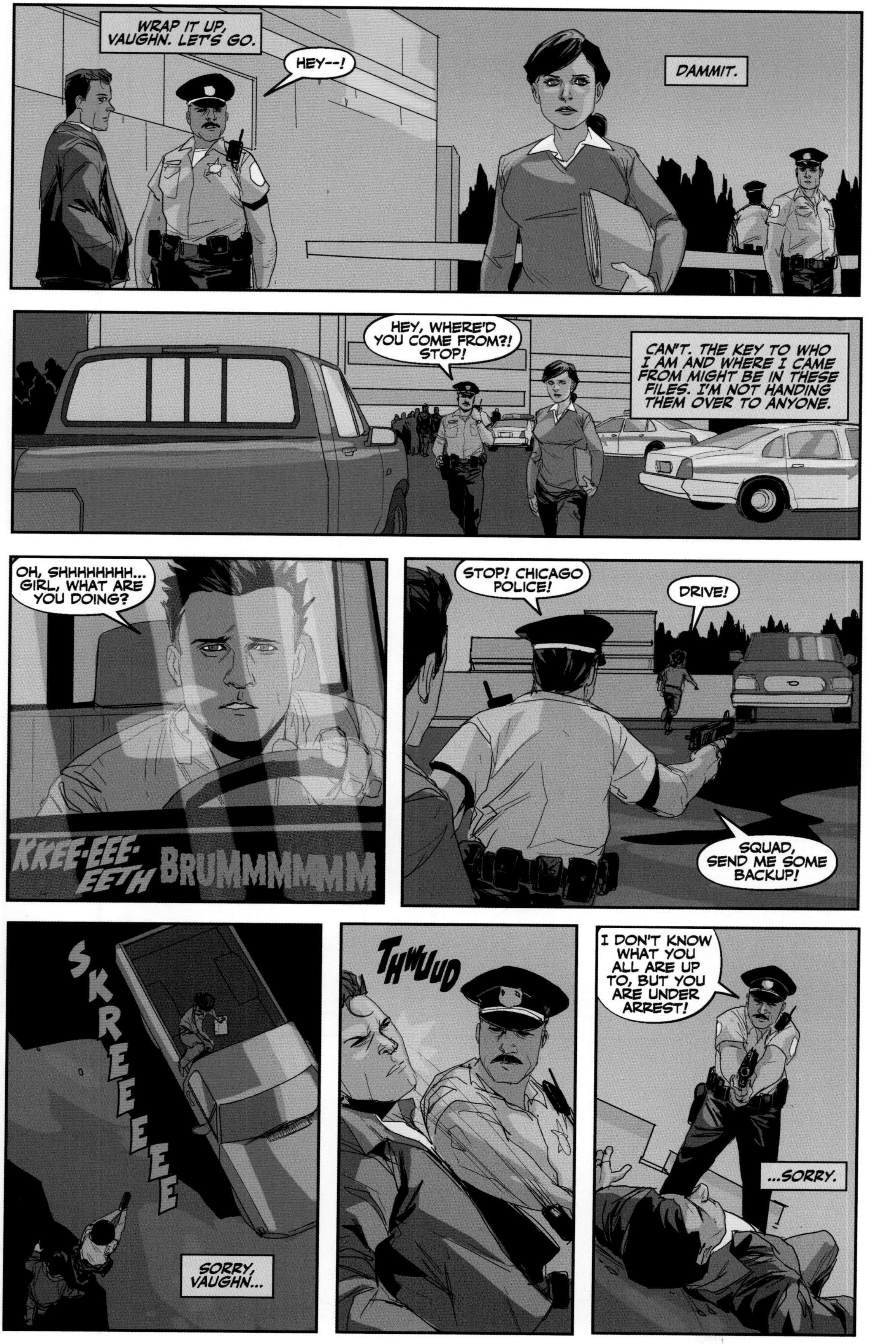
WRAP IT UP, VAUGHN. LET'S GO.
HEY--!
DAMMIT.
HEY, WHERE'D YOU COME FROM?! STOP!
CAN'T. THE KEY TO WHO I AM AND WHERE I CAME FROM MIGHT BE IN THESE FILES. I'M NOT HANDING THEM OVER TO ANYONE.
OH, SHHHHHHHH... GIRL, WHAT ARE YOU DOING?
KKEE-EEE-EETH
BRUMMMMMMM
STOP! CHICAGO POLICE!
DRIVE!
SQUAD, SEND ME SOME BACKUP!
SKREEEEEEE
SORRY, VAUGHN...
THWUUD
I DON'T KNOW WHAT YOU ALL ARE UP TO, BUT YOU ARE UNDER ARREST!
...SORRY.

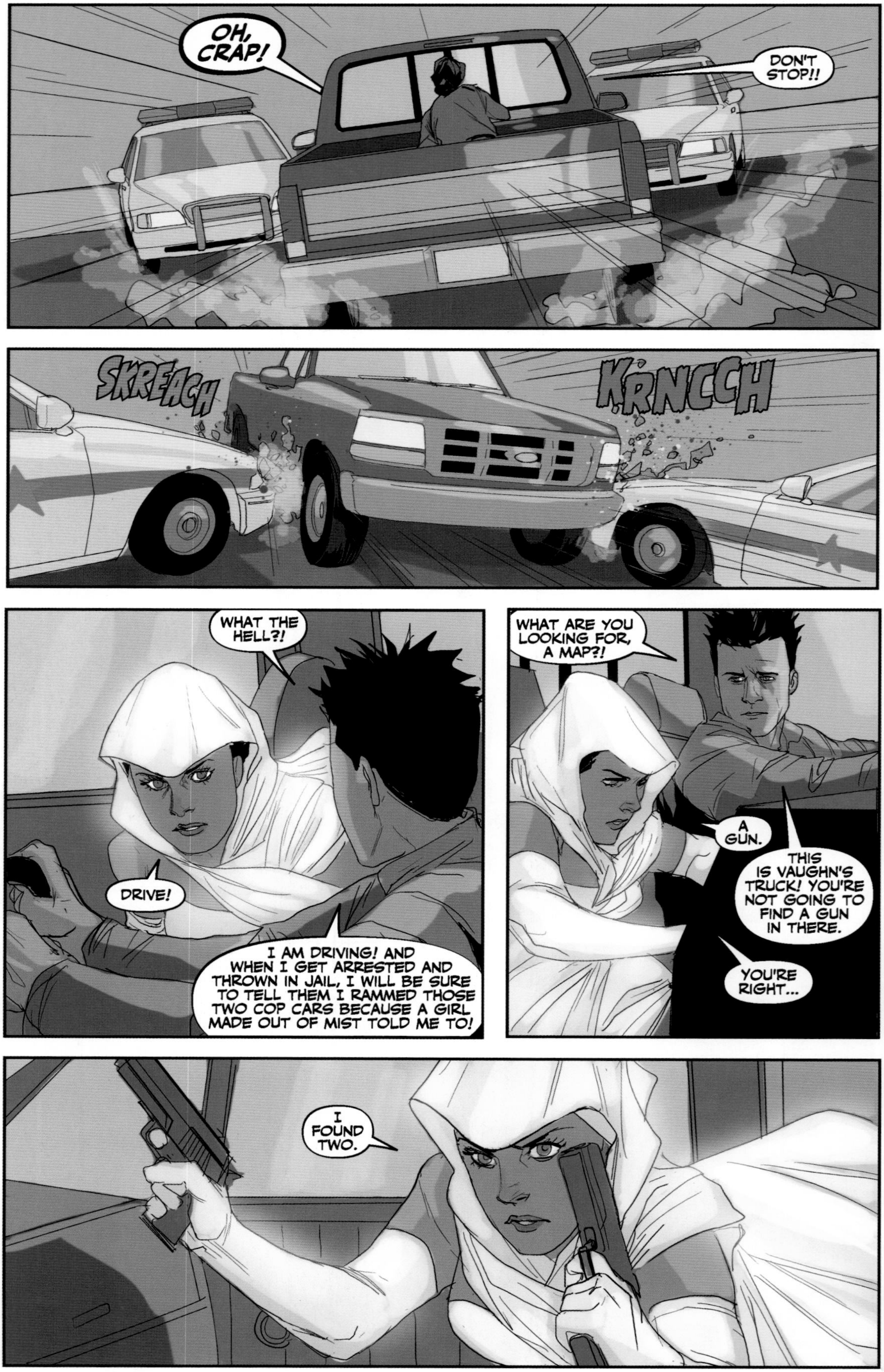
OH, CRAP!
DON'T STOP!!
SKREACH
KRNCCH
WHAT THE HELL?!
DRIVE!
I AM DRIVING! AND WHEN I GET ARRESTED AND THROWN IN JAIL, I WILL BE SURE TO TELL THEM I RAMMED THOSE TWO COP CARS BECAUSE A GIRL MADE OUT OF MIST TOLD ME TO!
WHAT ARE YOU LOOKING FOR, A MAP?!
A GUN.
THIS IS VAUGHN'S TRUCK! YOU'RE NOT GOING TO FIND A GUN IN THERE.
YOU'RE RIGHT...
I FOUND TWO.

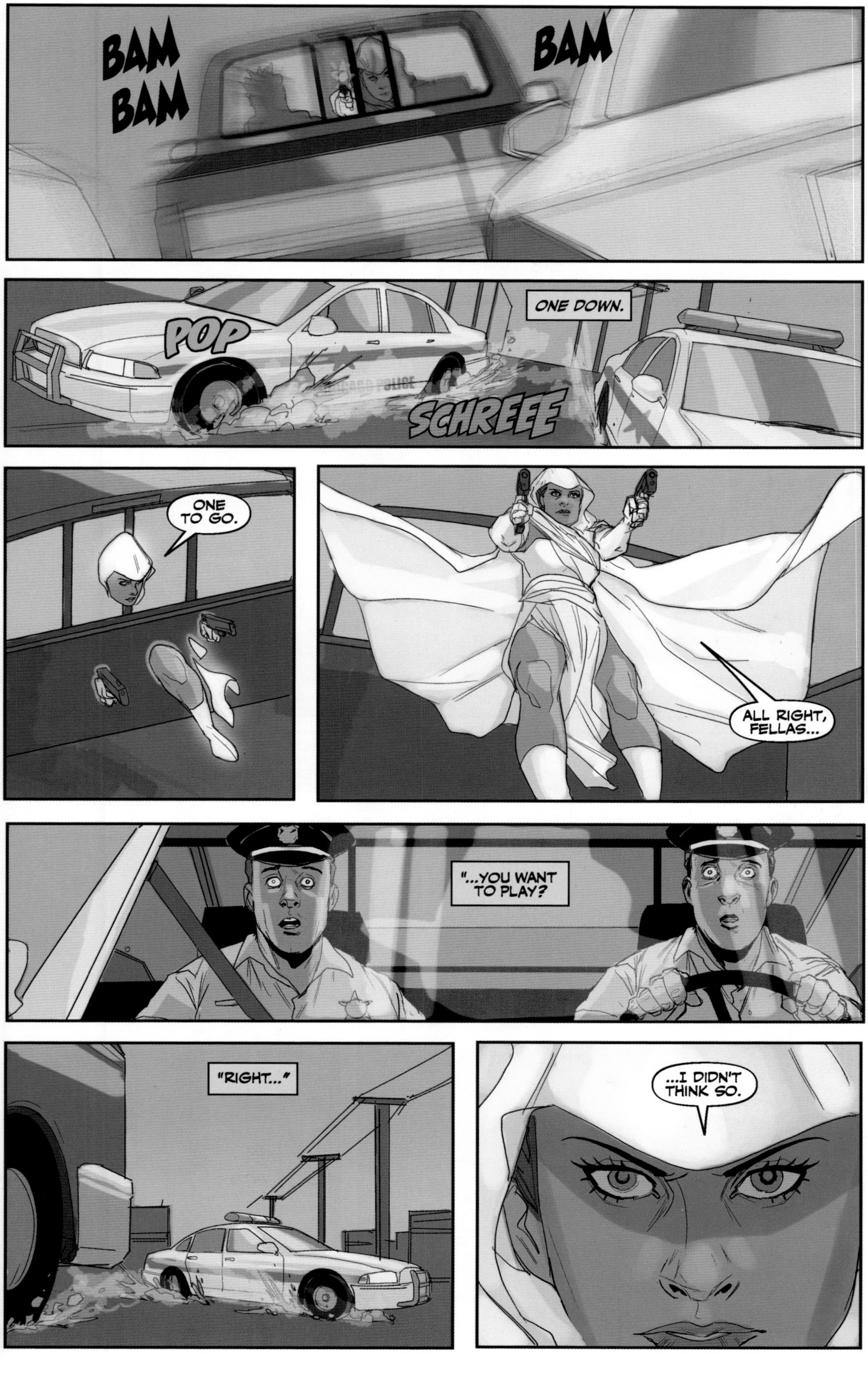
BAM
BAM
BAM
POP
ONE DOWN.
SCHREEE
ONE TO GO.
ALL RIGHT, FELLAS...
"...YOU WANT TO PLAY?
"RIGHT..."
...I DIDN'T THINK SO.

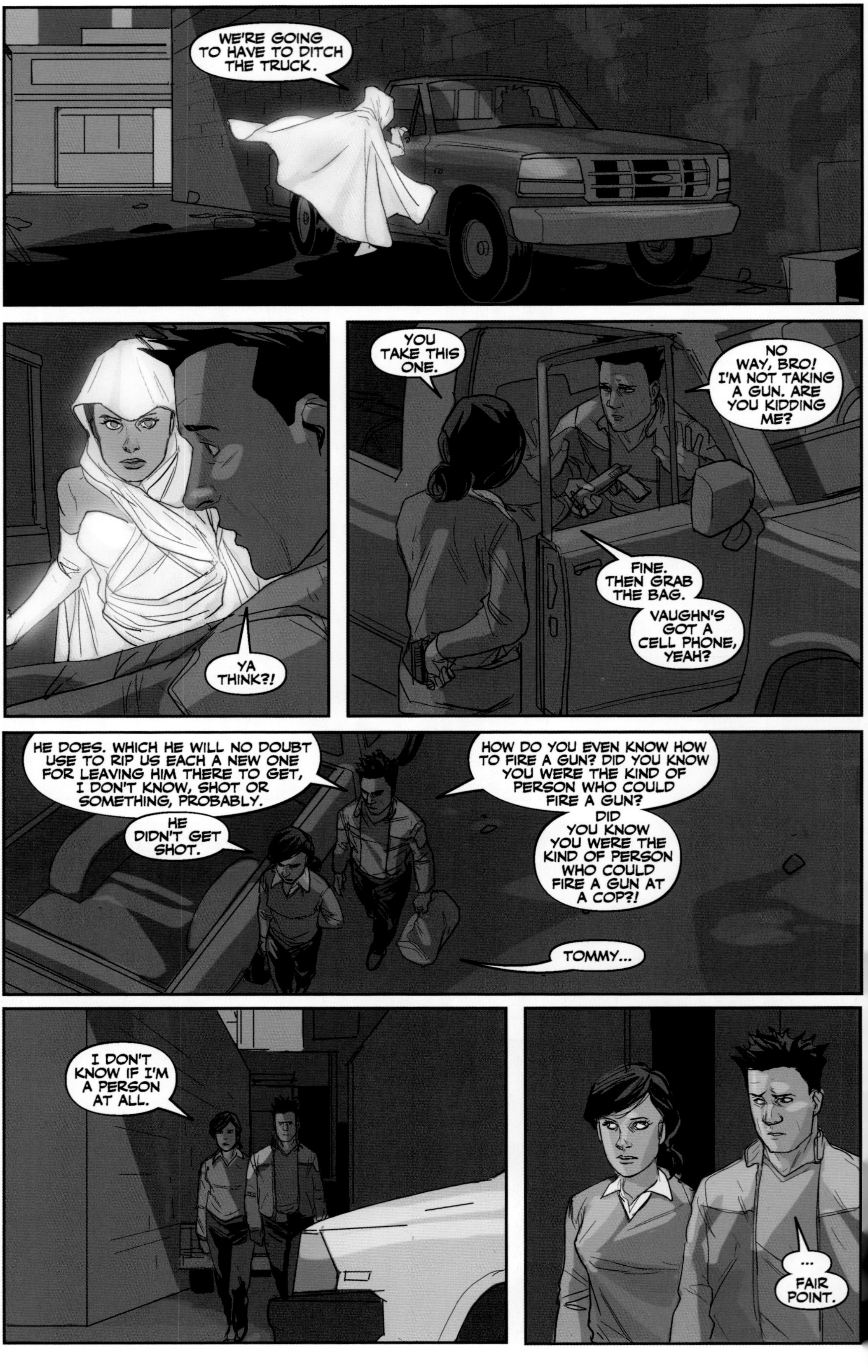
WE'RE GOING TO HAVE TO DITCH THE TRUCK.
YA THINK?!
YOU TAKE THIS ONE.
NO WAY, BRO! I'M NOT TAKING A GUN. ARE YOU KIDDING ME?
FINE. THEN GRAB THE BAG.
VAUGHN'S GOT A CELL PHONE, YEAH?
HE DOES. WHICH HE WILL NO DOUBT USE TO RIP US EACH A NEW ONE FOR LEAVING HIM THERE TO GET, I DON'T KNOW, SHOT OR SOMETHING, PROBABLY.
HE DIDN'T GET SHOT.
HOW DO YOU EVEN KNOW HOW TO FIRE A GUN? DID YOU KNOW YOU WERE THE KIND OF PERSON WHO COULD FIRE A GUN?
DID YOU KNOW YOU WERE THE KIND OF PERSON WHO COULD FIRE A GUN AT A COP?!
TOMMY...
I DON'T KNOW IF I'M A PERSON AT ALL.
... FAIR POINT.

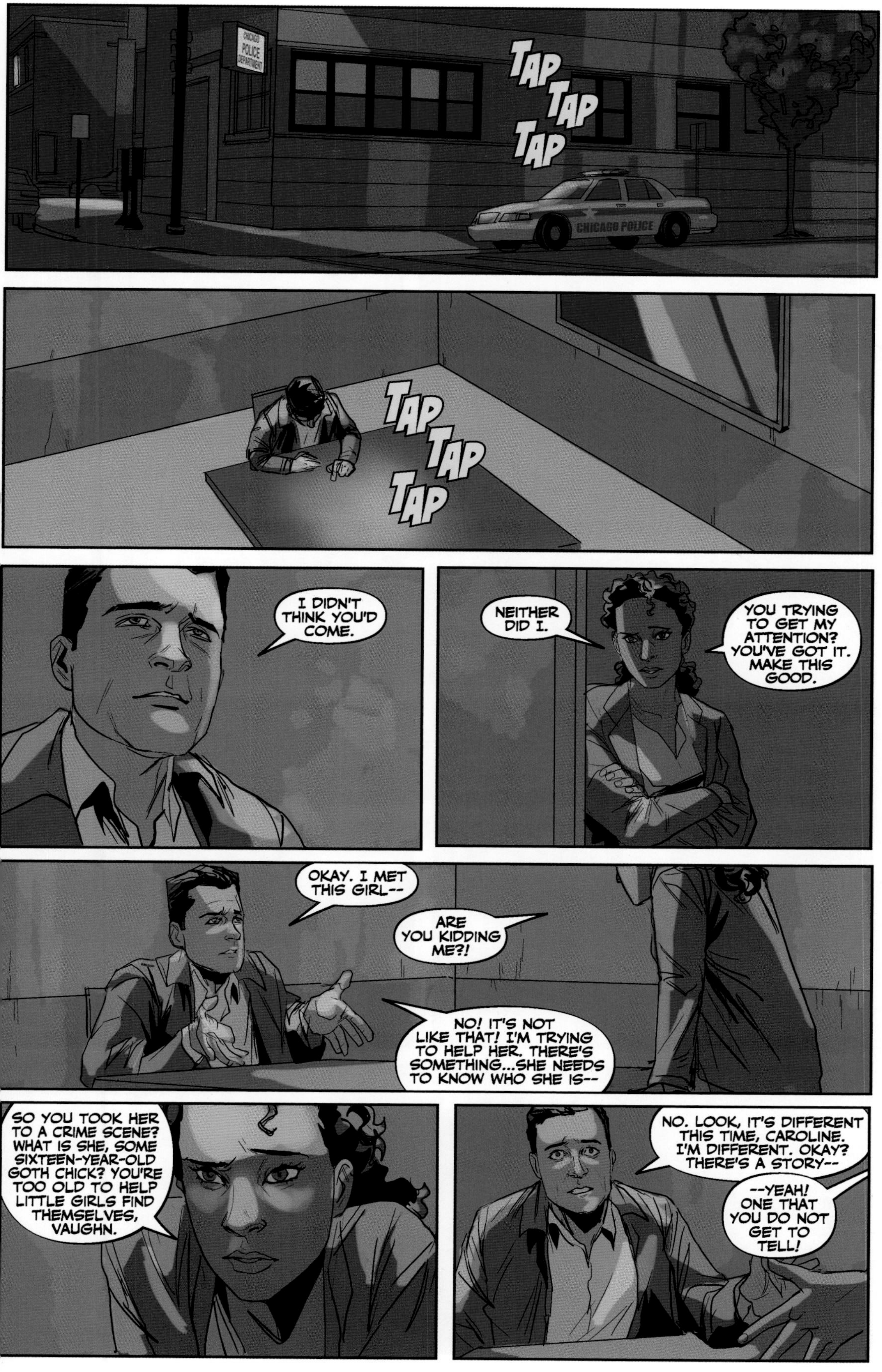
CHICAGO POLICE DEPARTMENT
TAP TAP TAP
CHICAGO POLICE
TAP TAP TAP
I DIDN'T THINK YOU'D COME.
NEITHER DID I.
YOU TRYING TO GET MY ATTENTION? YOU'VE GOT IT. MAKE THIS GOOD.
OKAY. I MET THIS GIRL--
ARE YOU KIDDING ME?!
NO! IT'S NOT LIKE THAT! I'M TRYING TO HELP HER. THERE'S SOMETHING...SHE NEEDS TO KNOW WHO SHE IS--
SO YOU TOOK HER TO A CRIME SCENE? WHAT IS SHE, SOME SIXTEEN-YEAR-OLD GOTH CHICK? YOU'RE TOO OLD TO HELP LITTLE GIRLS FIND THEMSELVES, VAUGHN.
NO. LOOK, IT'S DIFFERENT THIS TIME, CAROLINE. I'M DIFFERENT. OKAY? THERE'S A STORY--
--YEAH! ONE THAT YOU DO NOT GET TO TELL!

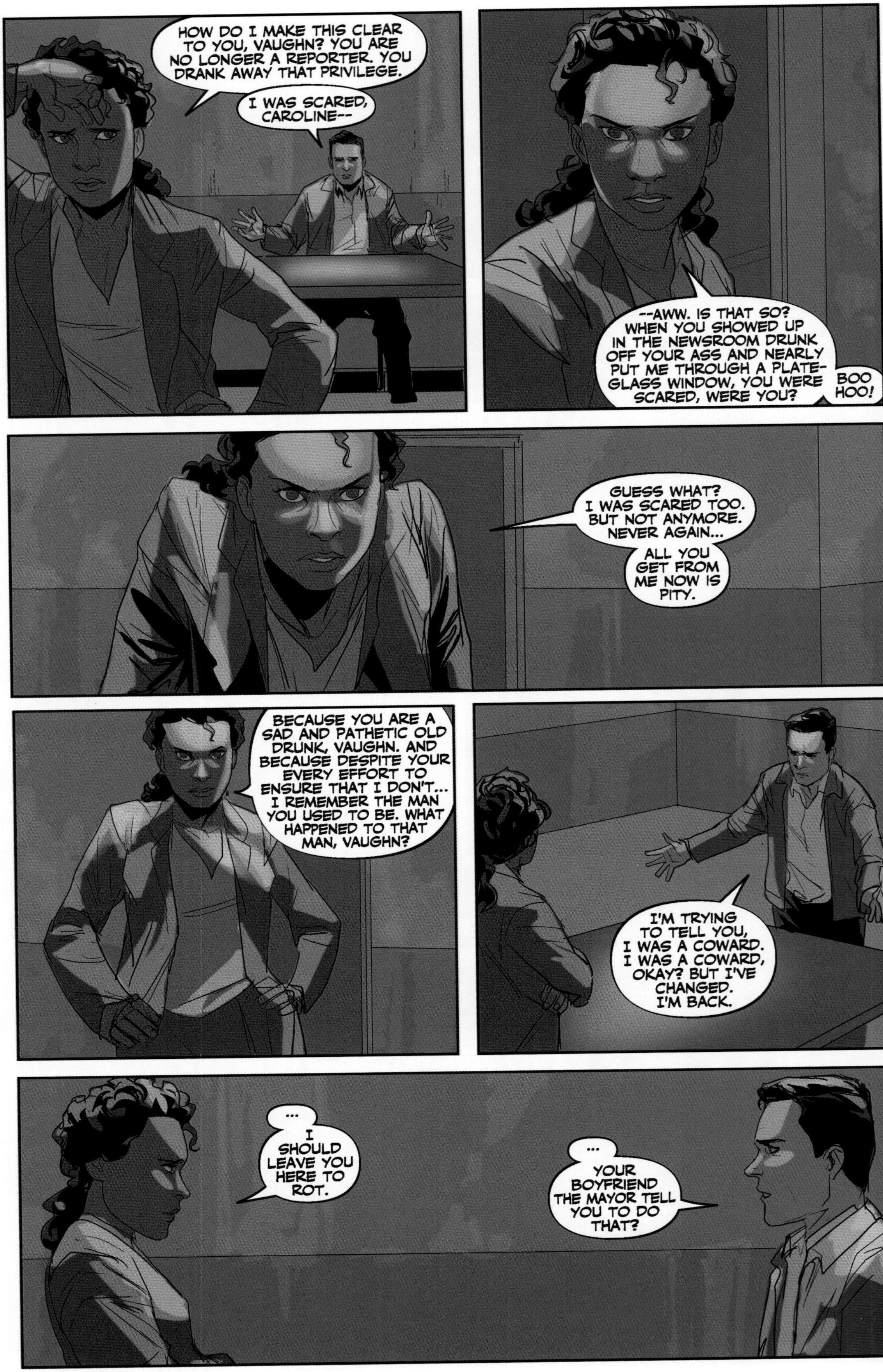
HOW DO I MAKE THIS CLEAR TO YOU, VAUGHN? YOU ARE NO LONGER A REPORTER. YOU DRANK AWAY THAT PRIVILEGE.
I WAS SCARED, CAROLINE--
--AWW. IS THAT SO? WHEN YOU SHOWED UP IN THE NEWSROOM DRUNK OFF YOUR ASS AND NEARLY PUT ME THROUGH A PLATE-GLASS WINDOW, YOU WERE SCARED, WERE YOU?
BOO HOO!
GUESS WHAT? I WAS SCARED TOO. BUT NOT ANYMORE. NEVER AGAIN...
ALL YOU GET FROM ME NOW IS PITY.
BECAUSE YOU ARE A SAD AND PATHETIC OLD DRUNK, VAUGHN. AND BECAUSE DESPITE YOUR EVERY EFFORT TO ENSURE THAT I DON'T... I REMEMBER THE MAN YOU USED TO BE. WHAT HAPPENED TO THAT MAN, VAUGHN?
I'M TRYING TO TELL YOU, I WAS A COWARD. I WAS A COWARD, OKAY? BUT I'VE CHANGED. I'M BACK.
...
I SHOULD LEAVE YOU HERE TO ROT.
...
YOUR BOYFRIEND THE MAYOR TELL YOU TO DO THAT?

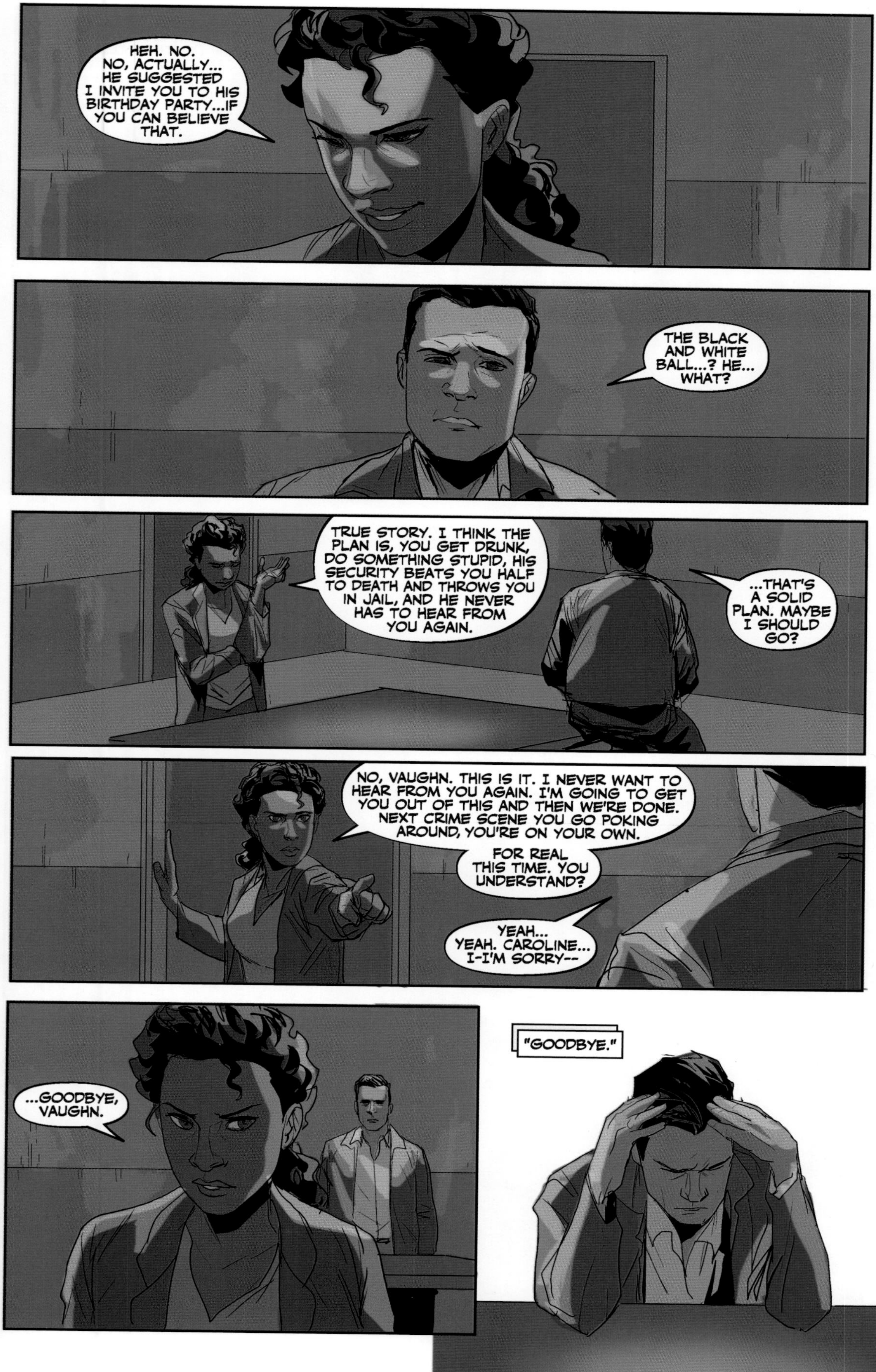
HEH. NO. NO, ACTUALLY... HE SUGGESTED I INVITE YOU TO HIS BIRTHDAY PARTY...IF YOU CAN BELIEVE THAT.
THE BLACK AND WHITE BALL...? HE... WHAT?
TRUE STORY. I THINK THE PLAN IS, YOU GET DRUNK, DO SOMETHING STUPID, HIS SECURITY BEATS YOU HALF TO DEATH AND THROWS YOU IN JAIL, AND HE NEVER HAS TO HEAR FROM YOU AGAIN.
...THAT'S A SOLID PLAN. MAYBE I SHOULD GO?
NO, VAUGHN. THIS IS IT. I NEVER WANT TO HEAR FROM YOU AGAIN. I'M GOING TO GET YOU OUT OF THIS AND THEN WE'RE DONE. NEXT CRIME SCENE YOU GO POKING AROUND, YOU'RE ON YOUR OWN.
FOR REAL THIS TIME. YOU UNDERSTAND?
YEAH... YEAH. CAROLINE... I-I'M SORRY--
...GOODBYE, VAUGHN.
"GOODBYE."

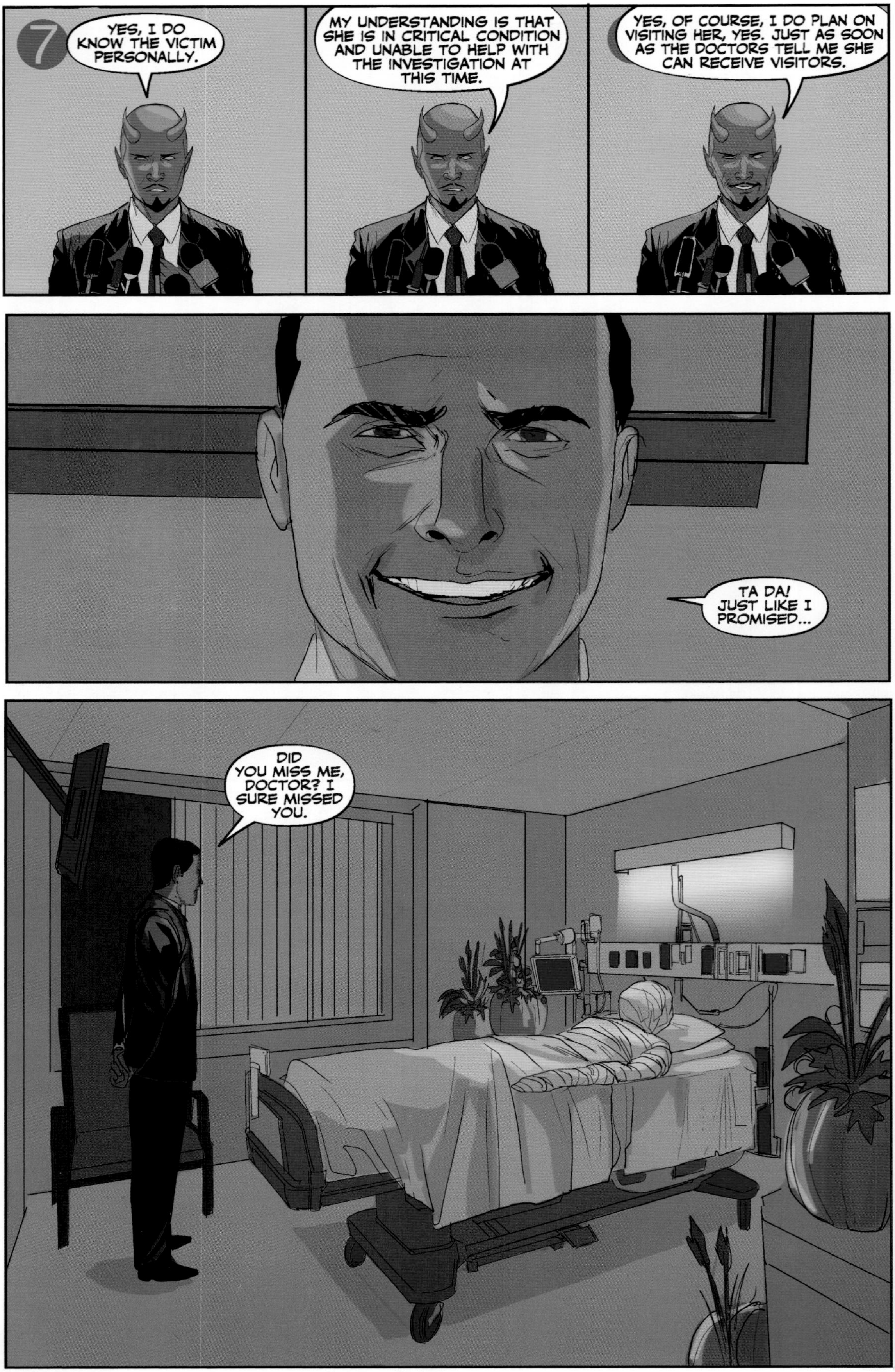
YES, I DO KNOW THE VICTIM PERSONALLY.
MY UNDERSTANDING IS THAT SHE IS IN CRITICAL CONDITION AND UNABLE TO HELP WITH THE INVESTIGATION AT THIS TIME.
YES, OF COURSE, I DO PLAN ON VISITING HER, YES. JUST AS SOON AS THE DOCTORS TELL ME SHE CAN RECEIVE VISITORS.
TA DA! JUST LIKE I PROMISED...
DID YOU MISS ME, DOCTOR? I SURE MISSED YOU.

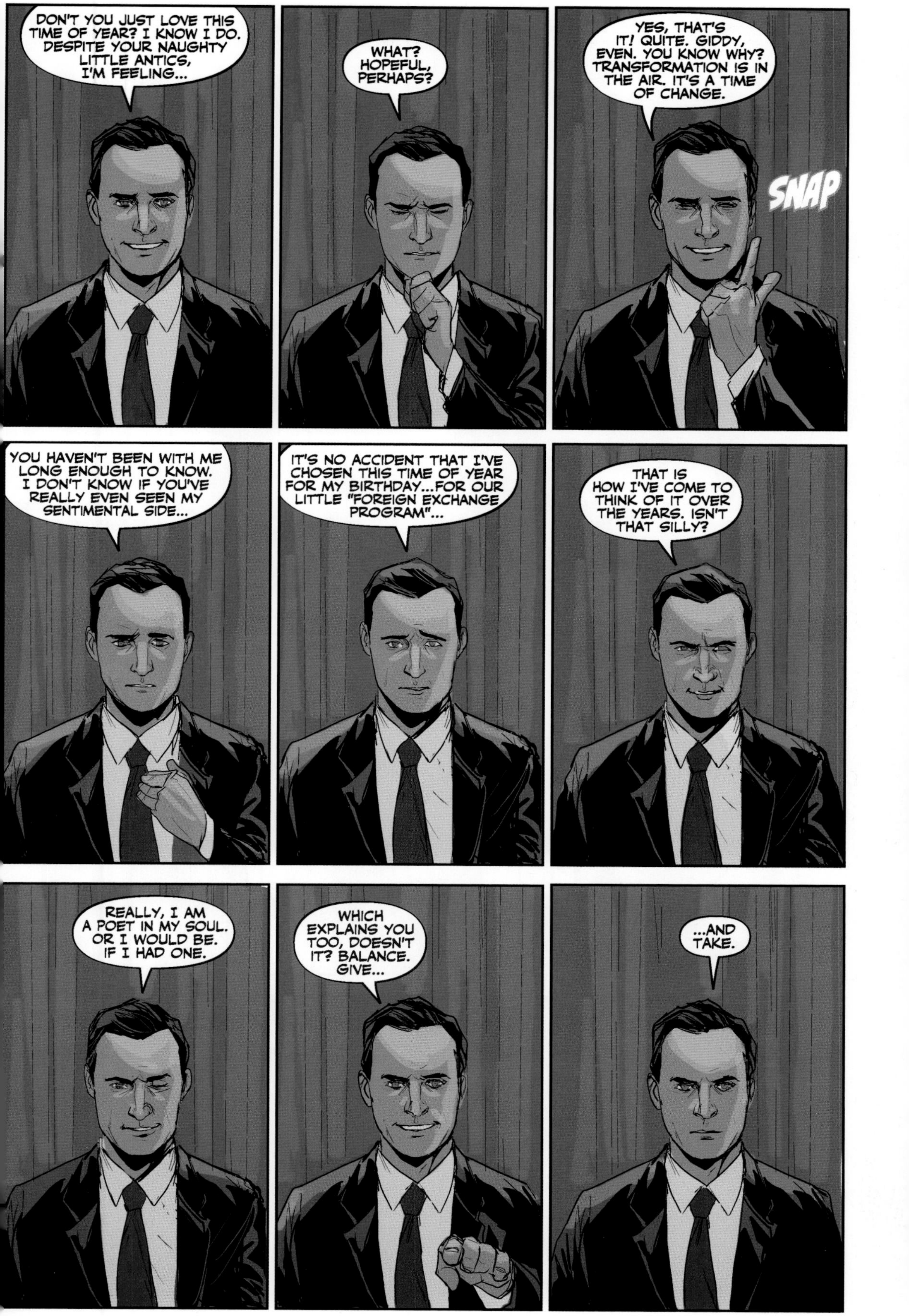
DON'T YOU JUST LOVE THIS TIME OF YEAR? I KNOW I DO. DESPITE YOUR NAUGHTY LITTLE ANTICS, I'M FEELING...
WHAT? HOPEFUL, PERHAPS?
YES, THAT'S IT! QUITE. GIDDY, EVEN. YOU KNOW WHY? TRANSFORMATION IS IN THE AIR. IT'S A TIME OF CHANGE.
SNAP
YOU HAVEN'T BEEN WITH ME LONG ENOUGH TO KNOW. I DON'T KNOW IF YOU'VE REALLY EVEN SEEN MY SENTIMENTAL SIDE...
IT'S NO ACCIDENT THAT I'VE CHOSEN THIS TIME OF YEAR FOR MY BIRTHDAY...FOR OUR LITTLE "FOREIGN EXCHANGE PROGRAM"...
THAT IS HOW I'VE COME TO THINK OF IT OVER THE YEARS. ISN'T THAT SILLY?
REALLY, I AM A POET IN MY SOUL. OR I WOULD BE. IF I HAD ONE.
WHICH EXPLAINS YOU TOO, DOESN'T IT? BALANCE. GIVE...
...AND TAKE.

I LOST MY DOCTOR...

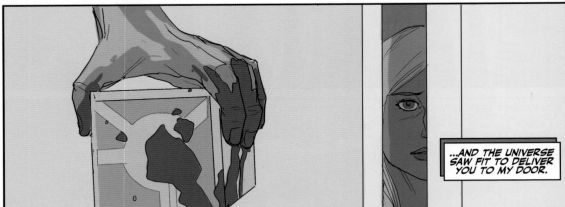

...AND THE UNIVERSE SAW FIT TO DELIVER YOU TO MY DOOR.

SO PRETTY...

...SO BROKEN...

...SO MAD.

AND THEN WITH A NAME LIKE "OCTOBER"?

WHAT AM I, MADE OF STEEL?

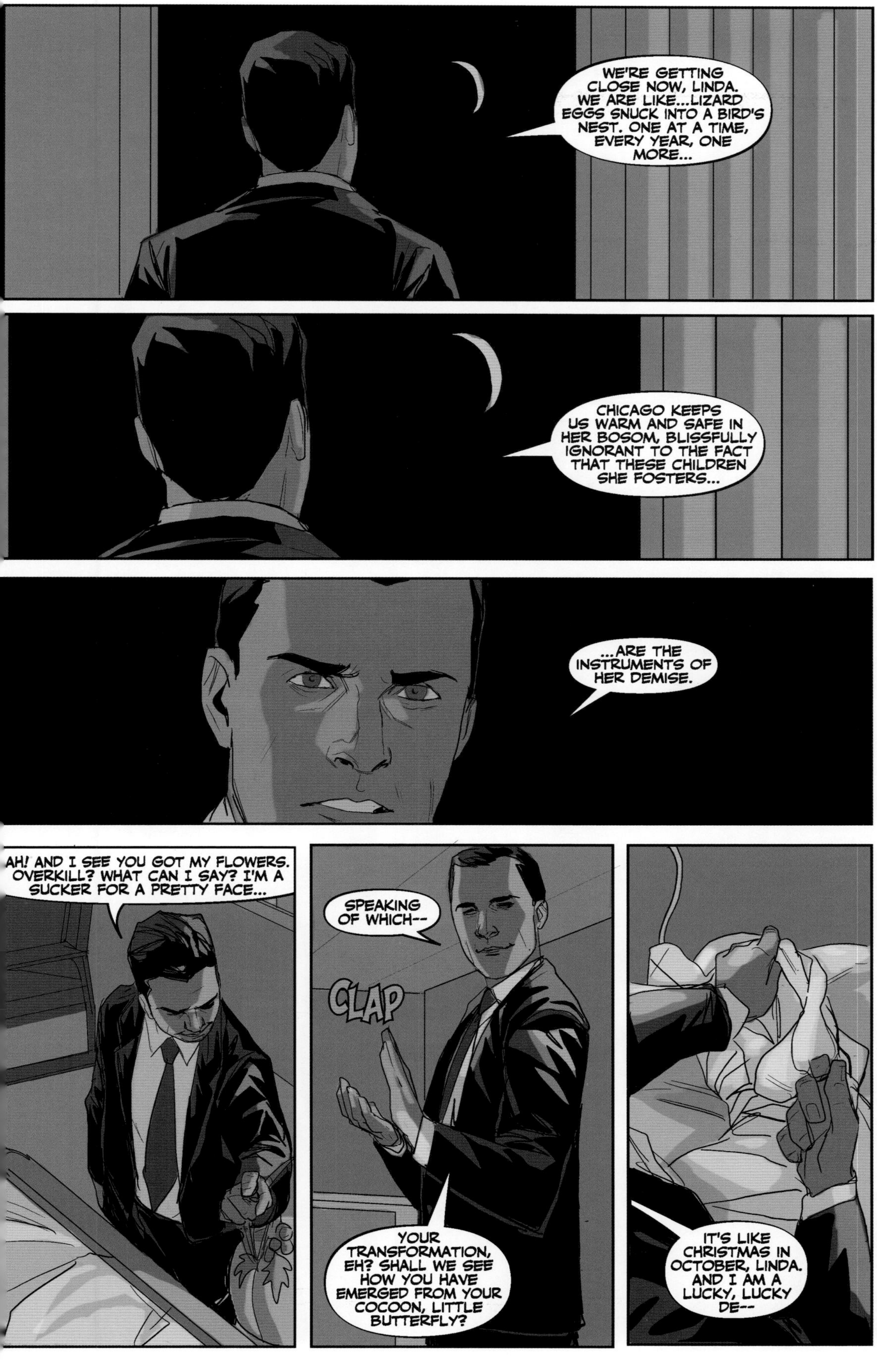
WE'RE GETTING CLOSE NOW, LINDA. WE ARE LIKE...LIZARD EGGS SNUCK INTO A BIRD'S NEST. ONE AT A TIME, EVERY YEAR, ONE MORE...
CHICAGO KEEPS US WARM AND SAFE IN HER BOSOM, BLISSFULLY IGNORANT TO THE FACT THAT THESE CHILDREN SHE FOSTERS...
...ARE THE INSTRUMENTS OF HER DEMISE.
AH! AND I SEE YOU GOT MY FLOWERS. OVERKILL? WHAT CAN I SAY? I'M A SUCKER FOR A PRETTY FACE...
SPEAKING OF WHICH--
CLAP
YOUR TRANSFORMATION, EH? SHALL WE SEE HOW YOU HAVE EMERGED FROM YOUR COCOON, LITTLE BUTTERFLY?
IT'S LIKE CHRISTMAS IN OCTOBER, LINDA. AND I AM A LUCKY, LUCKY DE--

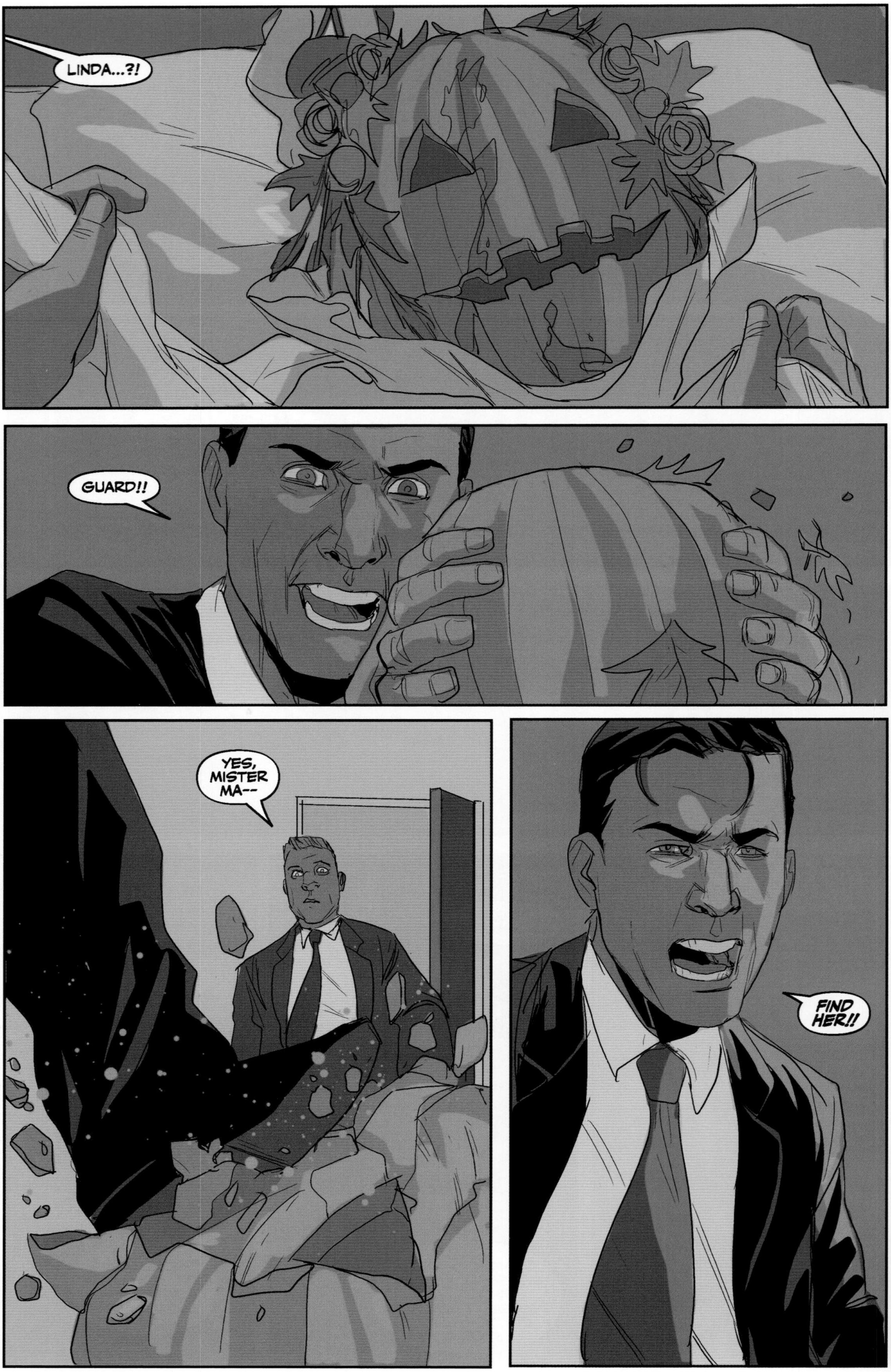
LINDA...?!
GUARD!!
YES, MISTER MA--
FIND HER!!

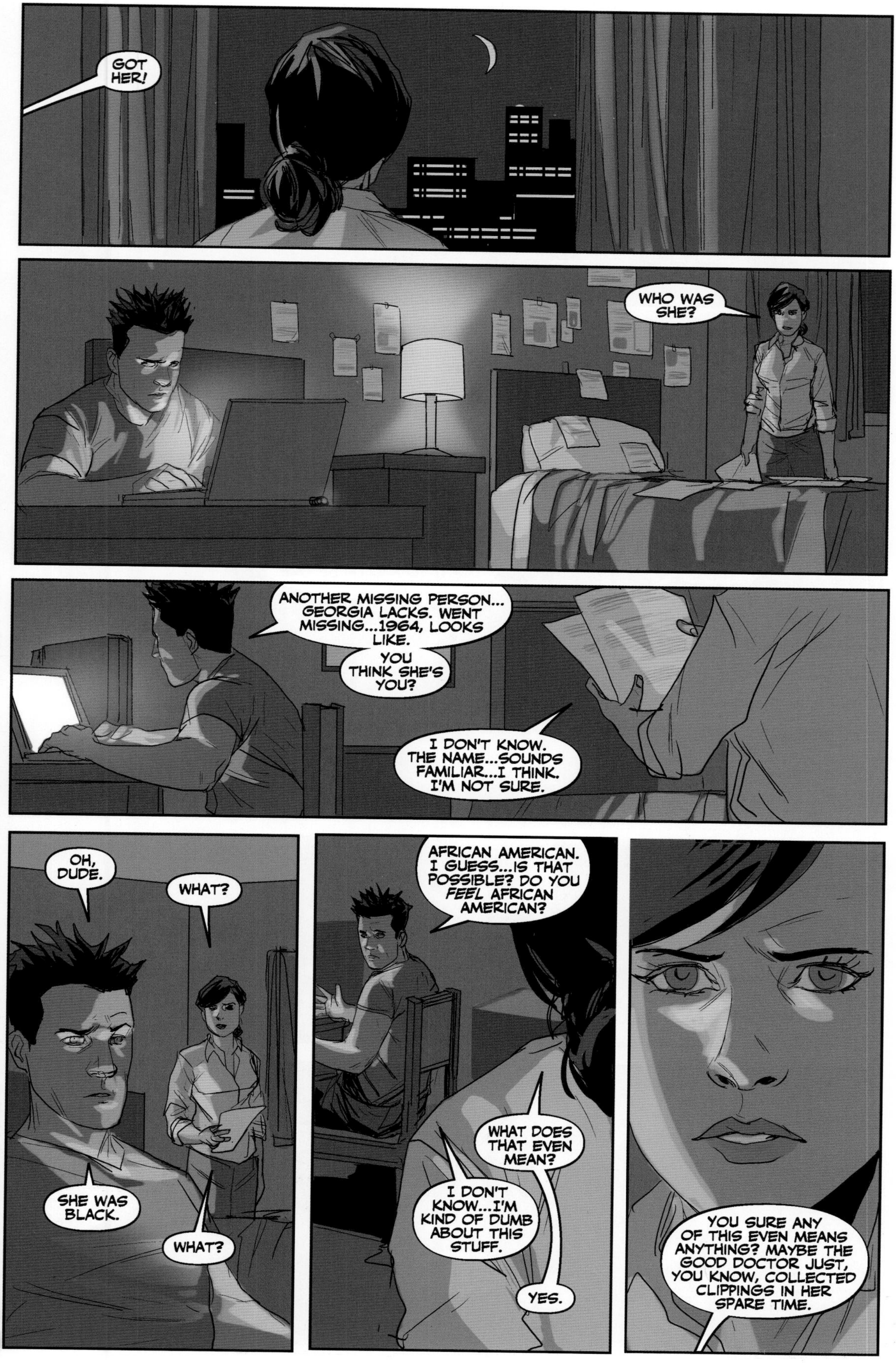
GOT HER!
WHO WAS SHE?
ANOTHER MISSING PERSON... GEORGIA LACKS. WENT MISSING...1964, LOOKS LIKE.
YOU THINK SHE'S YOU?
I DON'T KNOW. THE NAME...SOUNDS FAMILIAR...I THINK. I'M NOT SURE.
OH, DUDE.
WHAT?
SHE WAS BLACK.
WHAT?
AFRICAN AMERICAN. I GUESS...IS THAT POSSIBLE? DO YOU *FEEL* AFRICAN AMERICAN?
WHAT DOES THAT EVEN MEAN?
I DON'T KNOW...I'M KIND OF DUMB ABOUT THIS STUFF.
YES.
YOU SURE ANY OF THIS EVEN MEANS ANYTHING? MAYBE THE GOOD DOCTOR JUST, YOU KNOW, COLLECTED CLIPPINGS IN HER SPARE TIME.

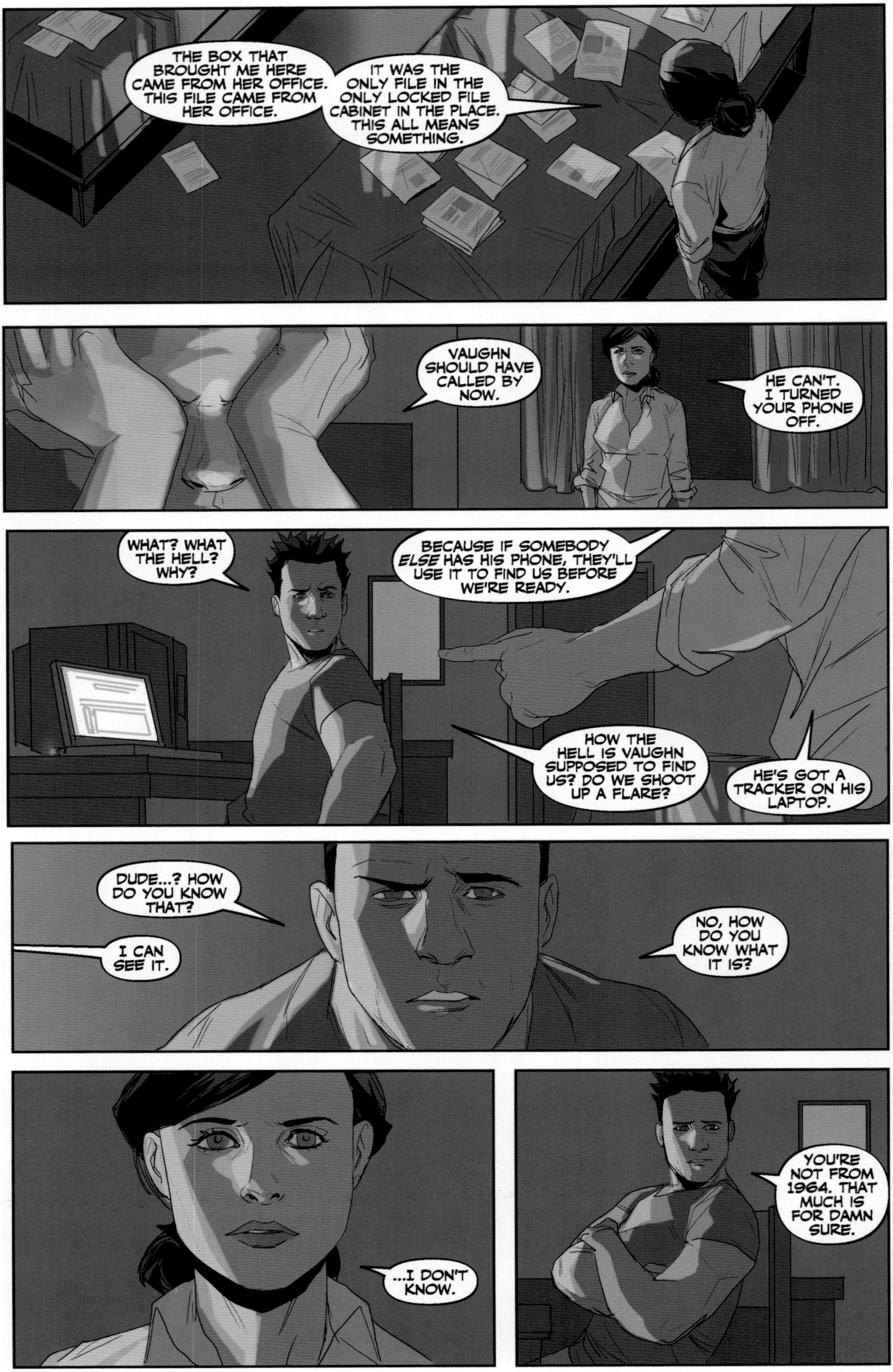
THE BOX THAT BROUGHT ME HERE CAME FROM HER OFFICE. THIS FILE CAME FROM HER OFFICE.
IT WAS THE ONLY FILE IN THE ONLY LOCKED FILE CABINET IN THE PLACE. THIS ALL MEANS SOMETHING.
VAUGHN SHOULD HAVE CALLED BY NOW.
HE CAN'T. I TURNED YOUR PHONE OFF.
WHAT? WHAT THE HELL? WHY?
BECAUSE IF SOMEBODY *ELSE* HAS HIS PHONE, THEY'LL USE IT TO FIND US BEFORE WE'RE READY.
HOW THE HELL IS VAUGHN SUPPOSED TO FIND US? DO WE SHOOT UP A FLARE?
HE'S GOT A TRACKER ON HIS LAPTOP.
DUDE...? HOW DO YOU KNOW THAT?
I CAN SEE IT.
NO, HOW DO YOU KNOW WHAT IT IS?
...I DON'T KNOW.
YOU'RE NOT FROM 1964. THAT MUCH IS FOR DAMN SURE.

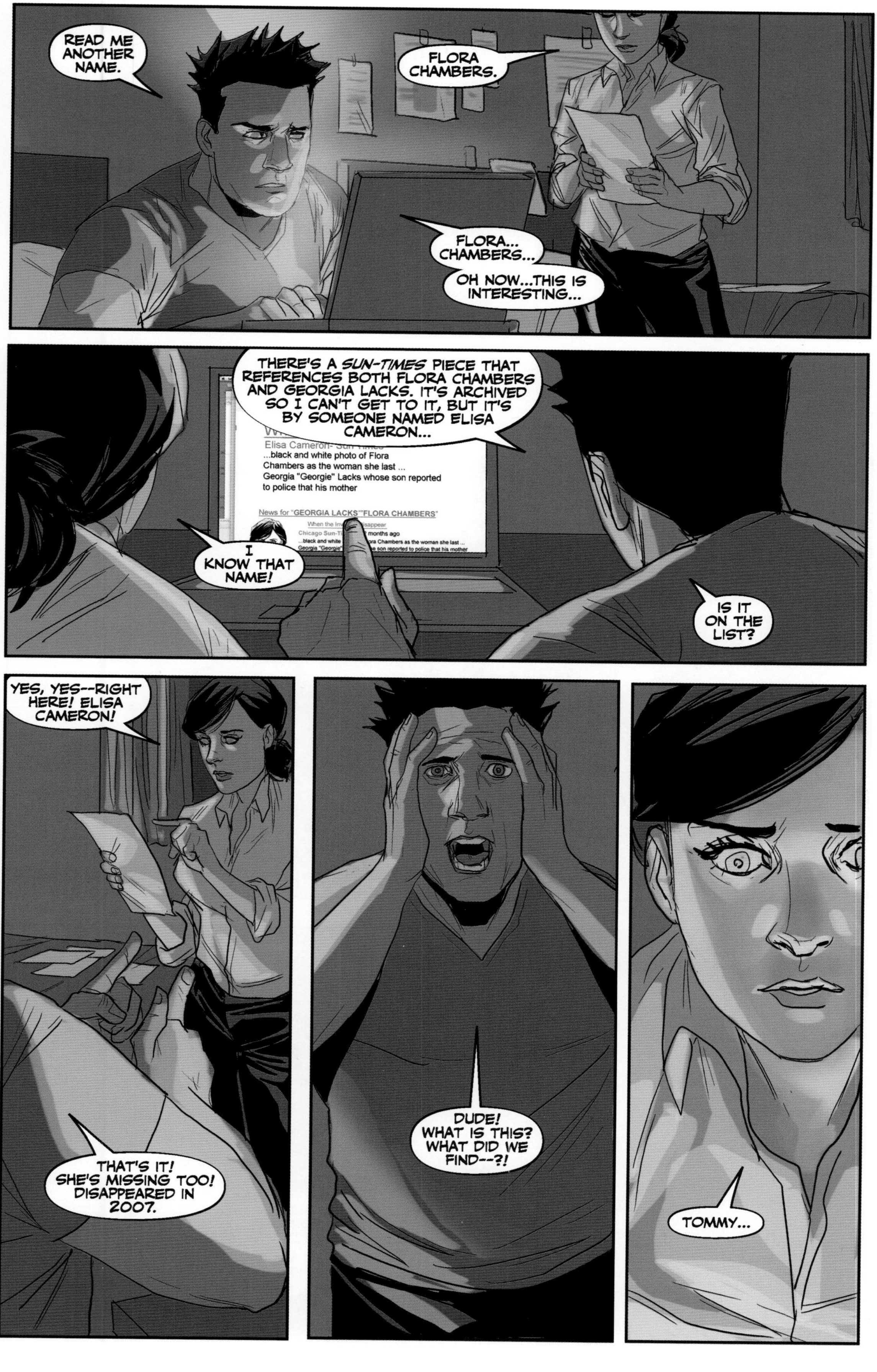
READ ME ANOTHER NAME.
FLORA CHAMBERS.
FLORA... CHAMBERS...
OH NOW...THIS IS INTERESTING...
THERE'S A SUN-TIMES PIECE THAT REFERENCES BOTH FLORA CHAMBERS AND GEORGIA LACKS. IT'S ARCHIVED SO I CAN'T GET TO IT, BUT IT'S BY SOMEONE NAMED ELISA CAMERON...
...black and white photo of Flora Chambers as the woman she last ... Georgia "Georgie" Lacks whose son reported to police that his mother
News for "GEORGIA LACKS" "FLORA CHAMBERS"
I KNOW THAT NAME!
IS IT ON THE LIST?
YES, YES--RIGHT HERE! ELISA CAMERON!
THAT'S IT! SHE'S MISSING TOO! DISAPPEARED IN 2007.
DUDE! WHAT IS THIS? WHAT DID WE FIND--?!
TOMMY...

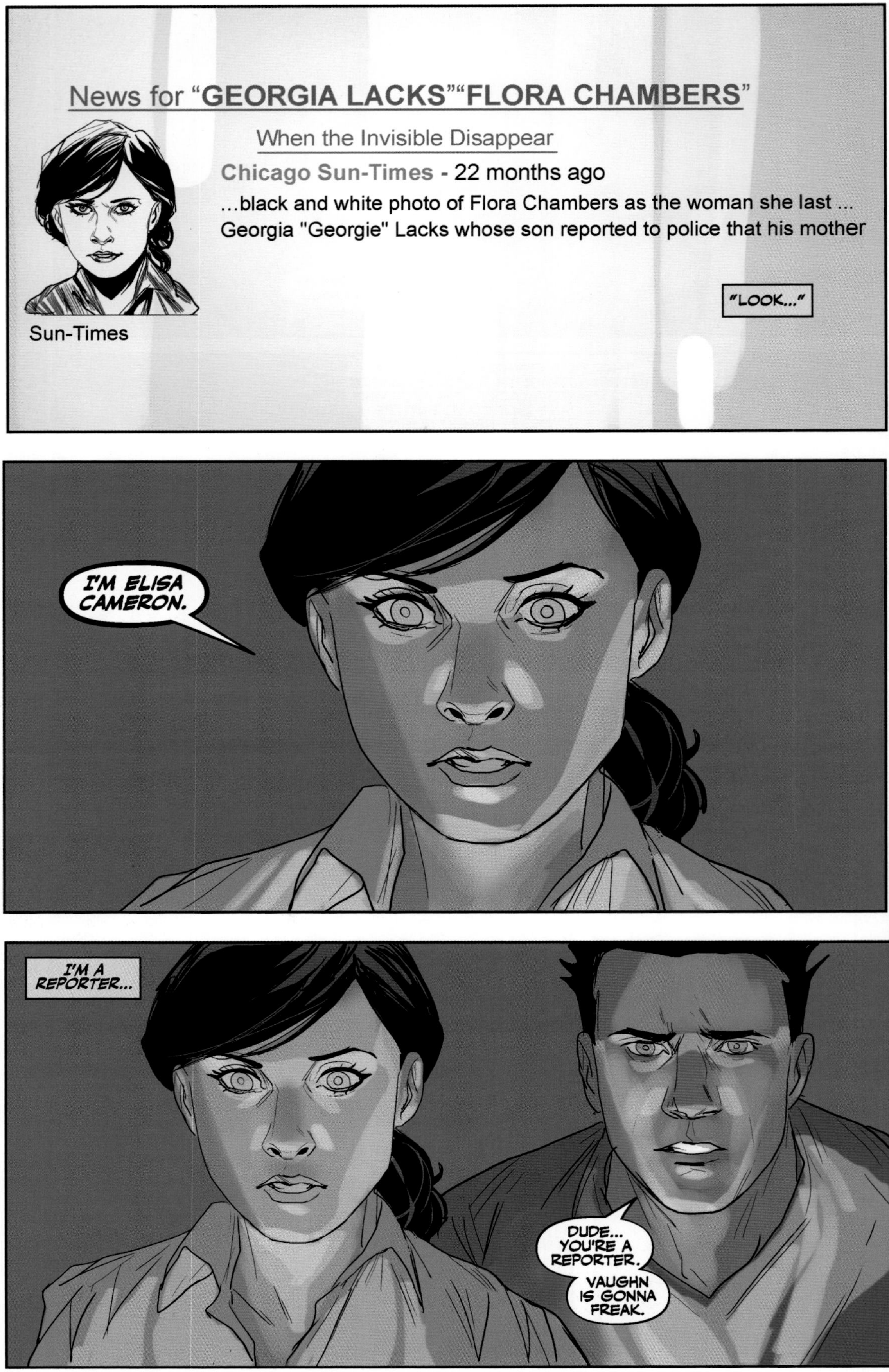
News for "GEORGIA LACKS""FLORA CHAMBERS"
When the Invisible Disappear
Chicago Sun-Times - 22 months ago
...black and white photo of Flora Chambers as the woman she last ...
Georgia "Georgie" Lacks whose son reported to police that his mother
Sun-Times
"LOOK..."
I'M ELISA CAMERON.
I'M A REPORTER...
DUDE... YOU'RE A REPORTER.
VAUGHN IS GONNA FREAK.

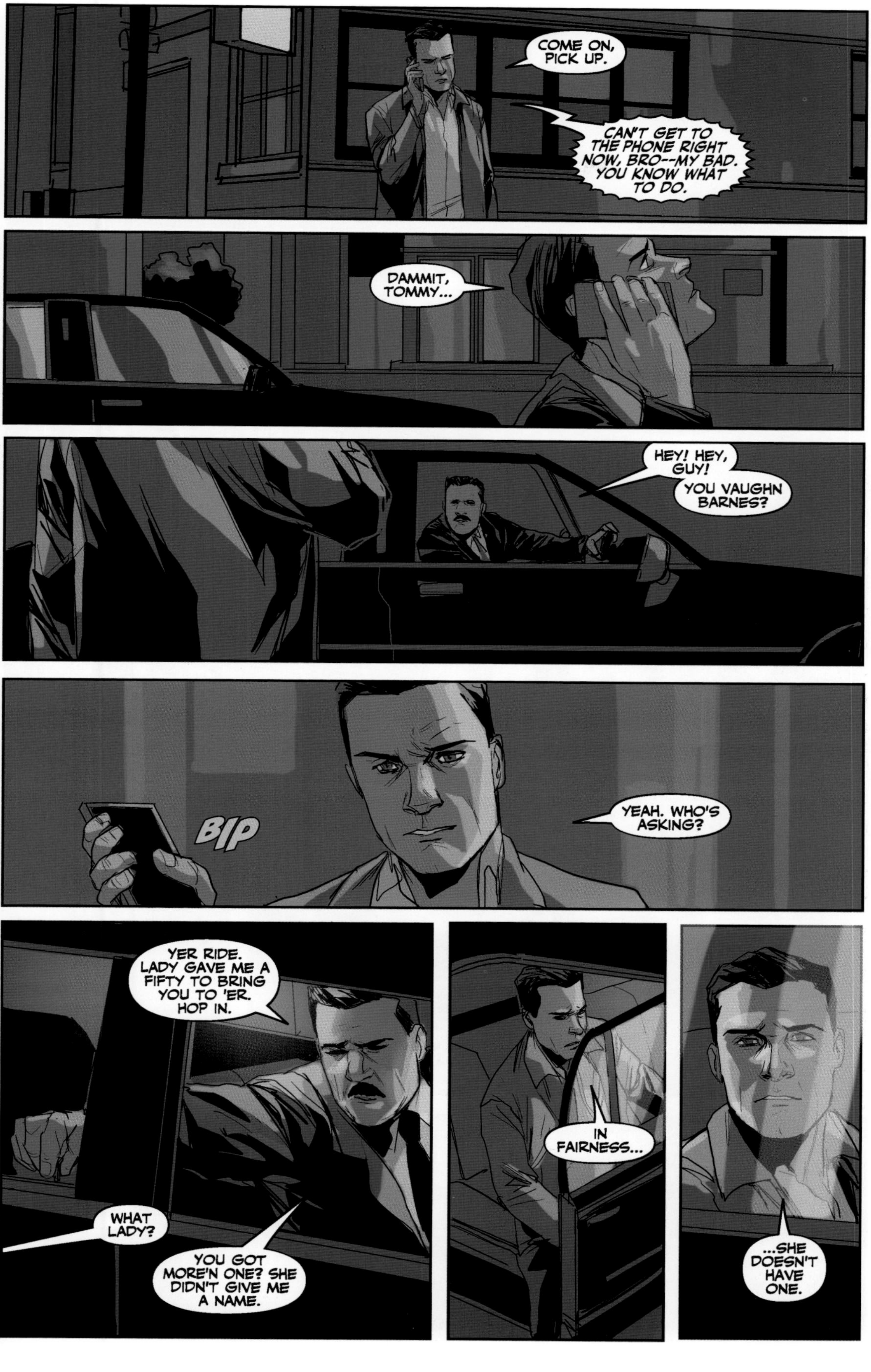
COME ON, PICK UP.
CAN'T GET TO THE PHONE RIGHT NOW, BRO--MY BAD. YOU KNOW WHAT TO DO.
DAMMIT, TOMMY...
HEY! HEY, GUY!
YOU VAUGHN BARNES?
BIP
YEAH. WHO'S ASKING?
YER RIDE. LADY GAVE ME A FIFTY TO BRING YOU TO 'ER. HOP IN.
WHAT LADY?
YOU GOT MORE'N ONE? SHE DIDN'T GIVE ME A NAME.
IN FAIRNESS...
...SHE DOESN'T HAVE ONE.

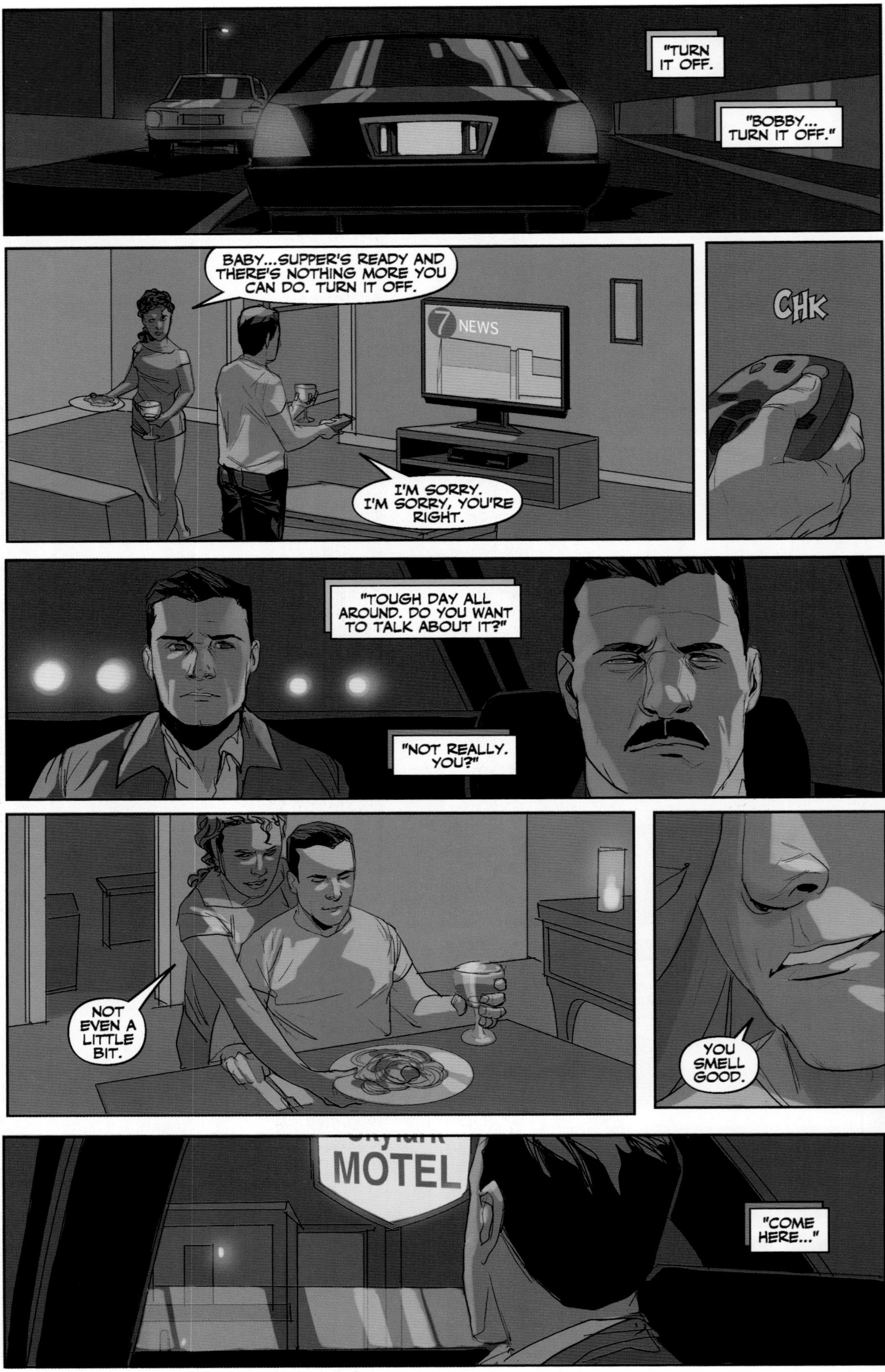
"TURN IT OFF.
"BOBBY... TURN IT OFF."
BABY...SUPPER'S READY AND THERE'S NOTHING MORE YOU CAN DO. TURN IT OFF.
7 NEWS
I'M SORRY. I'M SORRY, YOU'RE RIGHT.
CHK
"TOUGH DAY ALL AROUND. DO YOU WANT TO TALK ABOUT IT?"
"NOT REALLY. YOU?"
NOT EVEN A LITTLE BIT.
YOU SMELL GOOD.
MOTEL
"COME HERE..."

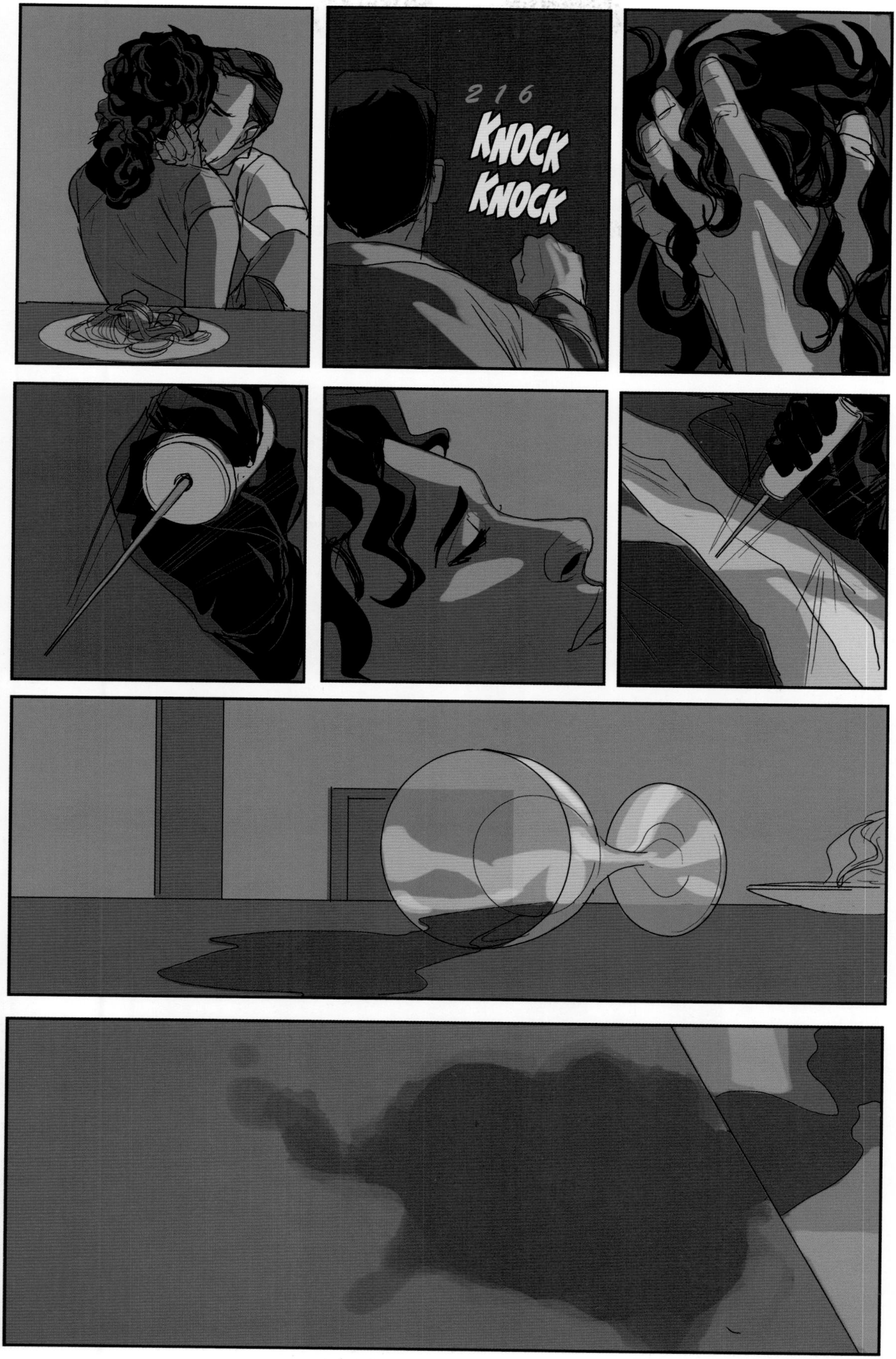
216
KNOCK
KNOCK

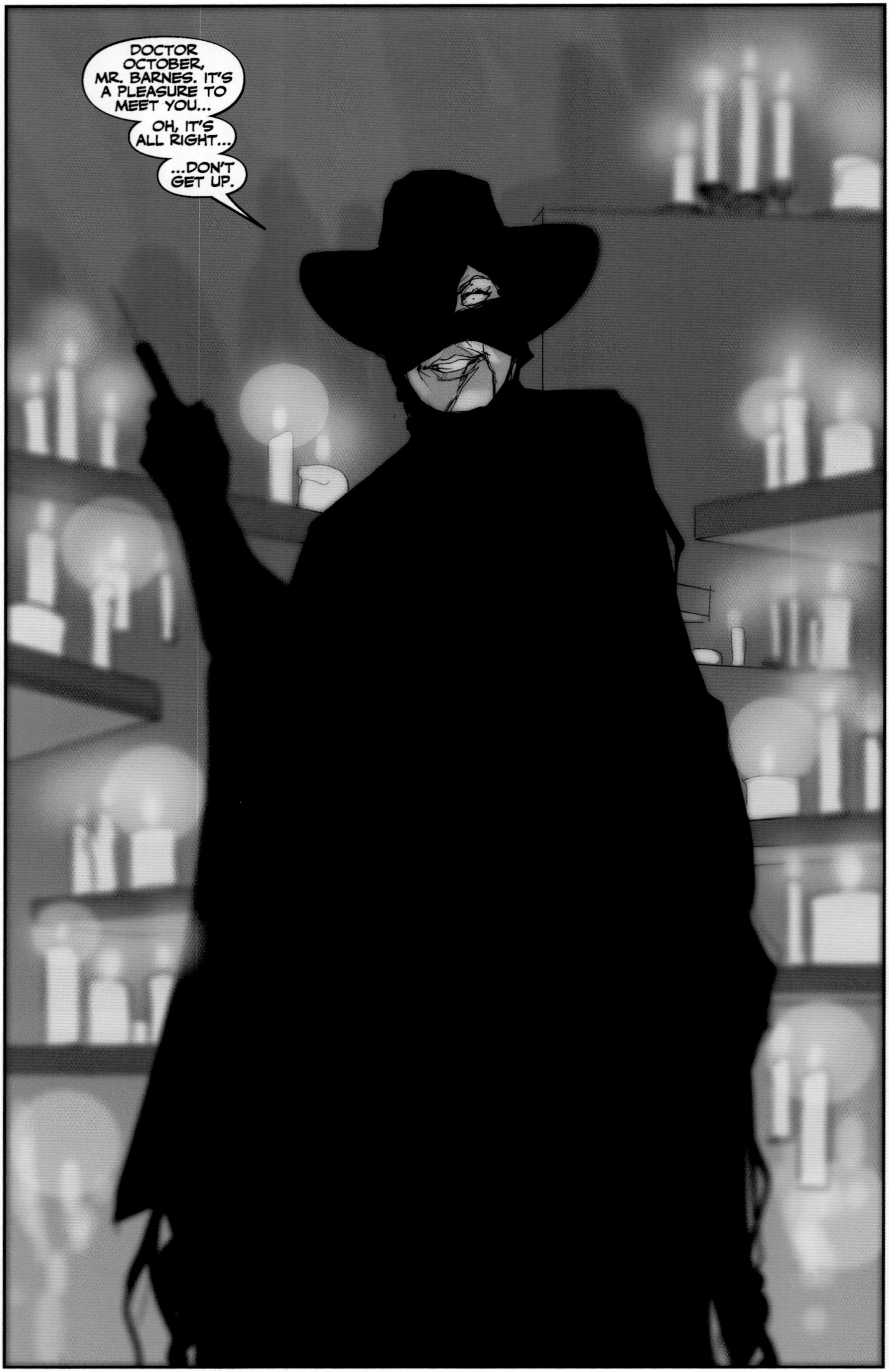
DOCTOR OCTOBER, MR. BARNES. IT'S A PLEASURE TO MEET YOU...
OH, IT'S ALL RIGHT...
...DON'T GET UP.

CHAPTER 3

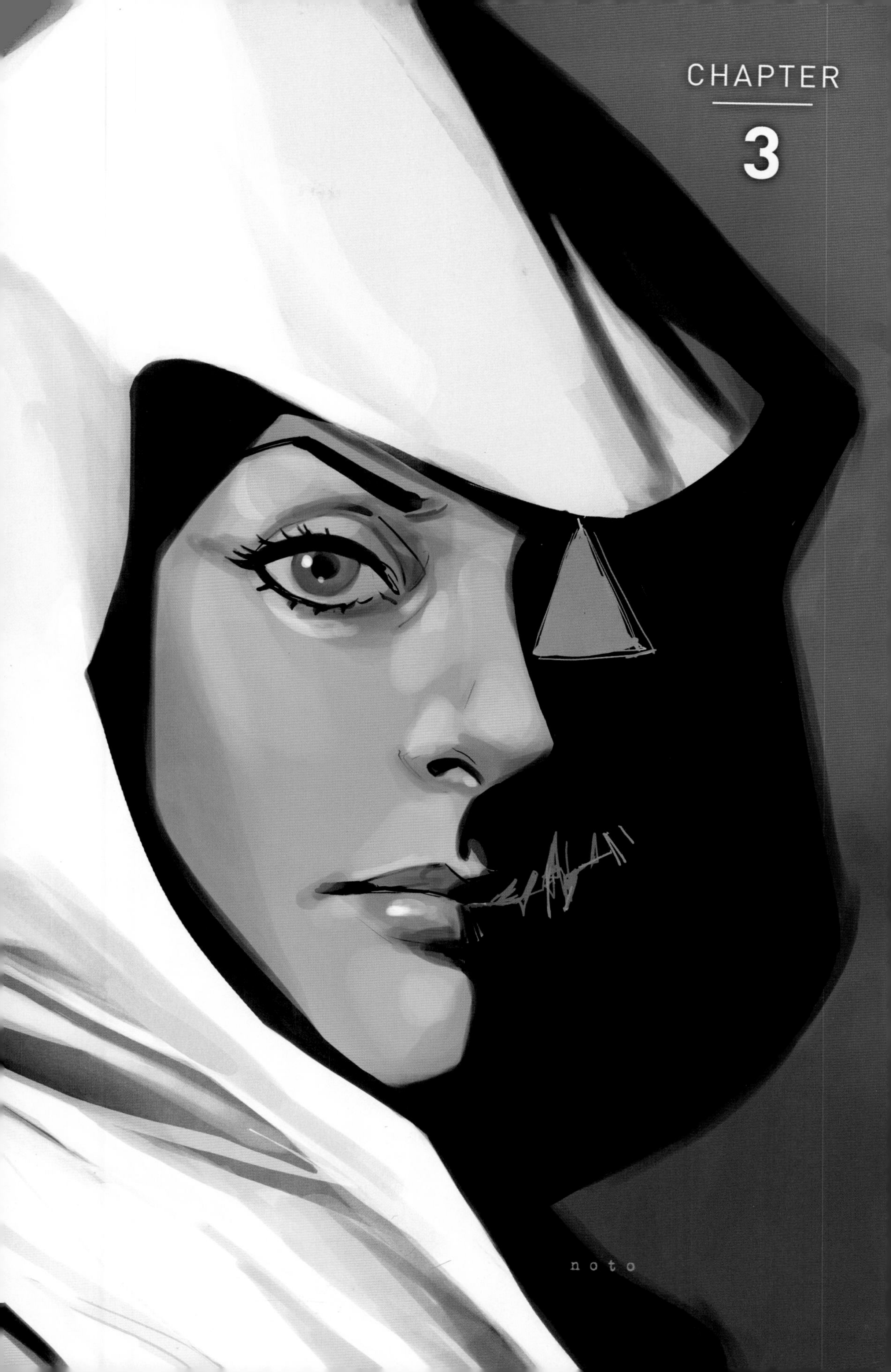
noto

"OF COURSE, NATURE DOES DEMAND BALANCE . . .
AND NATURE IS A CRUEL MISTRESS."

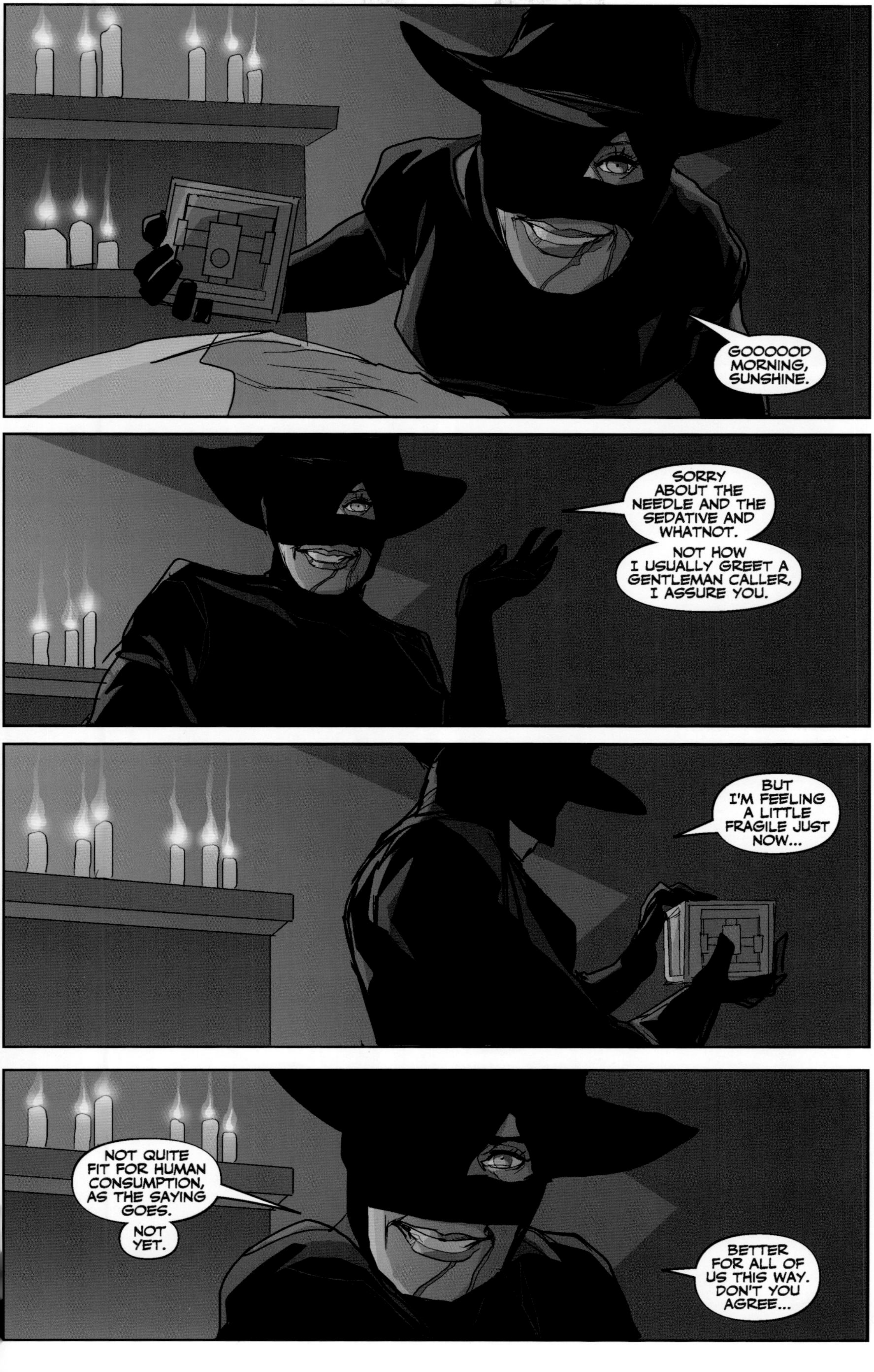
GOOOOOD MORNING, SUNSHINE.
SORRY ABOUT THE NEEDLE AND THE SEDATIVE AND WHATNOT.
NOT HOW I USUALLY GREET A GENTLEMAN CALLER, I ASSURE YOU.
BUT I'M FEELING A LITTLE FRAGILE JUST NOW...
NOT QUITE FIT FOR HUMAN CONSUMPTION, AS THE SAYING GOES.
NOT YET.
BETTER FOR ALL OF US THIS WAY. DON'T YOU AGREE...

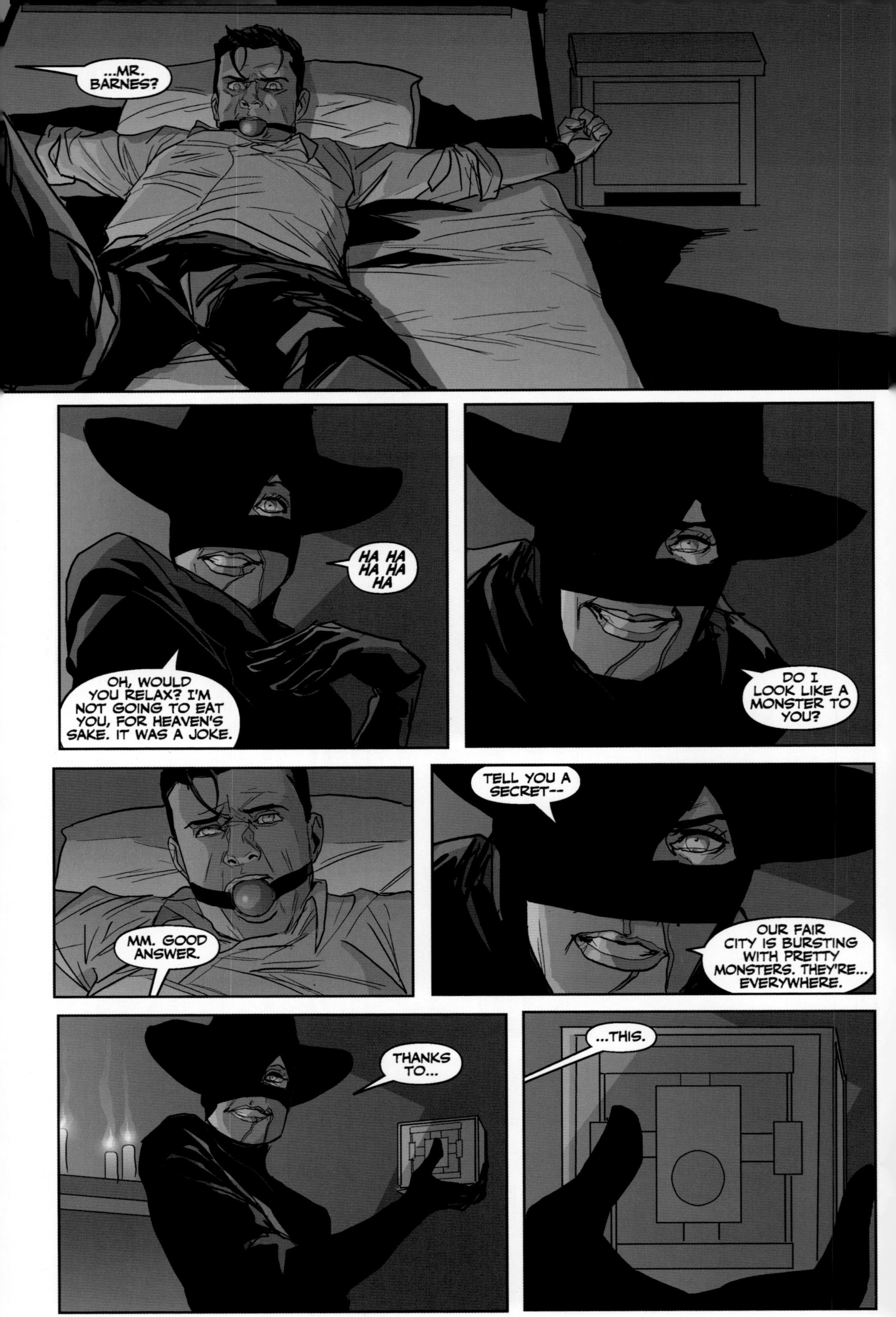
...MR. BARNES?
HA HA HA HA HA
OH, WOULD YOU RELAX? I'M NOT GOING TO EAT YOU, FOR HEAVEN'S SAKE. IT WAS A JOKE.
DO I LOOK LIKE A MONSTER TO YOU?
MM. GOOD ANSWER.
TELL YOU A SECRET--
OUR FAIR CITY IS BURSTING WITH PRETTY MONSTERS. THEY'RE... EVERYWHERE.
THANKS TO...
...THIS.

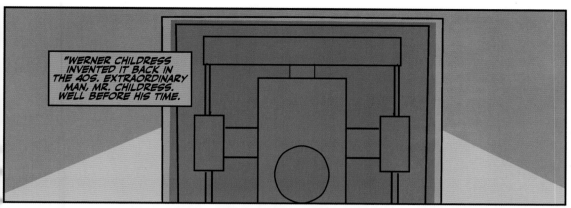

"WERNER CHILDRESS INVENTED IT BACK IN THE 40S. EXTRAORDINARY MAN, MR. CHILDRESS. WELL BEFORE HIS TIME.

"BIT PRONE TO SUPERSTITION, ALAS.

"THOUGHT HE'D WORKED OUT A WAY TO OPEN THE GATES OF HEAVEN...

"NOT SO MUCH.

"HE SHOULD HAVE KNOWN. NATURE AND SCIENCE BOTH DEMAND BALANCE.

"LAST WORDS WERE SOMETHING LIKE 'WAY TO GO, GRANDPA.' I BET.

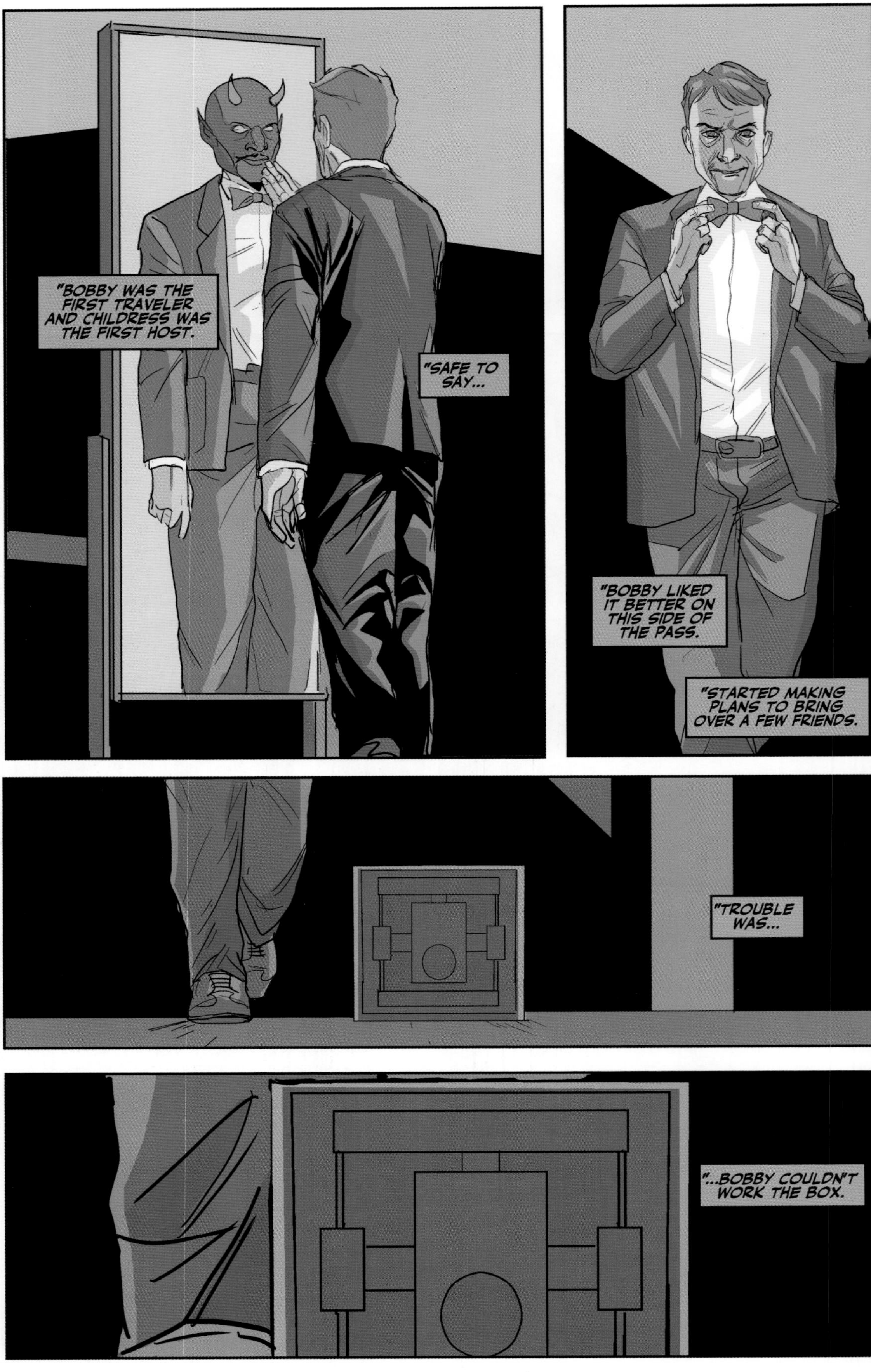
"BOBBY WAS THE FIRST TRAVELER AND CHILDRESS WAS THE FIRST HOST.
"SAFE TO SAY...
"BOBBY LIKED IT BETTER ON THIS SIDE OF THE PASS.
"STARTED MAKING PLANS TO BRING OVER A FEW FRIENDS.
"TROUBLE WAS...
"...BOBBY COULDN'T WORK THE BOX.

"DIDN'T LET THAT STOP HIM, THOUGH.

"BOBBY EXPLOITED EVERY CONNECTION THE OLD MAN HAD. INGRATIATED HIMSELF TO THE WEALTHY AND THE POWERFUL...

"WORKED HIS WAY UP, UNTIL...

"HE MADE HIS WAY INTO THE CHAMBERS FAMILY...

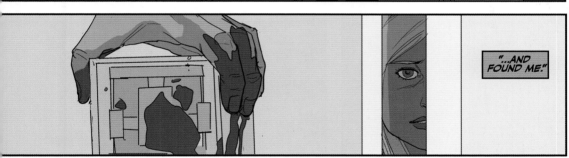

"..AND FOUND ME."

DID YOU KNOW THERE'S BEEN AT LEAST ONE CHAMBERS IN CITY HALL EVERY YEAR SINCE 1955?

"YOU EVER WONDER ABOUT THAT?

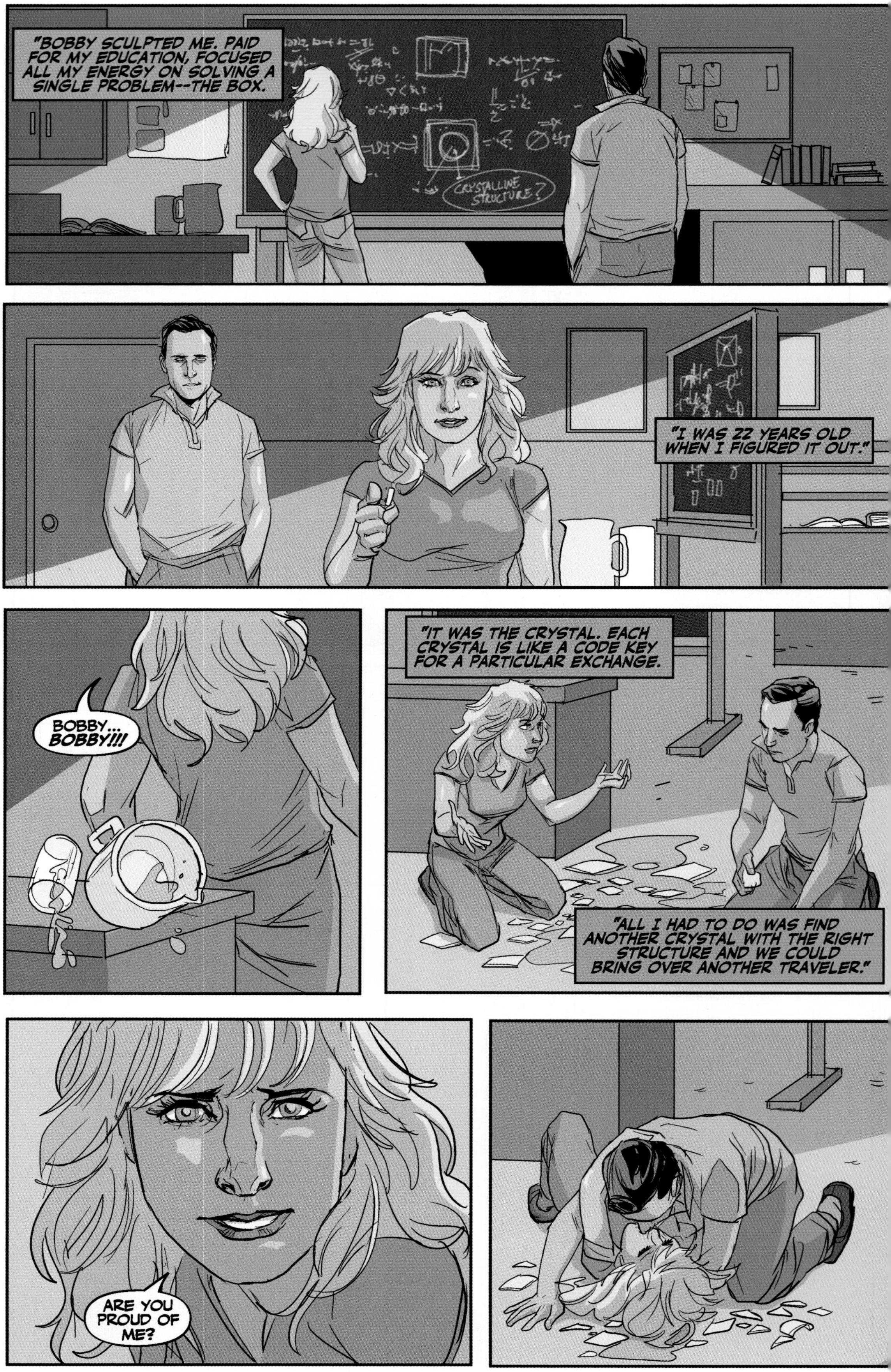
"BOBBY SCULPTED ME. PAID FOR MY EDUCATION, FOCUSED ALL MY ENERGY ON SOLVING A SINGLE PROBLEM--THE BOX.
CRYSTALLINE STRUCTURE?
"I WAS 22 YEARS OLD WHEN I FIGURED IT OUT."
BOBBY... BOBBY!!!
"IT WAS THE CRYSTAL. EACH CRYSTAL IS LIKE A CODE KEY FOR A PARTICULAR EXCHANGE.
"ALL I HAD TO DO WAS FIND ANOTHER CRYSTAL WITH THE RIGHT STRUCTURE AND WE COULD BRING OVER ANOTHER TRAVELER."
ARE YOU PROUD OF ME?

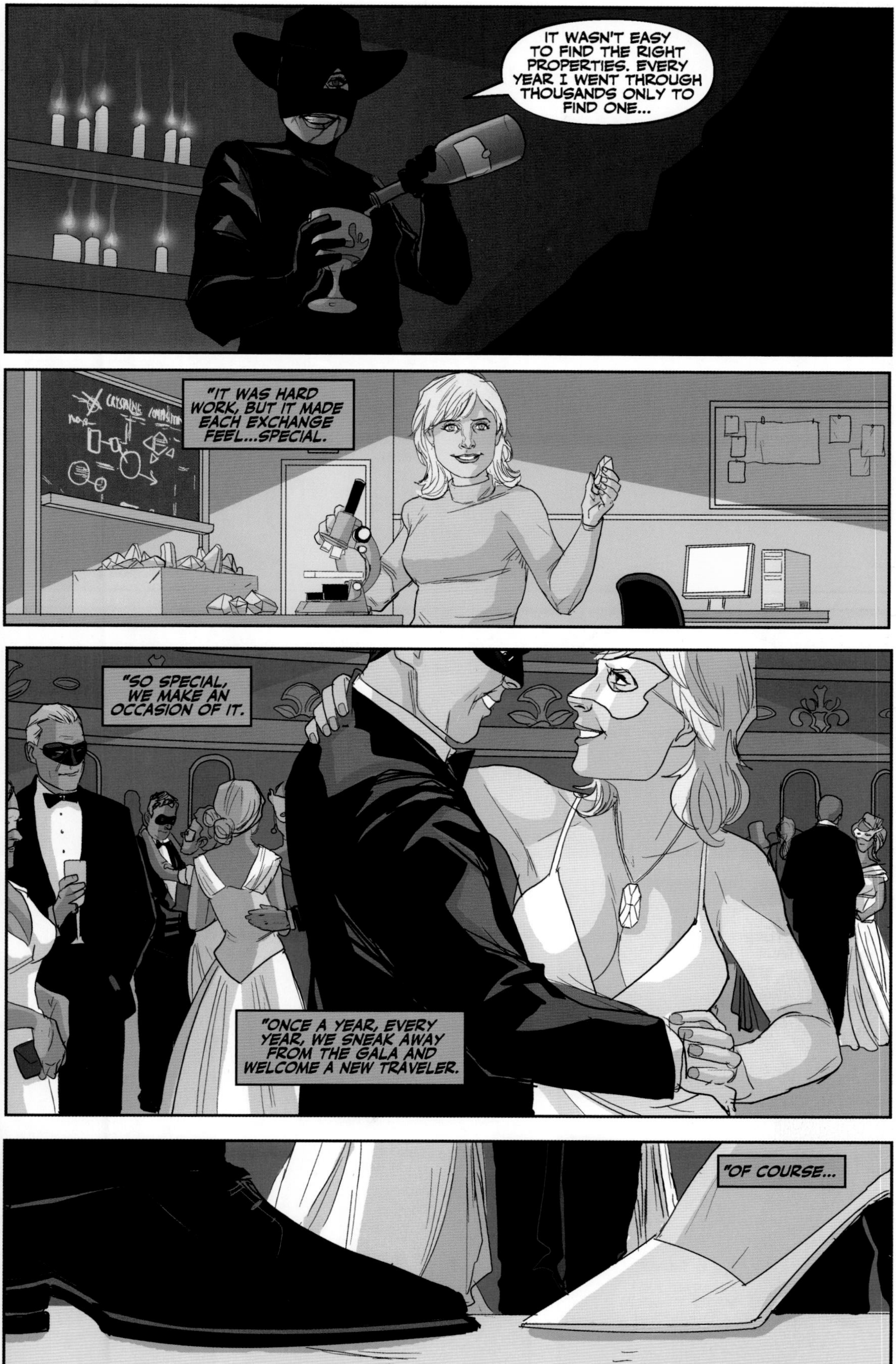
IT WASN'T EASY TO FIND THE RIGHT PROPERTIES. EVERY YEAR I WENT THROUGH THOUSANDS ONLY TO FIND ONE...
"IT WAS HARD WORK, BUT IT MADE EACH EXCHANGE FEEL...SPECIAL.
"SO SPECIAL, WE MAKE AN OCCASION OF IT.
"ONCE A YEAR, EVERY YEAR, WE SNEAK AWAY FROM THE GALA AND WELCOME A NEW TRAVELER.
"OF COURSE...

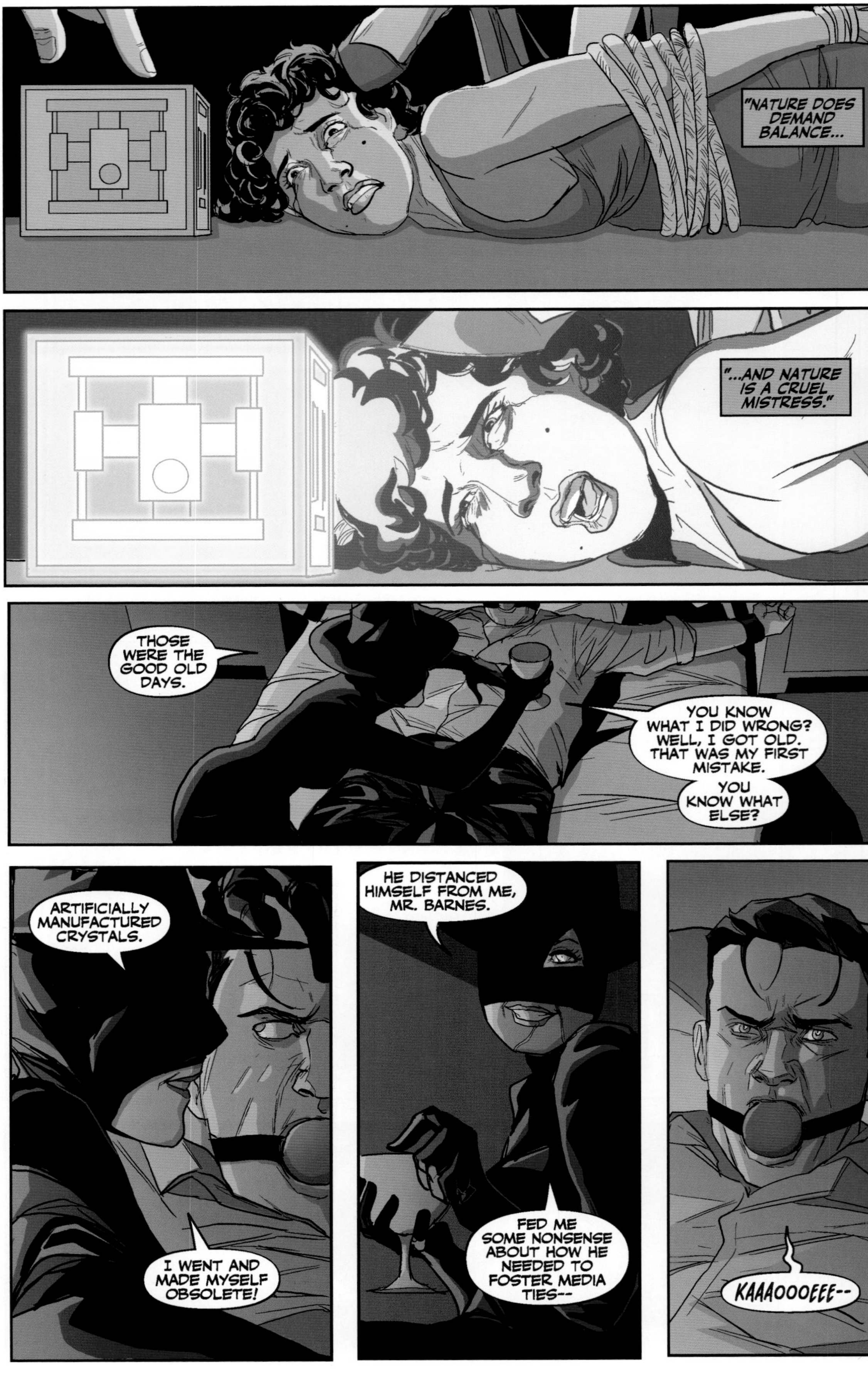
"NATURE DOES DEMAND BALANCE...
"...AND NATURE IS A CRUEL MISTRESS."
THOSE WERE THE GOOD OLD DAYS.
YOU KNOW WHAT I DID WRONG? WELL, I GOT OLD. THAT WAS MY FIRST MISTAKE.
YOU KNOW WHAT ELSE?
ARTIFICIALLY MANUFACTURED CRYSTALS.
I WENT AND MADE MYSELF OBSOLETE!
HE DISTANCED HIMSELF FROM ME, MR. BARNES.
FED ME SOME NONSENSE ABOUT HOW HE NEEDED TO FOSTER MEDIA TIES--
KAAAOOOEEE--

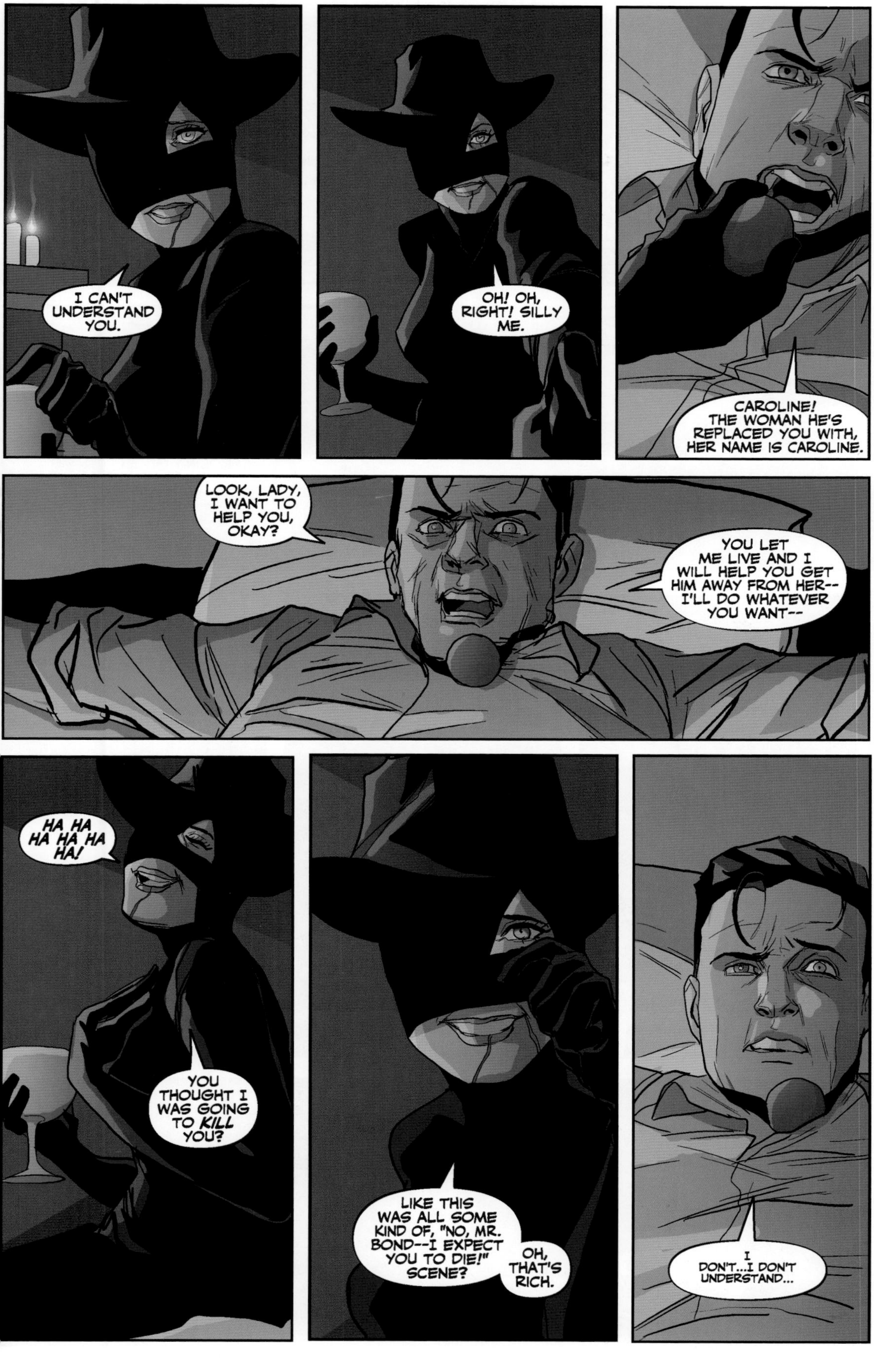
I CAN'T UNDERSTAND YOU.
OH! OH, RIGHT! SILLY ME.
CAROLINE! THE WOMAN HE'S REPLACED YOU WITH, HER NAME IS CAROLINE.
LOOK, LADY, I WANT TO HELP YOU, OKAY?
YOU LET ME LIVE AND I WILL HELP YOU GET HIM AWAY FROM HER-- I'LL DO WHATEVER YOU WANT--
HA HA HA HA HA HA!
YOU THOUGHT I WAS GOING TO KILL YOU?
LIKE THIS WAS ALL SOME KIND OF, "NO, MR. BOND--I EXPECT YOU TO DIE!" SCENE?
OH, THAT'S RICH.
I DON'T...I DON'T UNDERSTAND...

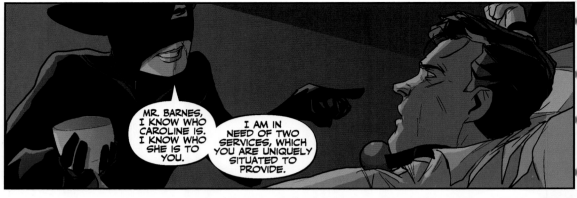

MR. BARNES, I KNOW WHO CAROLINE IS. I KNOW WHO SHE IS TO YOU.

I AM IN NEED OF TWO SERVICES, WHICH YOU ARE UNIQUELY SITUATED TO PROVIDE.

ONE, I NEED SOMETHING PRECIOUS TO MS. HITCHENS. SOMETHING I CAN TAKE FROM HER, THE WAY SHE TOOK MY BOBBY FROM ME--

I SWEAR, LADY, IF YOU THINK CAROLINE GIVES A RAT'S--

--AH AH!

DON'T ARGUE AGAINST YOUR OWN BEST INTERESTS, MR. BARNES.

AND TWO, I NEED A NEW PARTNER.

TALL, DARK, AND HANDSOME WOULD BE MY PREFERENCE, BUT YOU'LL DO.

BUT MOST IMPORTANTLY, I NEED HIM TO BE STRONG.

ARE YOU STRONG, MR. BARNES?

KRSH

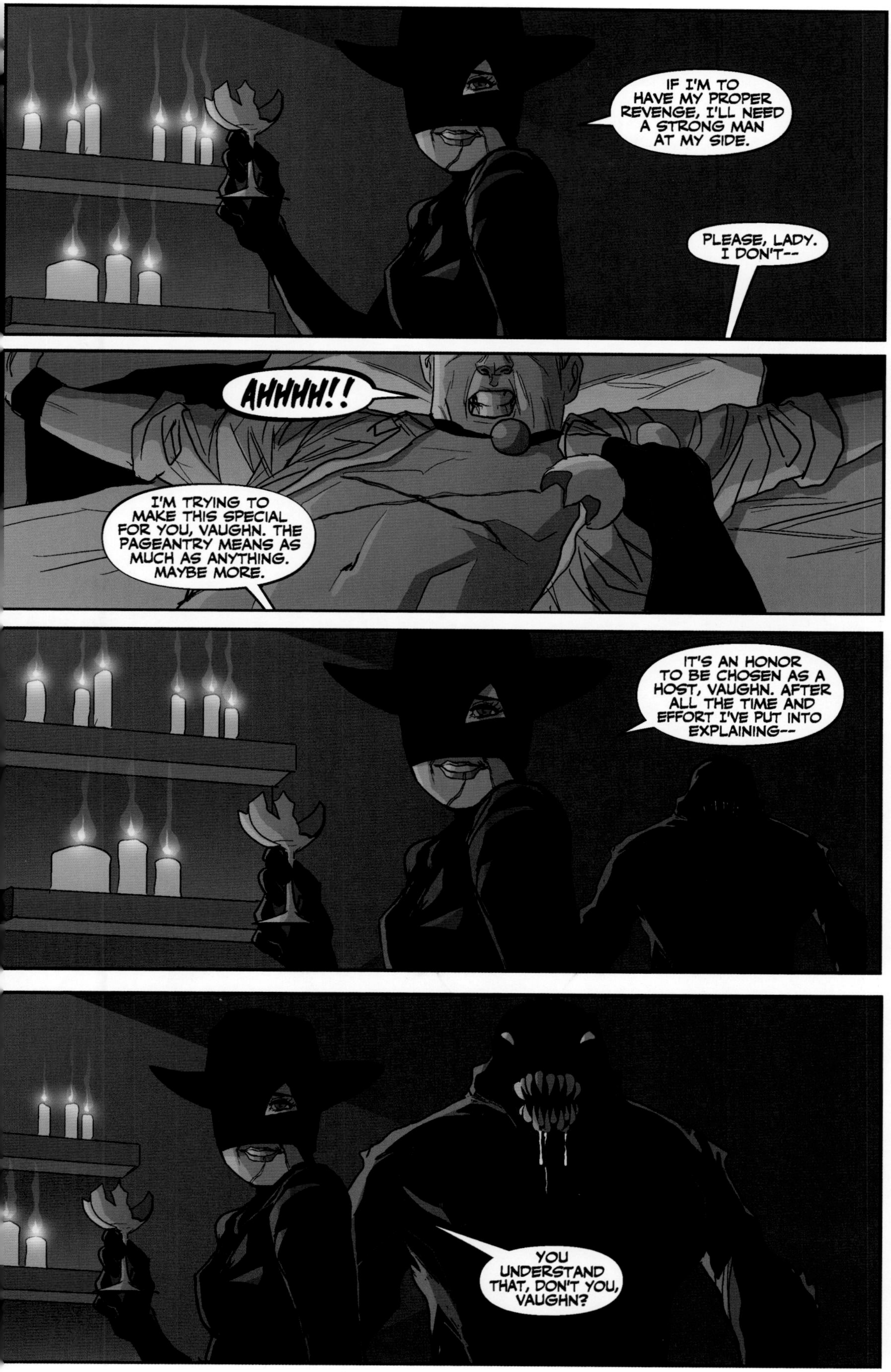
IF I'M TO HAVE MY PROPER REVENGE, I'LL NEED A STRONG MAN AT MY SIDE.
PLEASE, LADY. I DON'T--
AHHHH!!
I'M TRYING TO MAKE THIS SPECIAL FOR YOU, VAUGHN. THE PAGEANTRY MEANS AS MUCH AS ANYTHING. MAYBE MORE.
IT'S AN HONOR TO BE CHOSEN AS A HOST, VAUGHN. AFTER ALL THE TIME AND EFFORT I'VE PUT INTO EXPLAINING--
YOU UNDERSTAND THAT, DON'T YOU, VAUGHN?

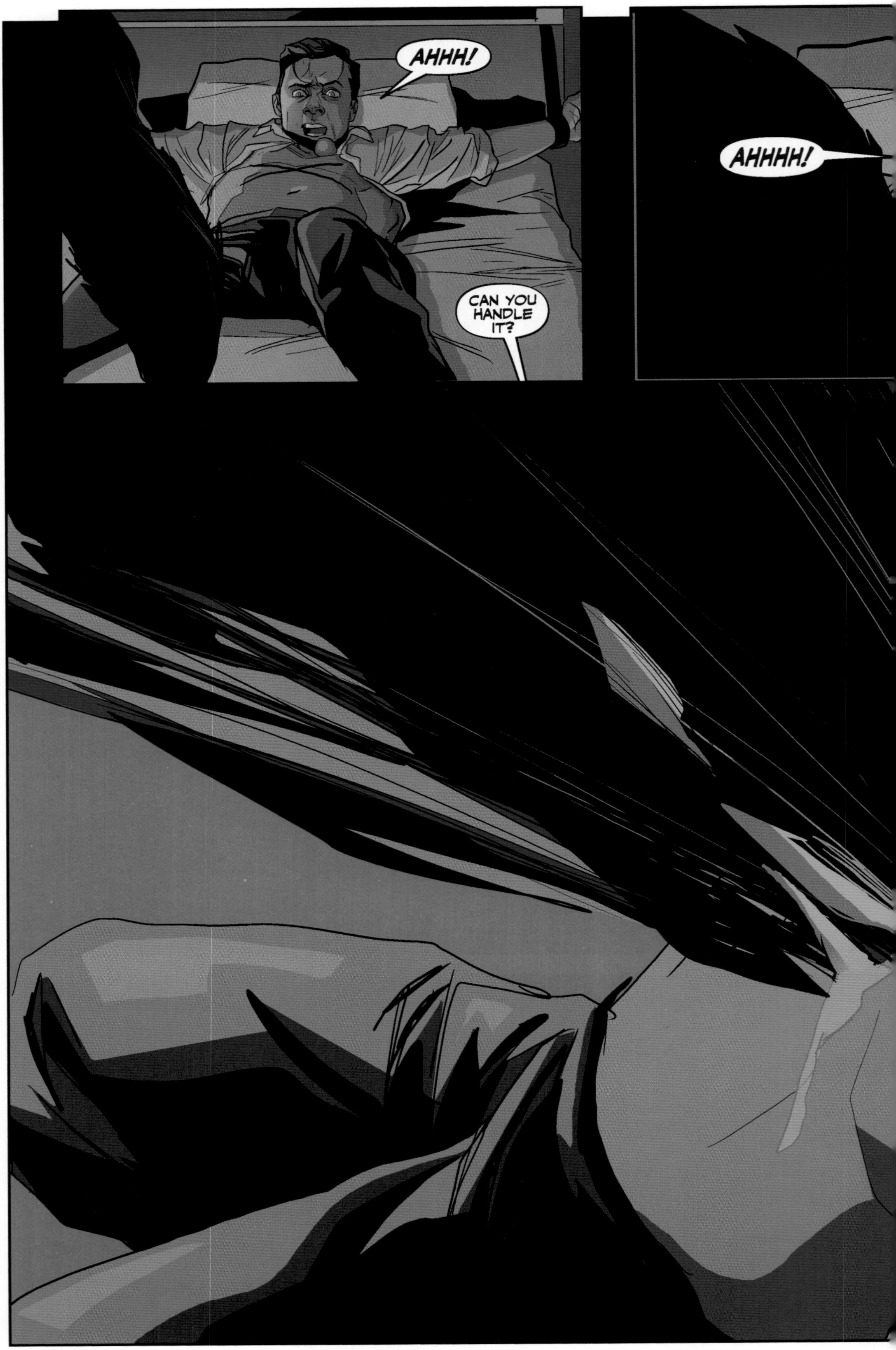
AHHH!
CAN YOU HANDLE IT?
AHHHH!

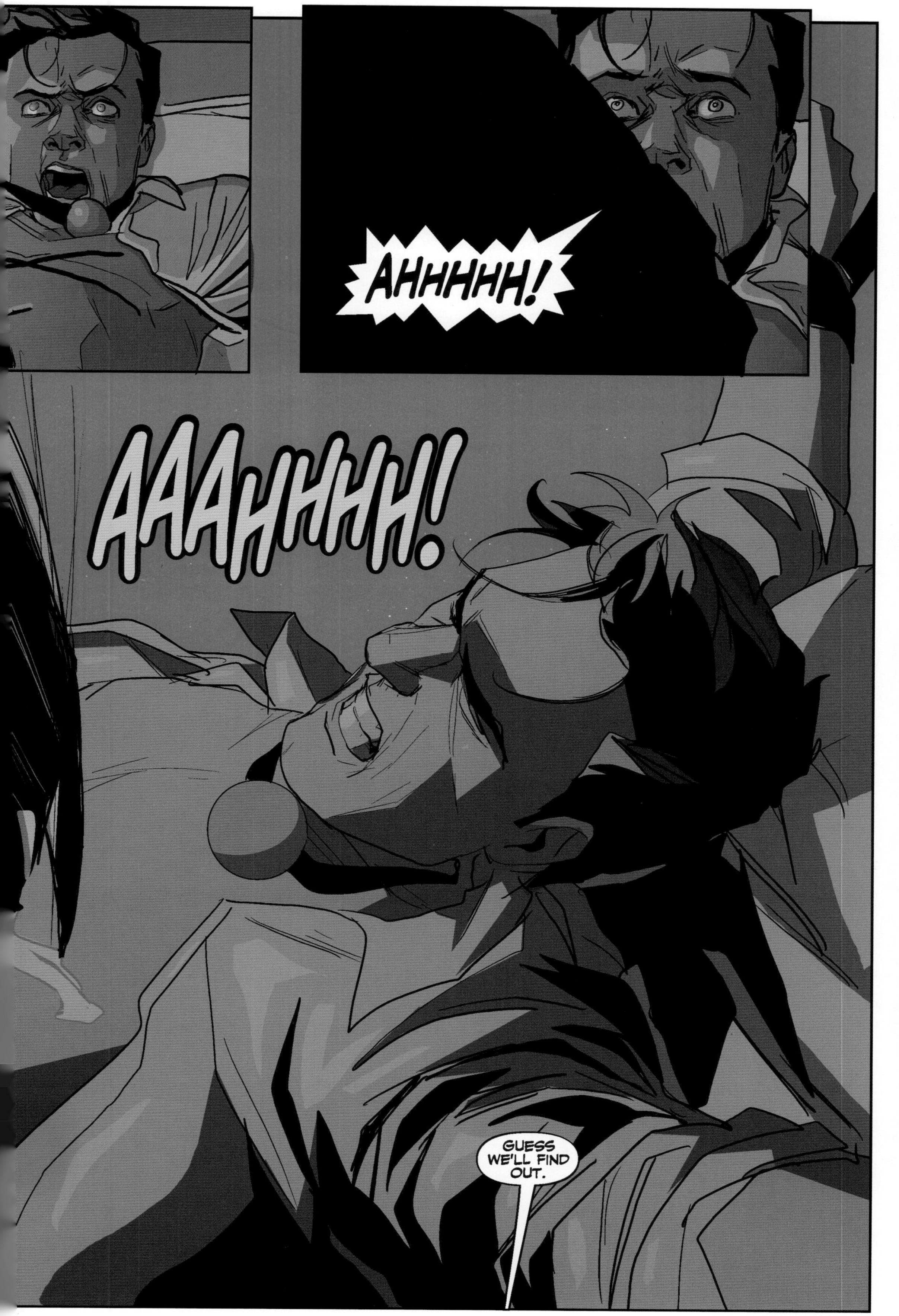
AHHHHH!
AAAHHHH!
GUESS WE'LL FIND OUT.

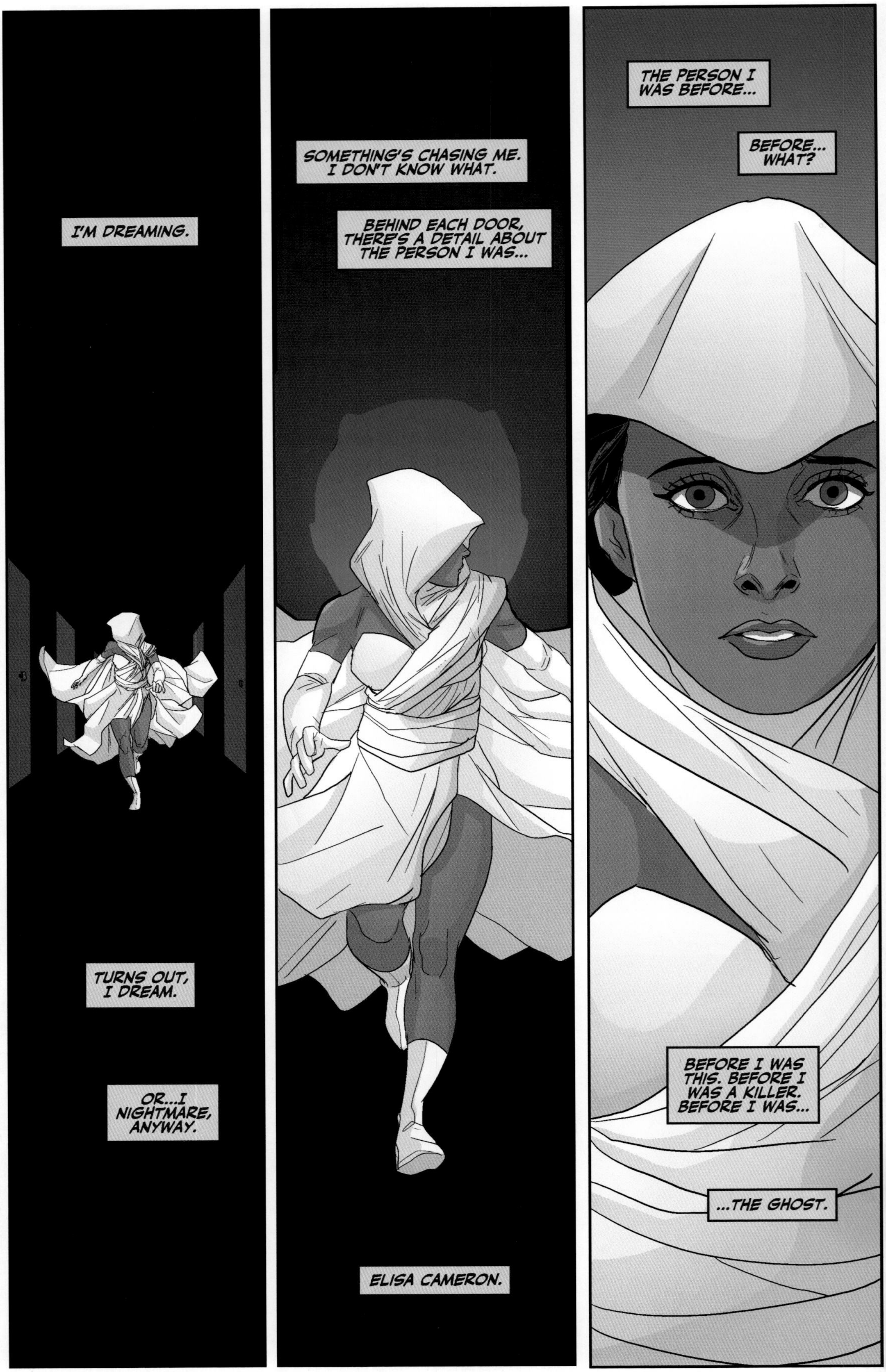
I'M DREAMING.
TURNS OUT, I DREAM.
OR...I NIGHTMARE, ANYWAY.
SOMETHING'S CHASING ME. I DON'T KNOW WHAT.
BEHIND EACH DOOR, THERE'S A DETAIL ABOUT THE PERSON I WAS...
ELISA CAMERON.
THE PERSON I WAS BEFORE...
BEFORE... WHAT?
BEFORE I WAS THIS. BEFORE I WAS A KILLER. BEFORE I WAS...
...THE GHOST.

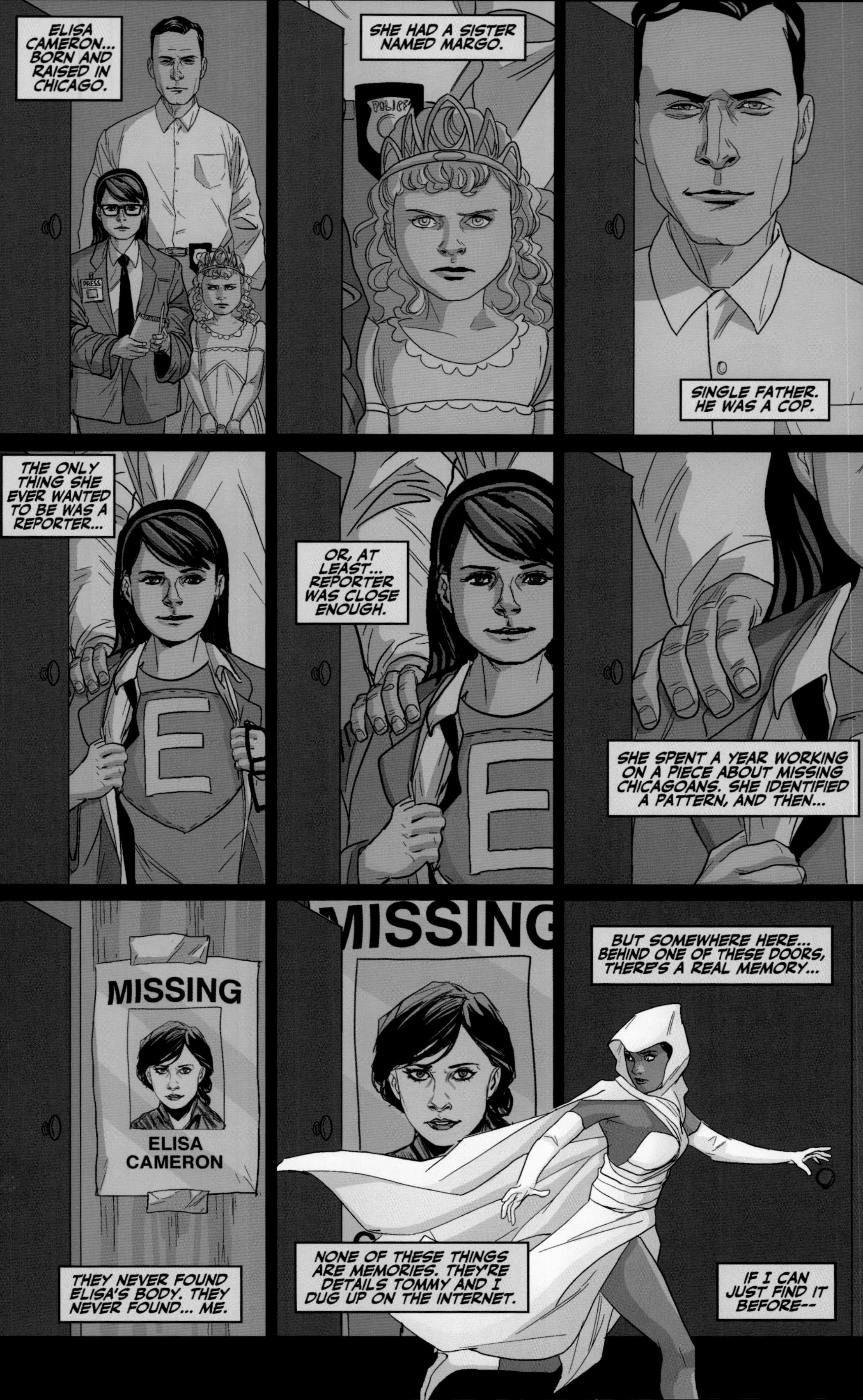
ELISA CAMERON... BORN AND RAISED IN CHICAGO.
PRESS
SHE HAD A SISTER NAMED MARGO.
POLICE
SINGLE FATHER. HE WAS A COP.
THE ONLY THING SHE EVER WANTED TO BE WAS A REPORTER...
OR, AT LEAST... REPORTER WAS CLOSE ENOUGH.
SHE SPENT A YEAR WORKING ON A PIECE ABOUT MISSING CHICAGOANS. SHE IDENTIFIED A PATTERN, AND THEN...
MISSING
ELISA CAMERON
THEY NEVER FOUND ELISA'S BODY. THEY NEVER FOUND... ME.
MISSING
NONE OF THESE THINGS ARE MEMORIES. THEY'RE DETAILS TOMMY AND I DUG UP ON THE INTERNET.
BUT SOMEWHERE HERE... BEHIND ONE OF THESE DOORS, THERE'S A REAL MEMORY...
IF I CAN JUST FIND IT BEFORE--

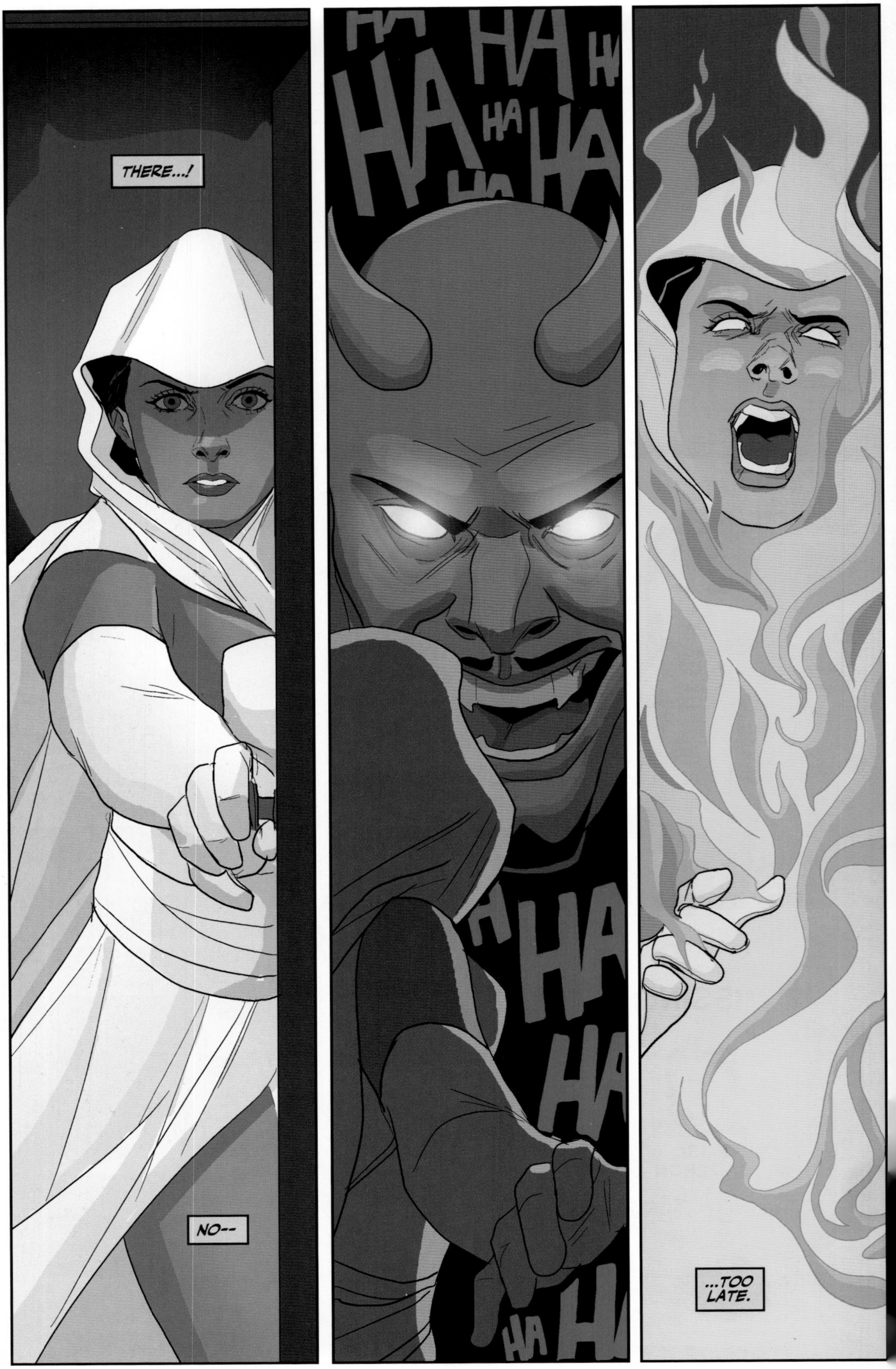
THERE...!
NO--
HA HA HA HA HA HA HA HA
HA HA HA HA
...TOO LATE.

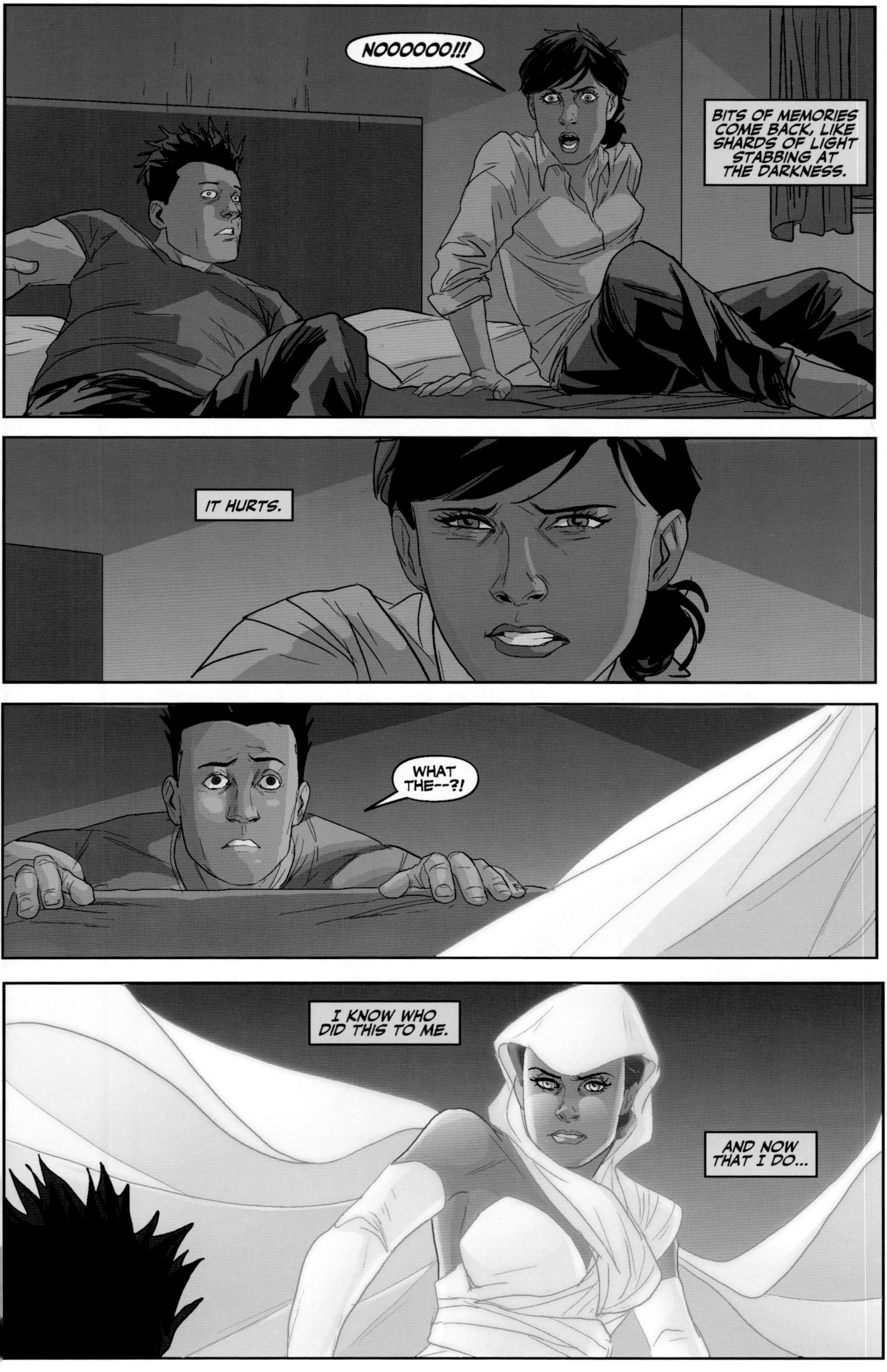
NOOOOOO!!!
BITS OF MEMORIES COME BACK, LIKE SHARDS OF LIGHT STABBING AT THE DARKNESS.
IT HURTS.
WHAT THE--?!
I KNOW WHO DID THIS TO ME.
AND NOW THAT I DO...

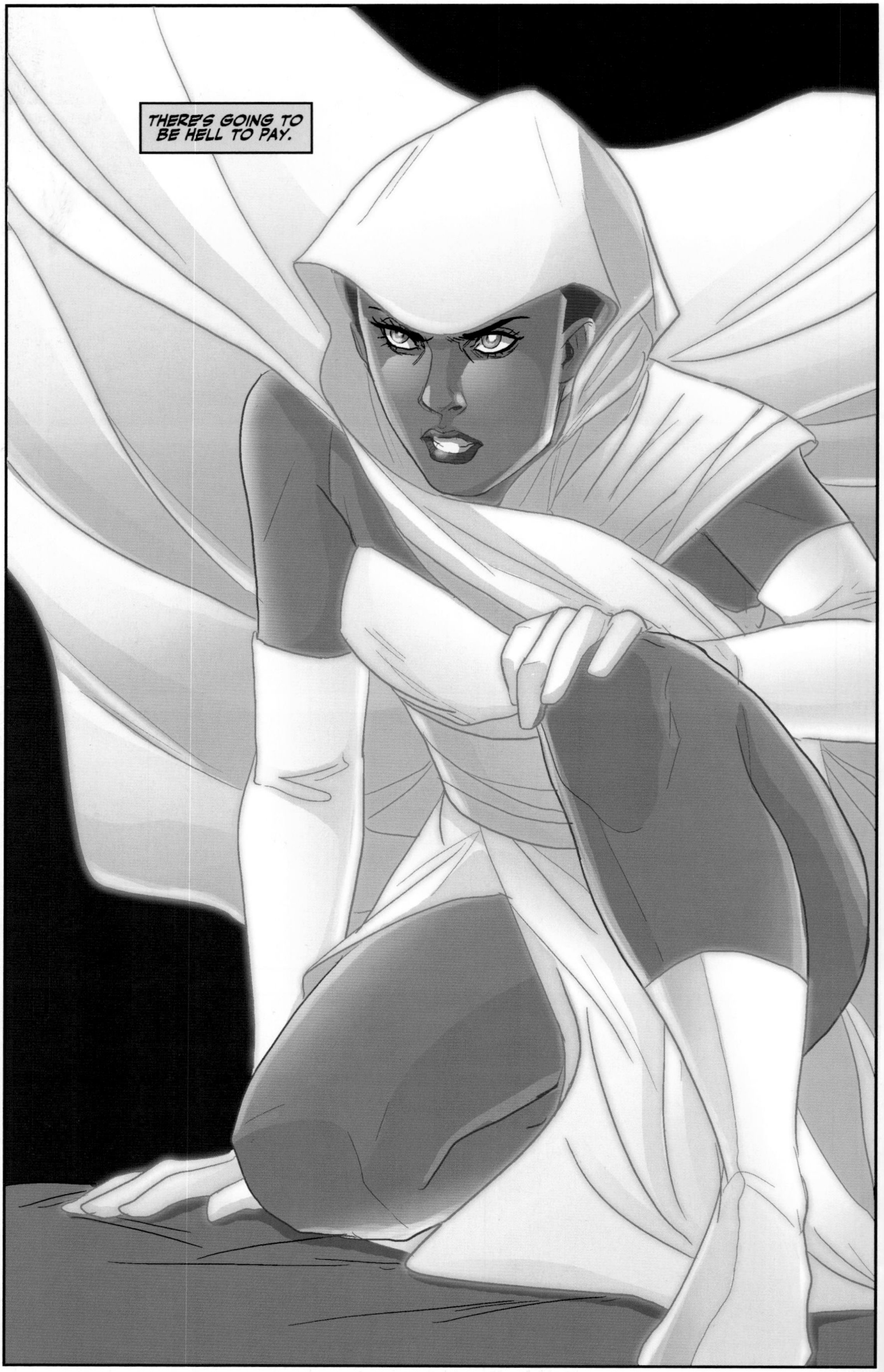
THERE'S GOING TO BE HELL TO PAY.

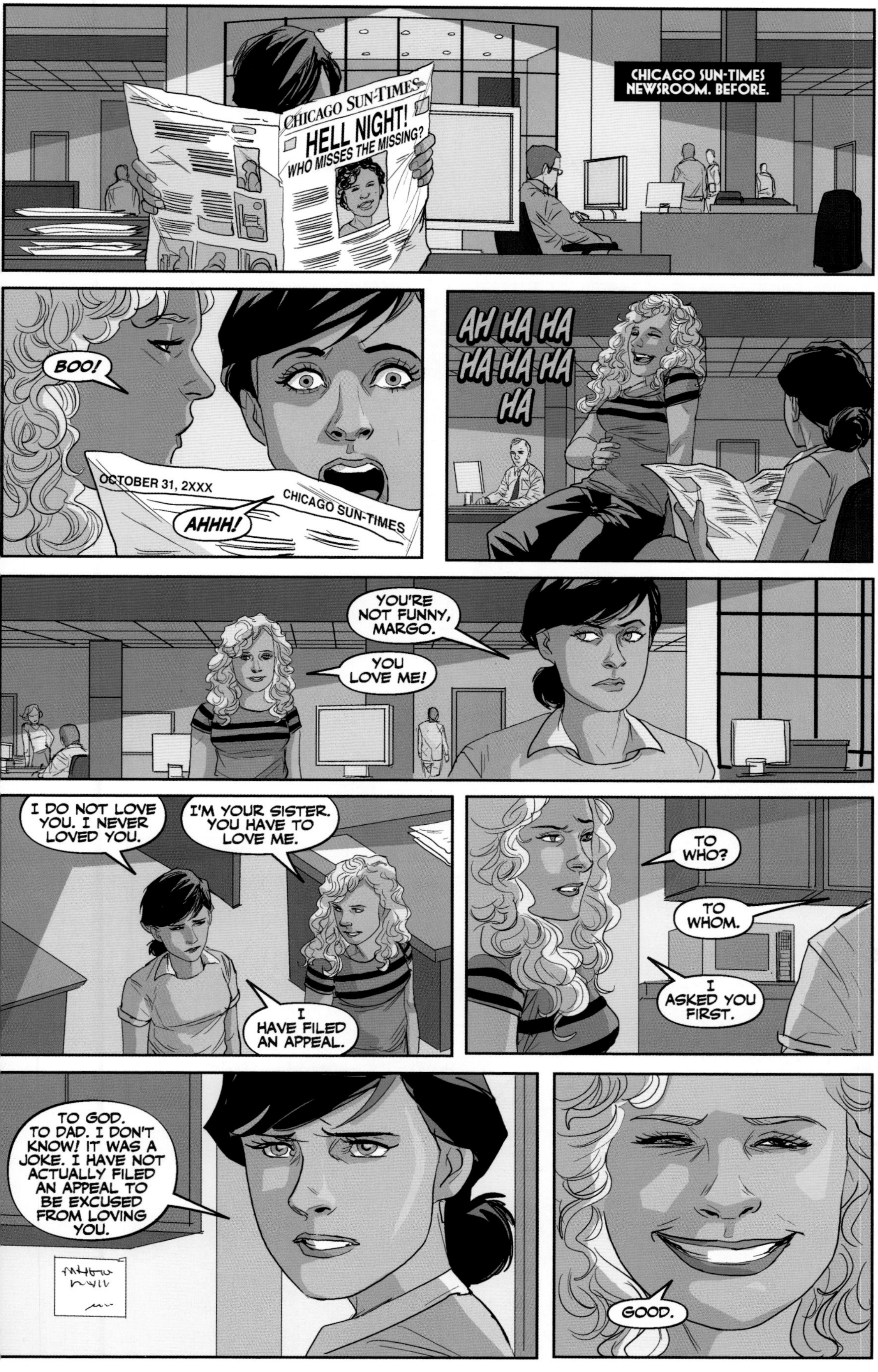
CHICAGO SUN-TIMES NEWSROOM. BEFORE.
CHICAGO SUN-TIMES
HELL NIGHT!
WHO MISSES THE MISSING?
BOO!
OCTOBER 31, 2XXX
CHICAGO SUN-TIMES
AHHH!
AH HA HA HA HA HA HA
YOU'RE NOT FUNNY, MARGO.
YOU LOVE ME!
I DO NOT LOVE YOU. I NEVER LOVED YOU.
I'M YOUR SISTER. YOU HAVE TO LOVE ME.
I HAVE FILED AN APPEAL.
TO WHO?
TO WHOM.
I ASKED YOU FIRST.
TO GOD. TO DAD. I DON'T KNOW! IT WAS A JOKE. I HAVE NOT ACTUALLY FILED AN APPEAL TO BE EXCUSED FROM LOVING YOU.
GOOD.

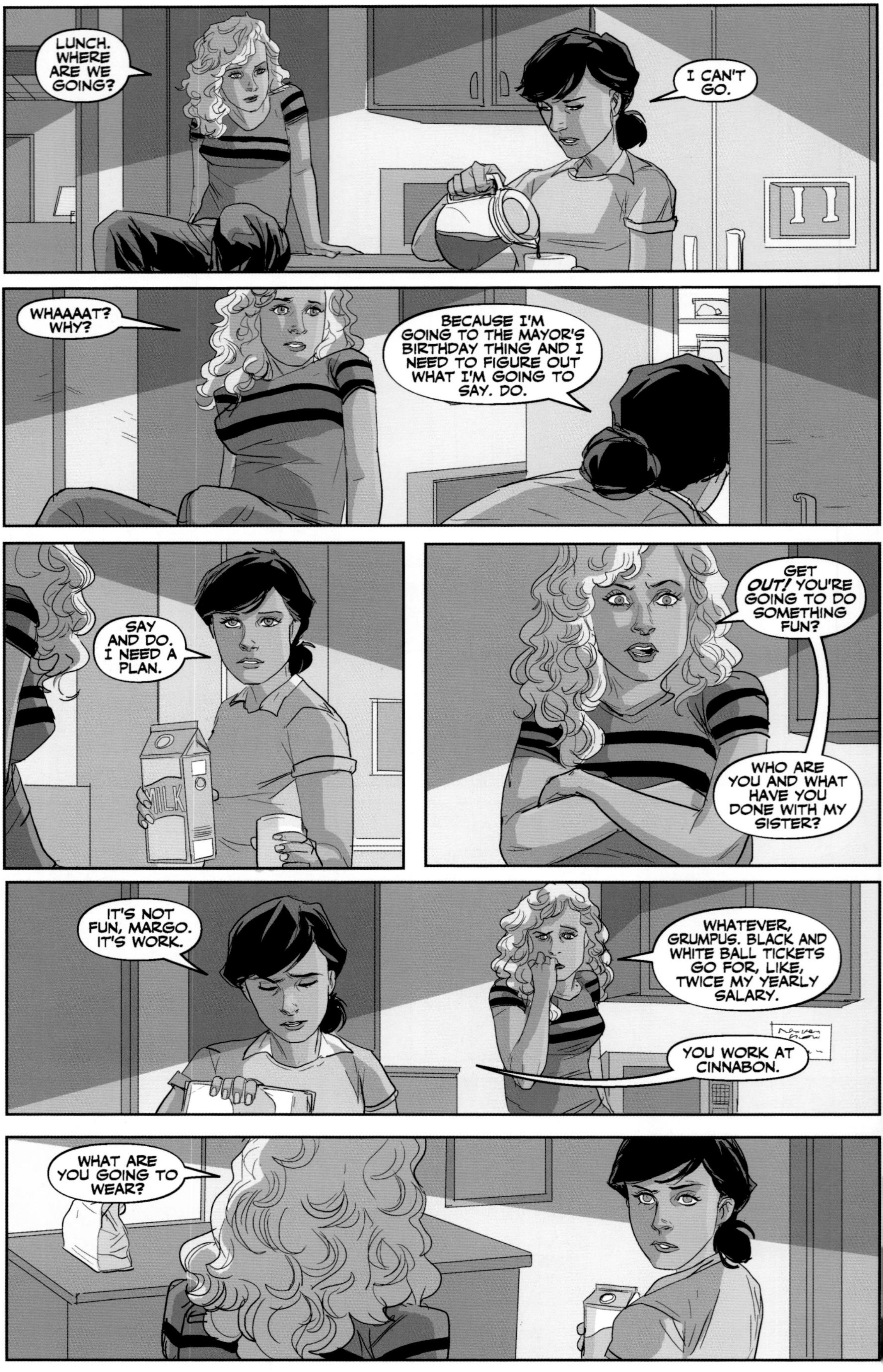
LUNCH. WHERE ARE WE GOING?
I CAN'T GO.
WHAAAAT? WHY?
BECAUSE I'M GOING TO THE MAYOR'S BIRTHDAY THING AND I NEED TO FIGURE OUT WHAT I'M GOING TO SAY. DO.
SAY AND DO. I NEED A PLAN.
MILK
GET *OUT!* YOU'RE GOING TO DO SOMETHING FUN?
WHO ARE YOU AND WHAT HAVE YOU DONE WITH MY SISTER?
IT'S NOT FUN, MARGO. IT'S WORK.
WHATEVER, GRUMPUS. BLACK AND WHITE BALL TICKETS GO FOR, LIKE, TWICE MY YEARLY SALARY.
YOU WORK AT CINNABON.
WHAT ARE YOU GOING TO WEAR?

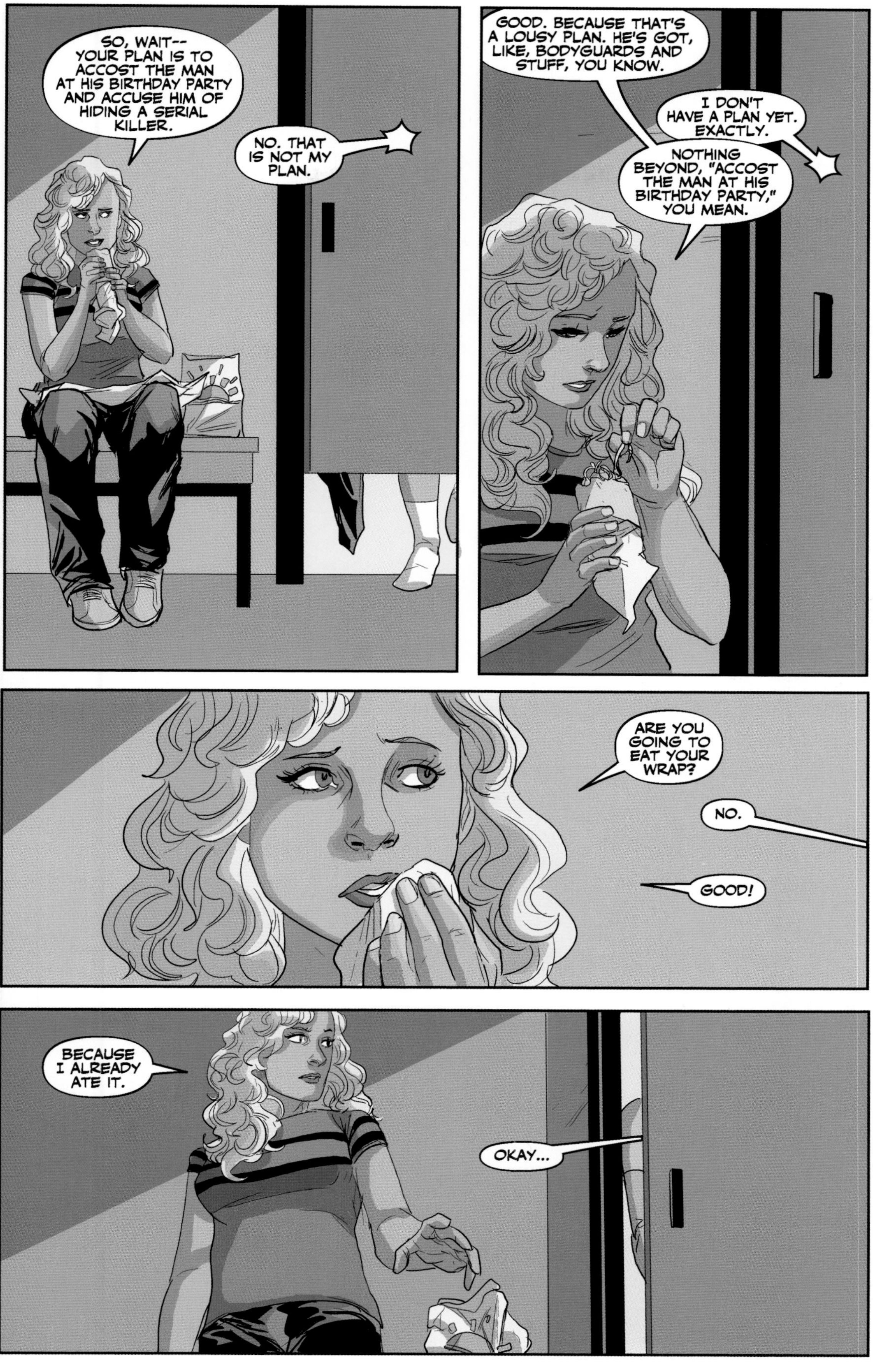
SO, WAIT-- YOUR PLAN IS TO ACCOST THE MAN AT HIS BIRTHDAY PARTY AND ACCUSE HIM OF HIDING A SERIAL KILLER.
NO. THAT IS NOT MY PLAN.
GOOD. BECAUSE THAT'S A LOUSY PLAN. HE'S GOT, LIKE, BODYGUARDS AND STUFF, YOU KNOW.
I DON'T HAVE A PLAN YET. EXACTLY.
NOTHING BEYOND, "ACCOST THE MAN AT HIS BIRTHDAY PARTY," YOU MEAN.
ARE YOU GOING TO EAT YOUR WRAP?
NO.
GOOD!
BECAUSE I ALREADY ATE IT.
OKAY...

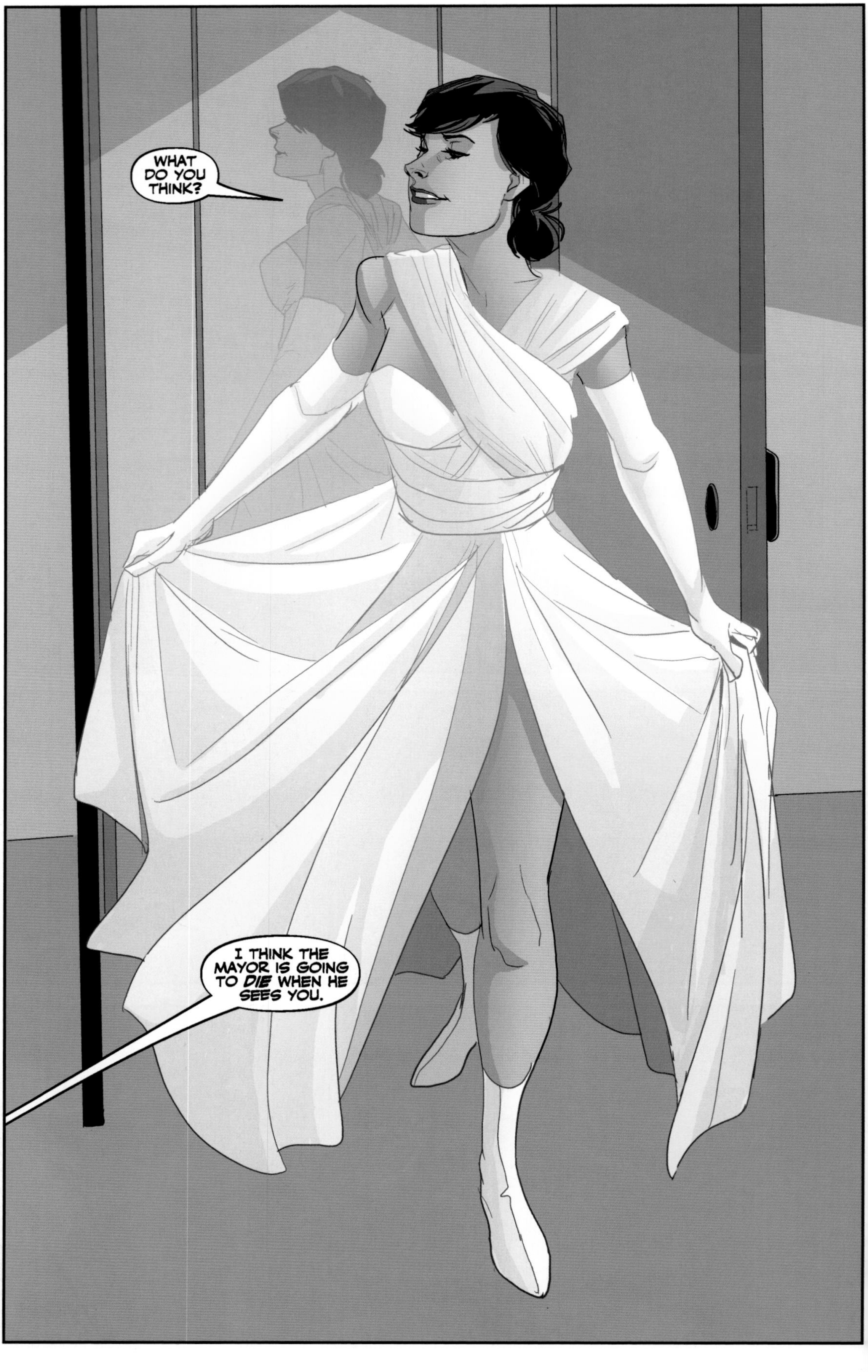
WHAT DO YOU THINK?
I THINK THE MAYOR IS GOING TO *DIE* WHEN HE SEES YOU.

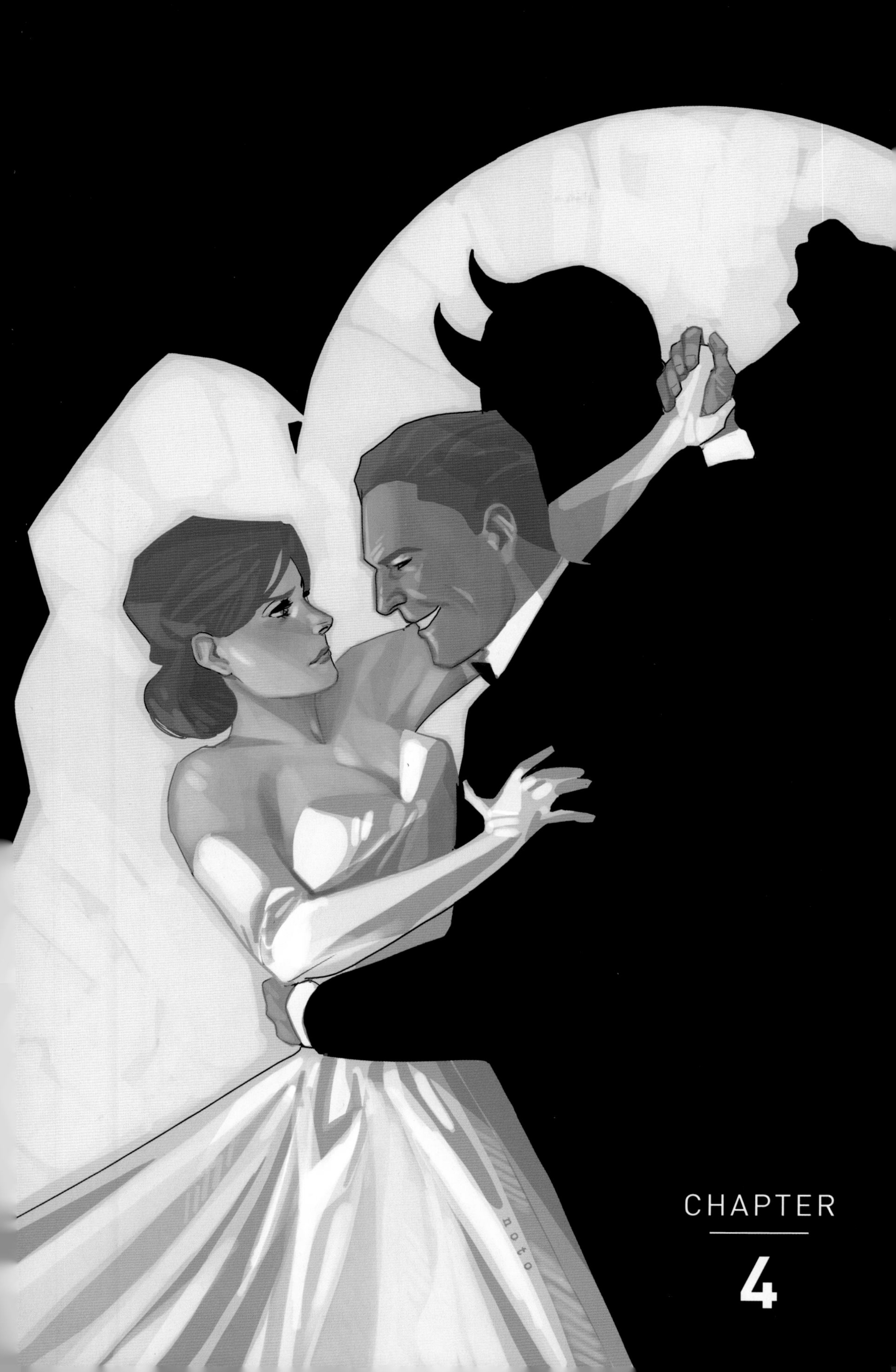
noto

CHAPTER 4

"I HAD MORE GUTS THAN BRAINS. I WANTED TO BE A HERO, A VOICE FOR THE VOICELESS, A REPRESENTATIVE OF THE DEAD. CAREFUL WHAT YOU WISH FOR, KID."

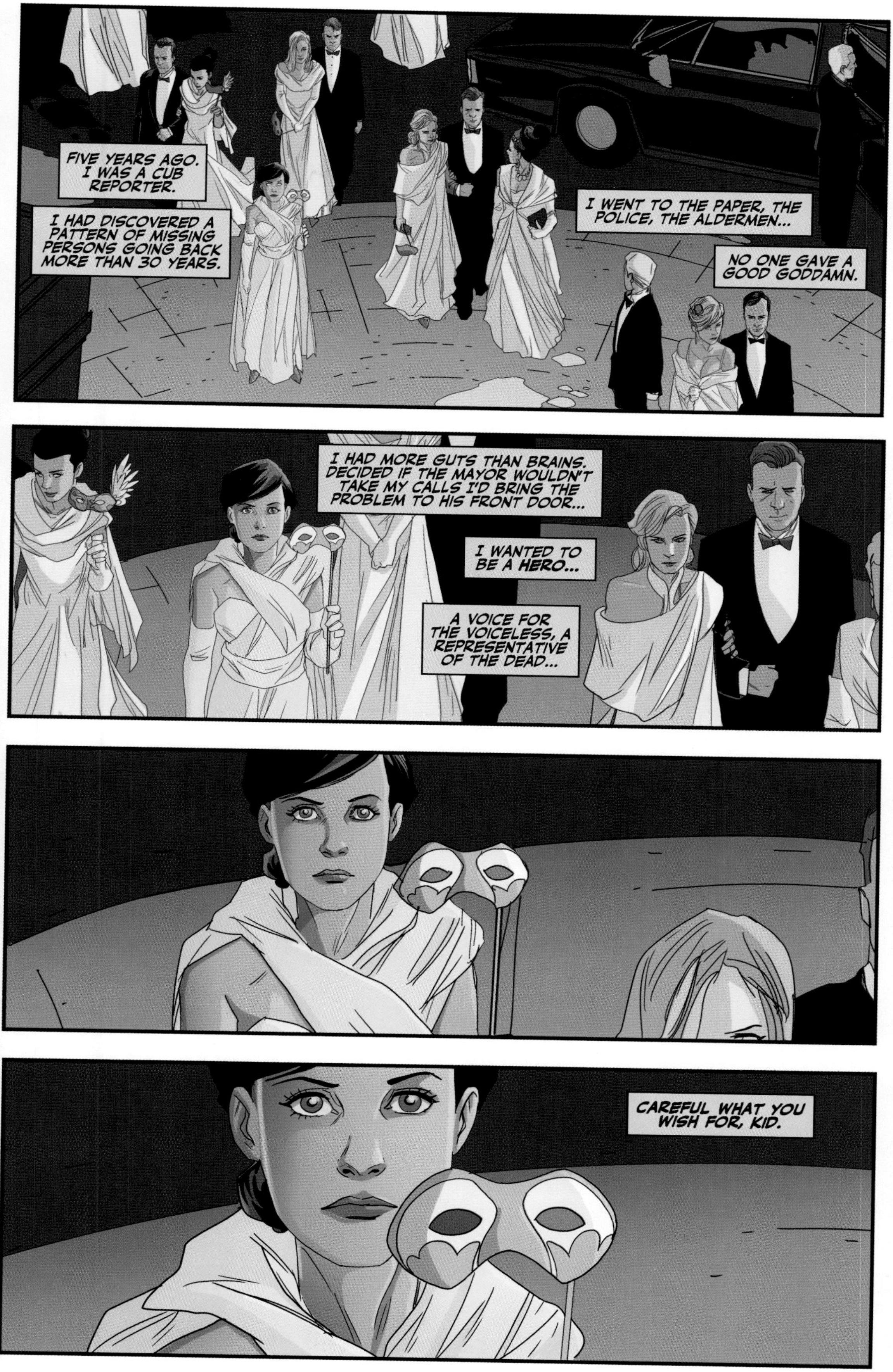
FIVE YEARS AGO. I WAS A CUB REPORTER.
I HAD DISCOVERED A PATTERN OF MISSING PERSONS GOING BACK MORE THAN 30 YEARS.
I WENT TO THE PAPER, THE POLICE, THE ALDERMEN...
NO ONE GAVE A GOOD GODDAMN.
I HAD MORE GUTS THAN BRAINS. DECIDED IF THE MAYOR WOULDN'T TAKE MY CALLS I'D BRING THE PROBLEM TO HIS FRONT DOOR...
I WANTED TO BE A HERO...
A VOICE FOR THE VOICELESS, A REPRESENTATIVE OF THE DEAD...
CAREFUL WHAT YOU WISH FOR, KID.

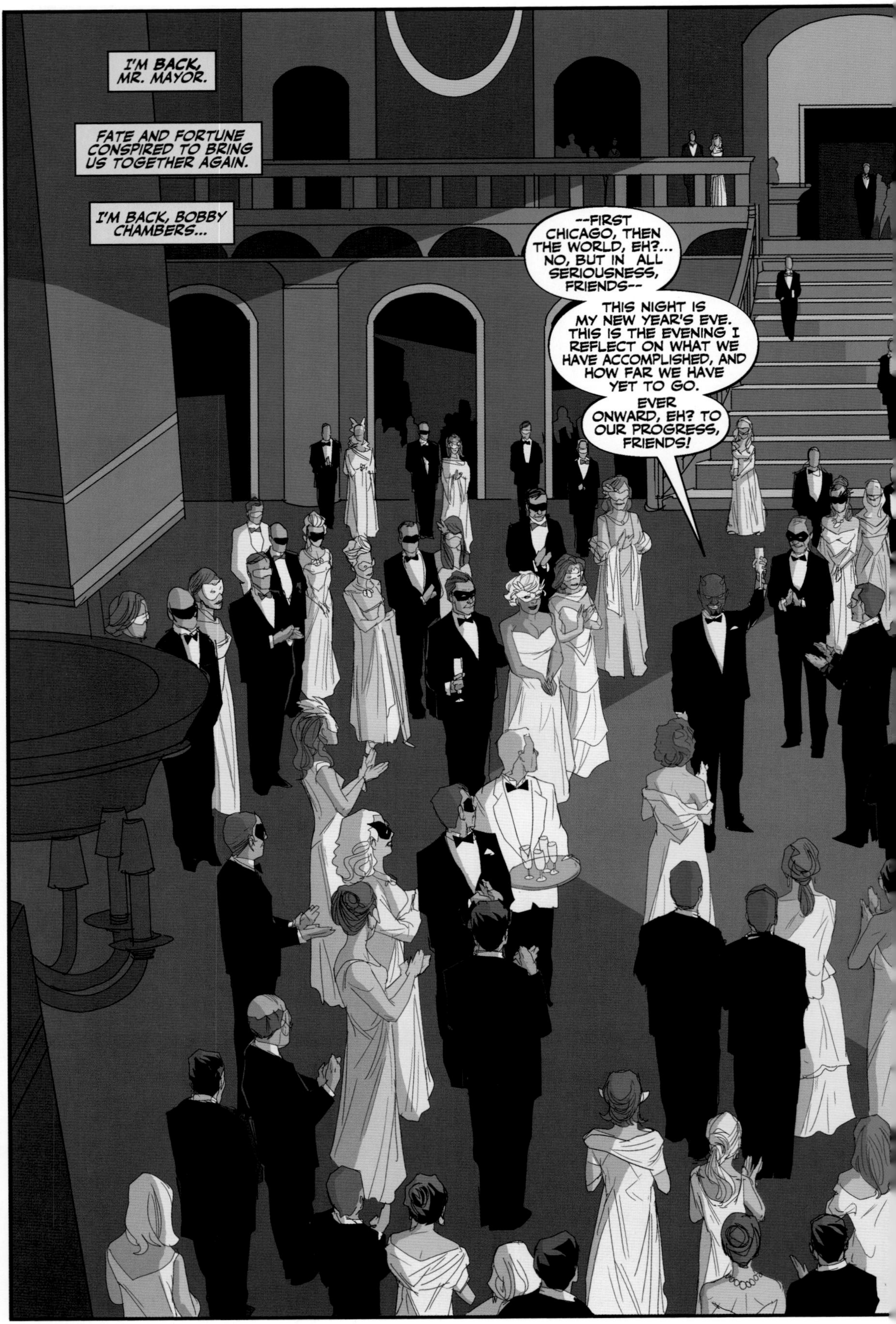
I'M BACK, MR. MAYOR.
FATE AND FORTUNE CONSPIRED TO BRING US TOGETHER AGAIN.
I'M BACK, BOBBY CHAMBERS...
--FIRST CHICAGO, THEN THE WORLD, EH?... NO, BUT IN ALL SERIOUSNESS, FRIENDS--
THIS NIGHT IS MY NEW YEAR'S EVE. THIS IS THE EVENING I REFLECT ON WHAT WE HAVE ACCOMPLISHED, AND HOW FAR WE HAVE YET TO GO.
EVER ONWARD, EH? TO OUR PROGRESS, FRIENDS!

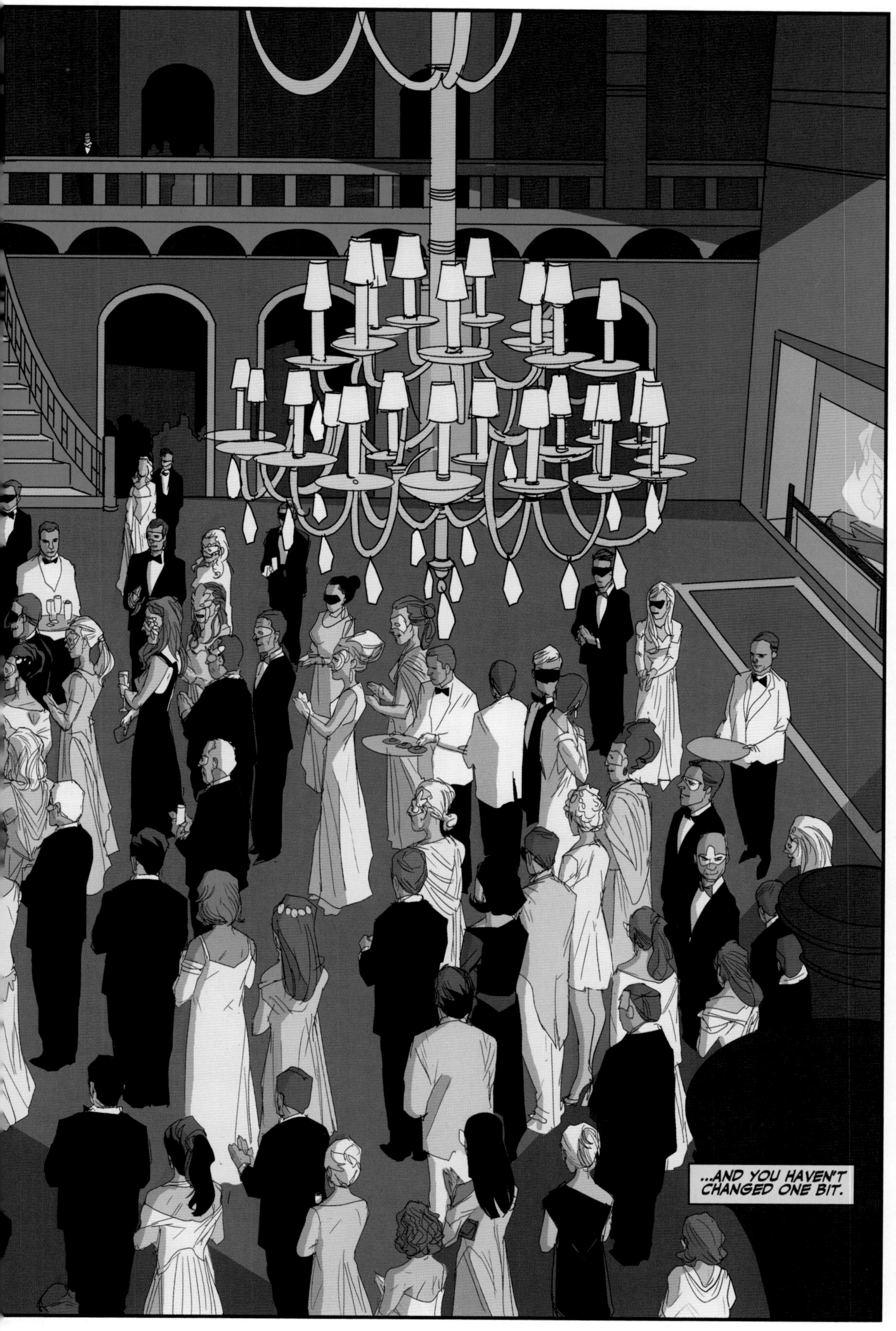
...AND YOU HAVEN'T CHANGED ONE BIT.

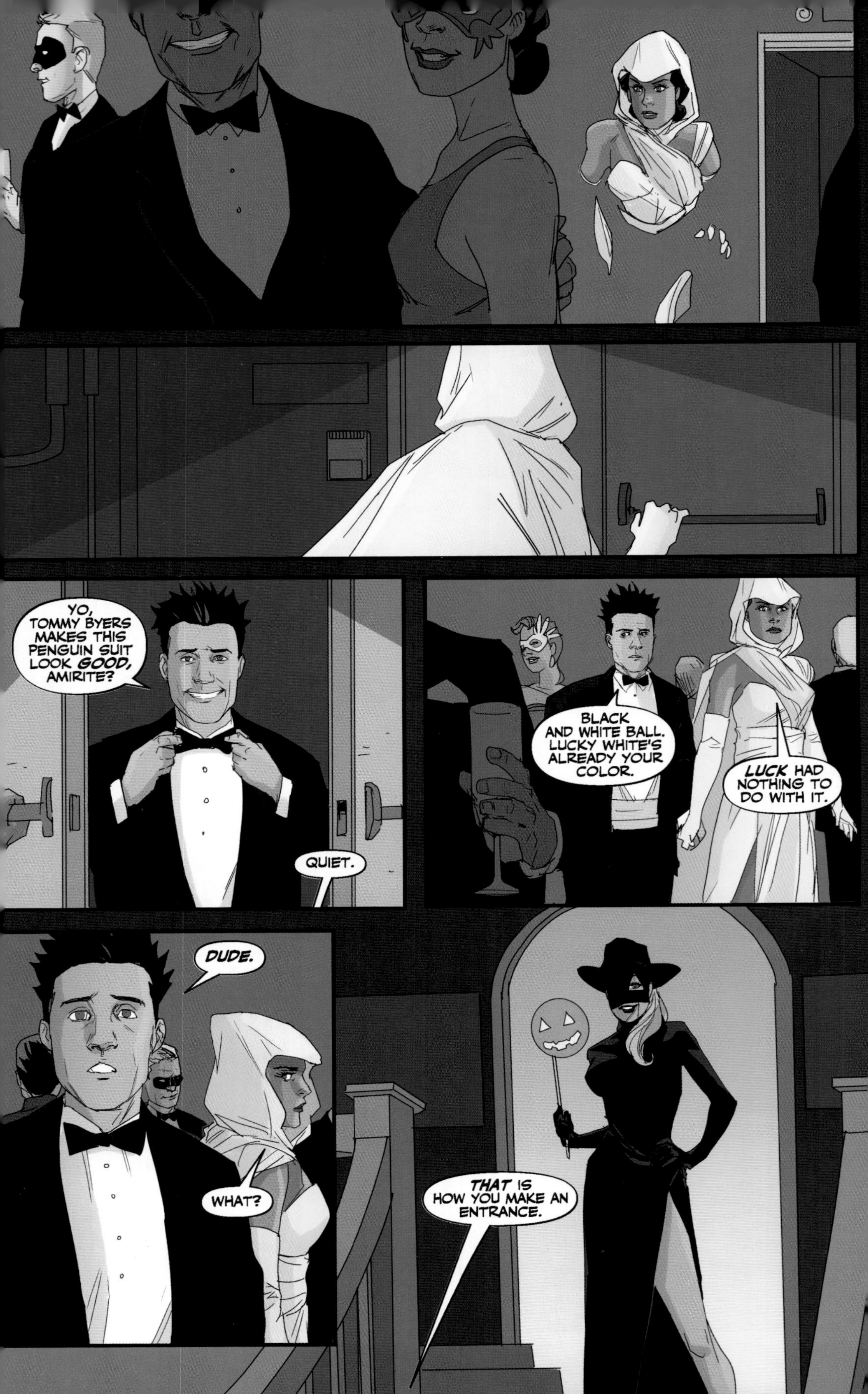
YO, TOMMY BYERS MAKES THIS PENGUIN SUIT LOOK *GOOD*, AMIRITE?
QUIET.
BLACK AND WHITE BALL. LUCKY WHITE'S ALREADY YOUR COLOR.
LUCK HAD NOTHING TO DO WITH IT.
DUDE.
WHAT?
THAT IS HOW YOU MAKE AN ENTRANCE.

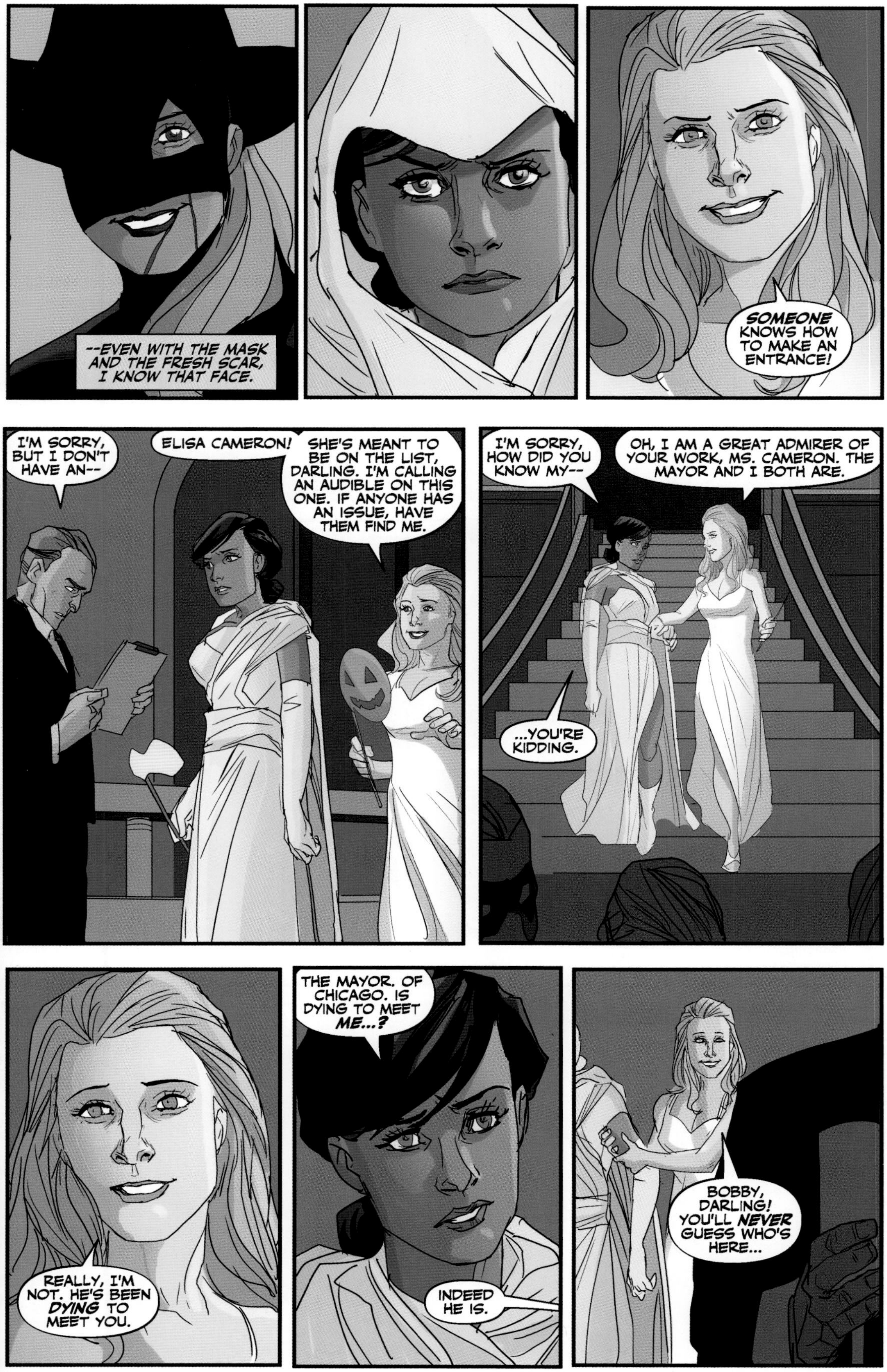
--EVEN WITH THE MASK AND THE FRESH SCAR, I KNOW THAT FACE.
SOMEONE KNOWS HOW TO MAKE AN ENTRANCE!
I'M SORRY, BUT I DON'T HAVE AN--
ELISA CAMERON!
SHE'S MEANT TO BE ON THE LIST, DARLING. I'M CALLING AN AUDIBLE ON THIS ONE. IF ANYONE HAS AN ISSUE, HAVE THEM FIND ME.
I'M SORRY, HOW DID YOU KNOW MY--
OH, I AM A GREAT ADMIRER OF YOUR WORK, MS. CAMERON. THE MAYOR AND I BOTH ARE.
...YOU'RE KIDDING.
REALLY, I'M NOT. HE'S BEEN DYING TO MEET YOU.
THE MAYOR. OF CHICAGO. IS DYING TO MEET ME...?
INDEED HE IS.
BOBBY, DARLING! YOU'LL NEVER GUESS WHO'S HERE...

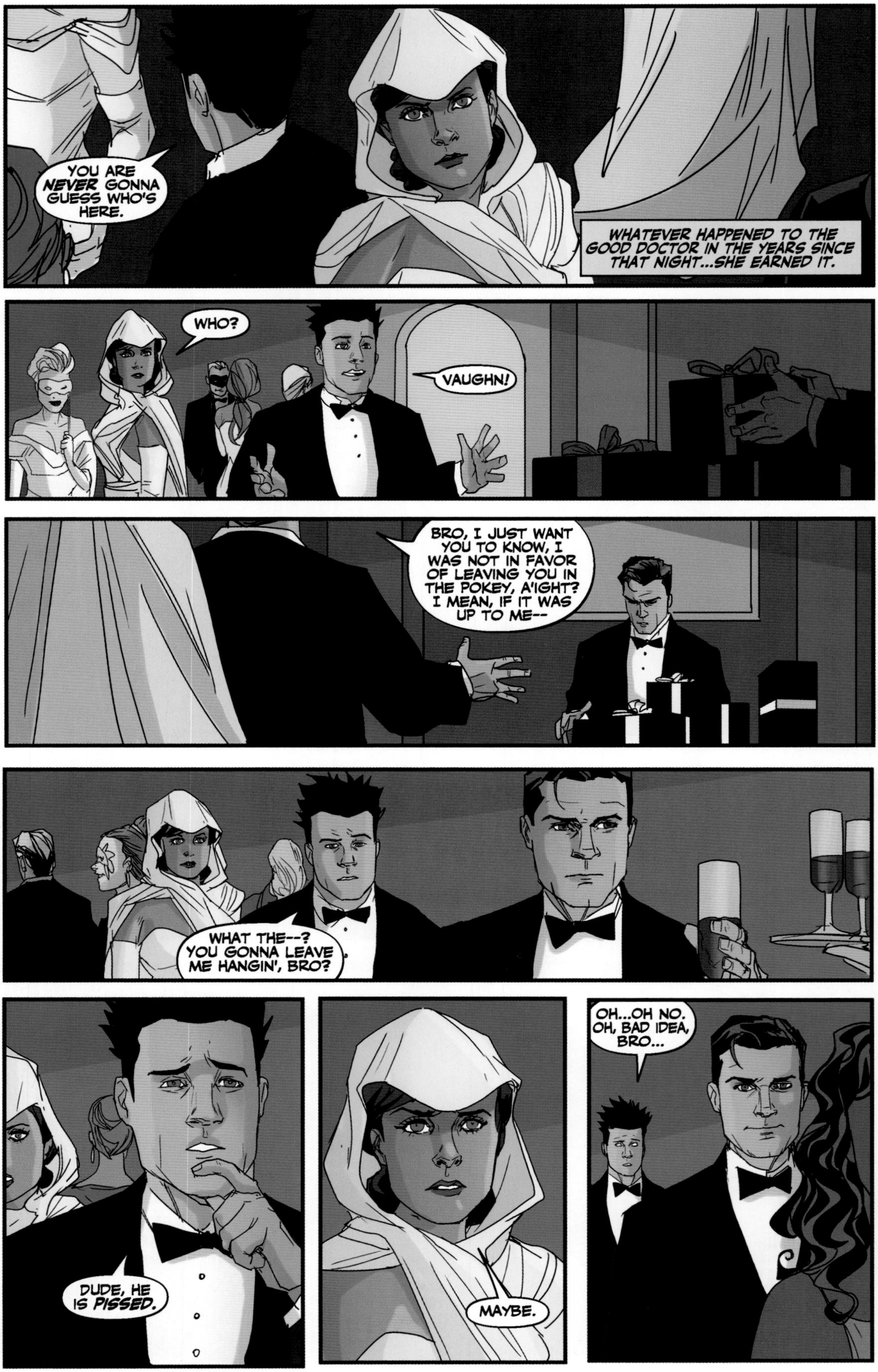
YOU ARE *NEVER* GONNA GUESS WHO'S HERE.
WHATEVER HAPPENED TO THE GOOD DOCTOR IN THE YEARS SINCE THAT NIGHT...SHE EARNED IT.
WHO?
VAUGHN!
BRO, I JUST WANT YOU TO KNOW, I WAS NOT IN FAVOR OF LEAVING YOU IN THE POKEY, A'IGHT? I MEAN, IF IT WAS UP TO ME--
WHAT THE--? YOU GONNA LEAVE ME HANGIN', BRO?
DUDE, HE IS *PISSED*.
MAYBE.
OH...OH NO. OH, BAD IDEA, BRO...

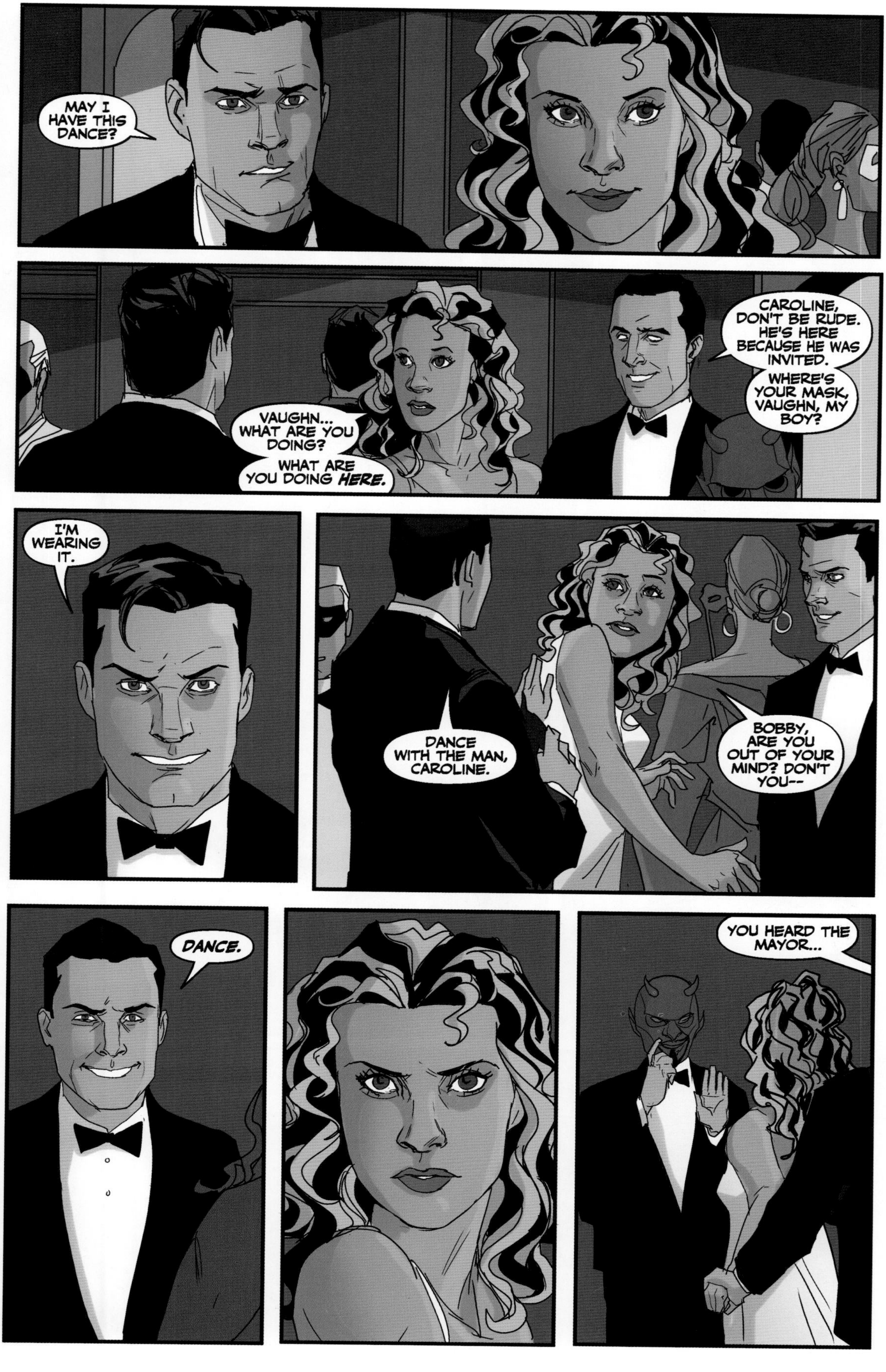
MAY I HAVE THIS DANCE?
VAUGHN... WHAT ARE YOU DOING?
WHAT ARE YOU DOING *HERE*.
CAROLINE, DON'T BE RUDE. HE'S HERE BECAUSE HE WAS INVITED.
WHERE'S YOUR MASK, VAUGHN, MY BOY?
I'M WEARING IT.
DANCE WITH THE MAN, CAROLINE.
BOBBY, ARE YOU OUT OF YOUR MIND? DON'T YOU--
DANCE.
YOU HEARD THE MAYOR...

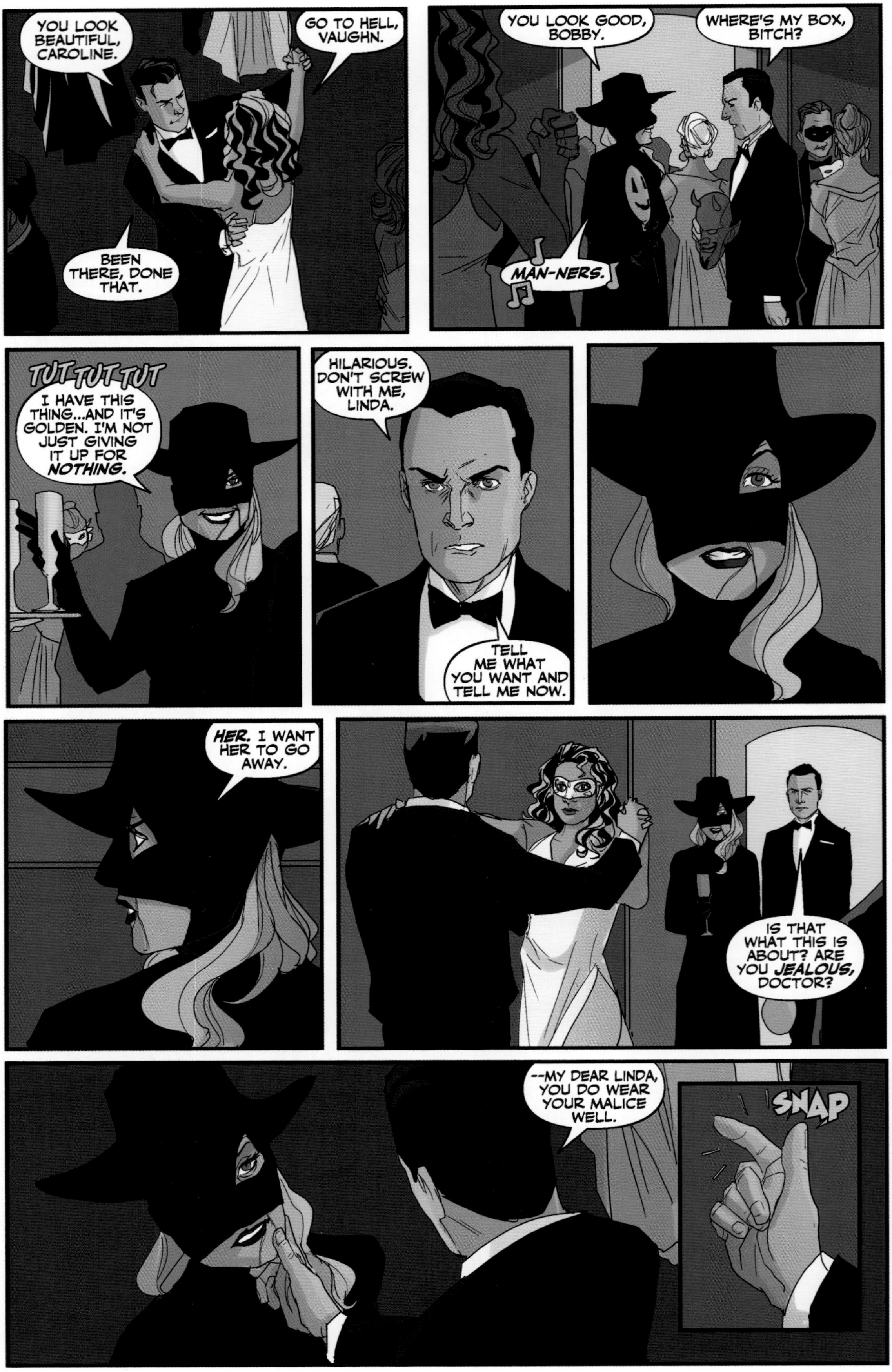
YOU LOOK BEAUTIFUL, CAROLINE.
GO TO HELL, VAUGHN.
BEEN THERE, DONE THAT.
YOU LOOK GOOD, BOBBY.
WHERE'S MY BOX, BITCH?
MAN-NERS.
TUT TUT TUT
I HAVE THIS THING...AND IT'S GOLDEN. I'M NOT JUST GIVING IT UP FOR NOTHING.
HILARIOUS. DON'T SCREW WITH ME, LINDA.
TELL ME WHAT YOU WANT AND TELL ME NOW.
HER. I WANT HER TO GO AWAY.
IS THAT WHAT THIS IS ABOUT? ARE YOU JEALOUS, DOCTOR?
--MY DEAR LINDA, YOU DO WEAR YOUR MALICE WELL.
SNAP

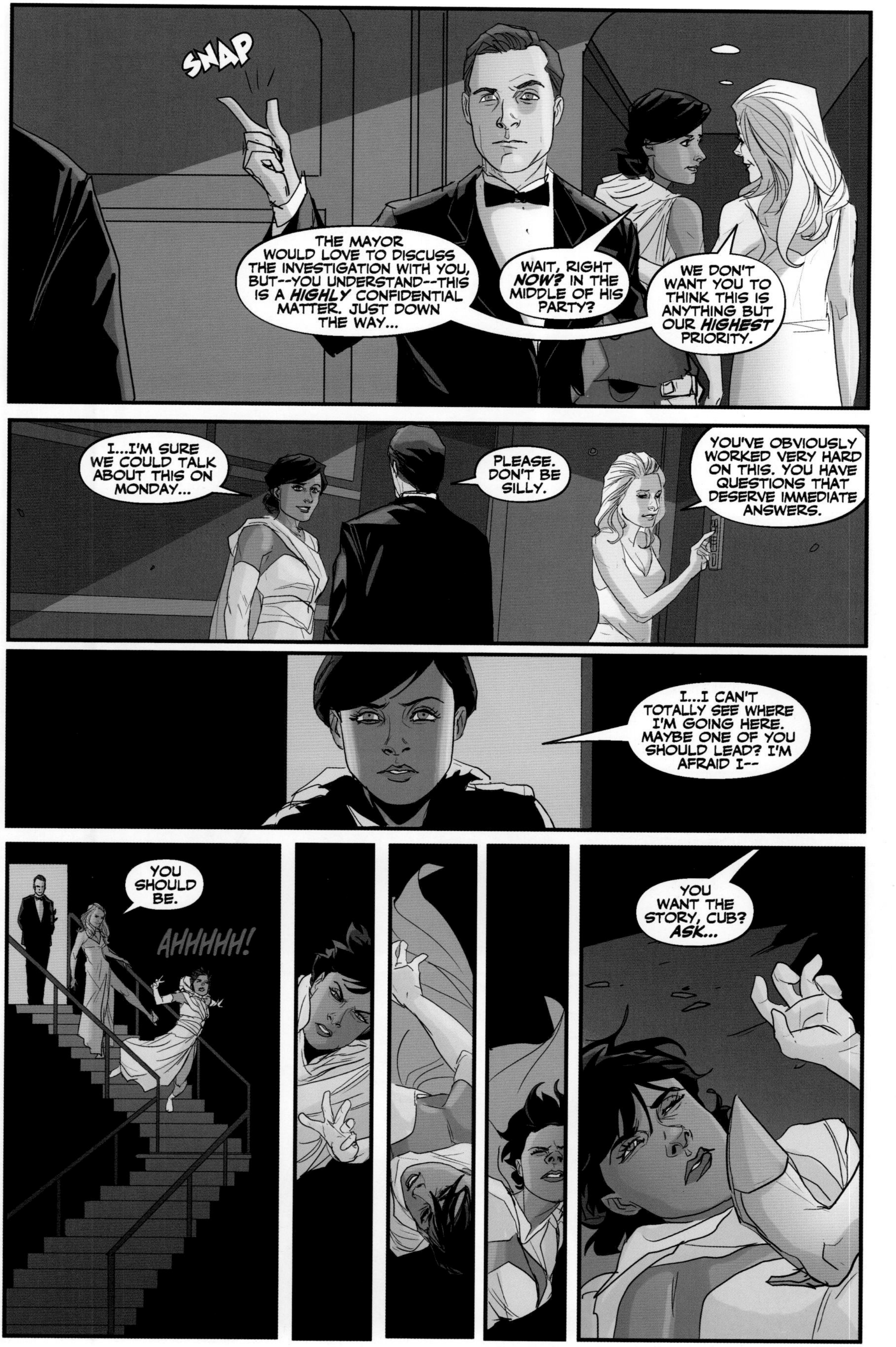
SNAP
THE MAYOR WOULD LOVE TO DISCUSS THE INVESTIGATION WITH YOU, BUT--YOU UNDERSTAND--THIS IS A HIGHLY CONFIDENTIAL MATTER. JUST DOWN THE WAY...
WAIT, RIGHT NOW? IN THE MIDDLE OF HIS PARTY?
WE DON'T WANT YOU TO THINK THIS IS ANYTHING BUT OUR HIGHEST PRIORITY.
I...I'M SURE WE COULD TALK ABOUT THIS ON MONDAY...
PLEASE. DON'T BE SILLY.
YOU'VE OBVIOUSLY WORKED VERY HARD ON THIS. YOU HAVE QUESTIONS THAT DESERVE IMMEDIATE ANSWERS.
I...I CAN'T TOTALLY SEE WHERE I'M GOING HERE. MAYBE ONE OF YOU SHOULD LEAD? I'M AFRAID I--
YOU SHOULD BE.
AHHHHH!
YOU WANT THE STORY, CUB? ASK...

...AND YE SHALL RECEIVE.

BOBBY, YOU'RE HURTING ME! WHAT IS THIS? WHAT'S HAPPENING?!

THE BOX. NOW, LINDA.

IT'S GONE--!

WHAT DO YOU MEAN, "IT'S GONE"?

I HID IT ON THE GIFT TABLE LIKE YOU SAID--AND NOW IT'S GONE.

FOOLS!!

MR. MAYOR, ARE YOU LOOKING FOR SOMETHING IN PART--

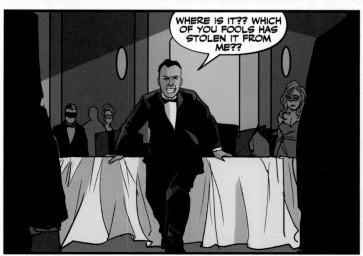

WHERE IS IT?? WHICH OF YOU FOOLS HAS STOLEN IT FROM ME??

BOBBY...

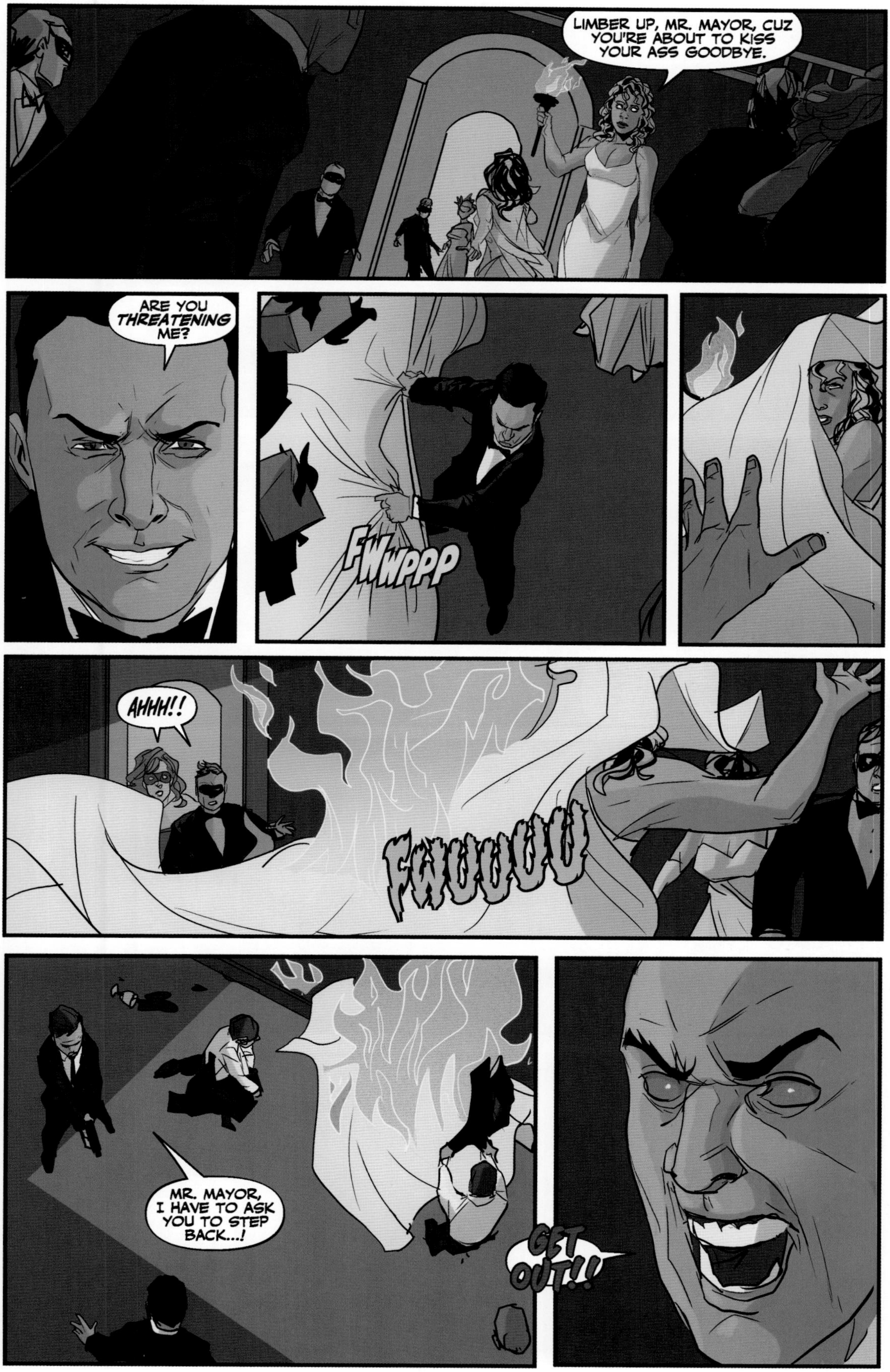
LIMBER UP, MR. MAYOR, CUZ YOU'RE ABOUT TO KISS YOUR ASS GOODBYE.
ARE YOU *THREATENING* ME?
FWWPPP
AHHH!!
FWUUUU
MR. MAYOR, I HAVE TO ASK YOU TO STEP BACK...!
GET OUT!!

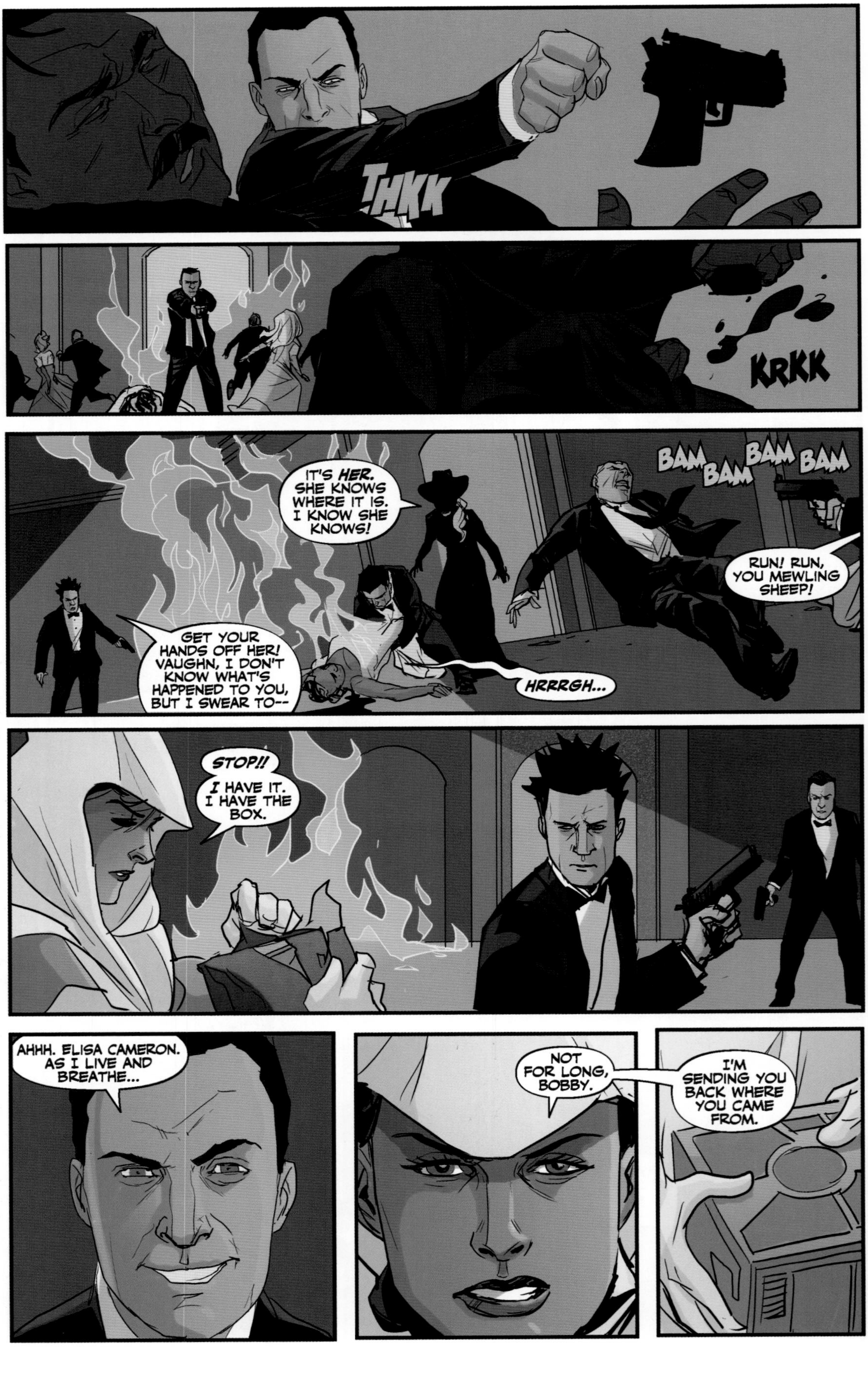
THKK
KRKK
BAM BAM BAM BAM
IT'S HER. SHE KNOWS WHERE IT IS. I KNOW SHE KNOWS!
RUN! RUN, YOU MEWLING SHEEP!
GET YOUR HANDS OFF HER! VAUGHN, I DON'T KNOW WHAT'S HAPPENED TO YOU, BUT I SWEAR TO--
HRRRGH...
STOP!!
I HAVE IT. I HAVE THE BOX.
AHHH. ELISA CAMERON. AS I LIVE AND BREATHE...
NOT FOR LONG, BOBBY.
I'M SENDING YOU BACK WHERE YOU CAME FROM.

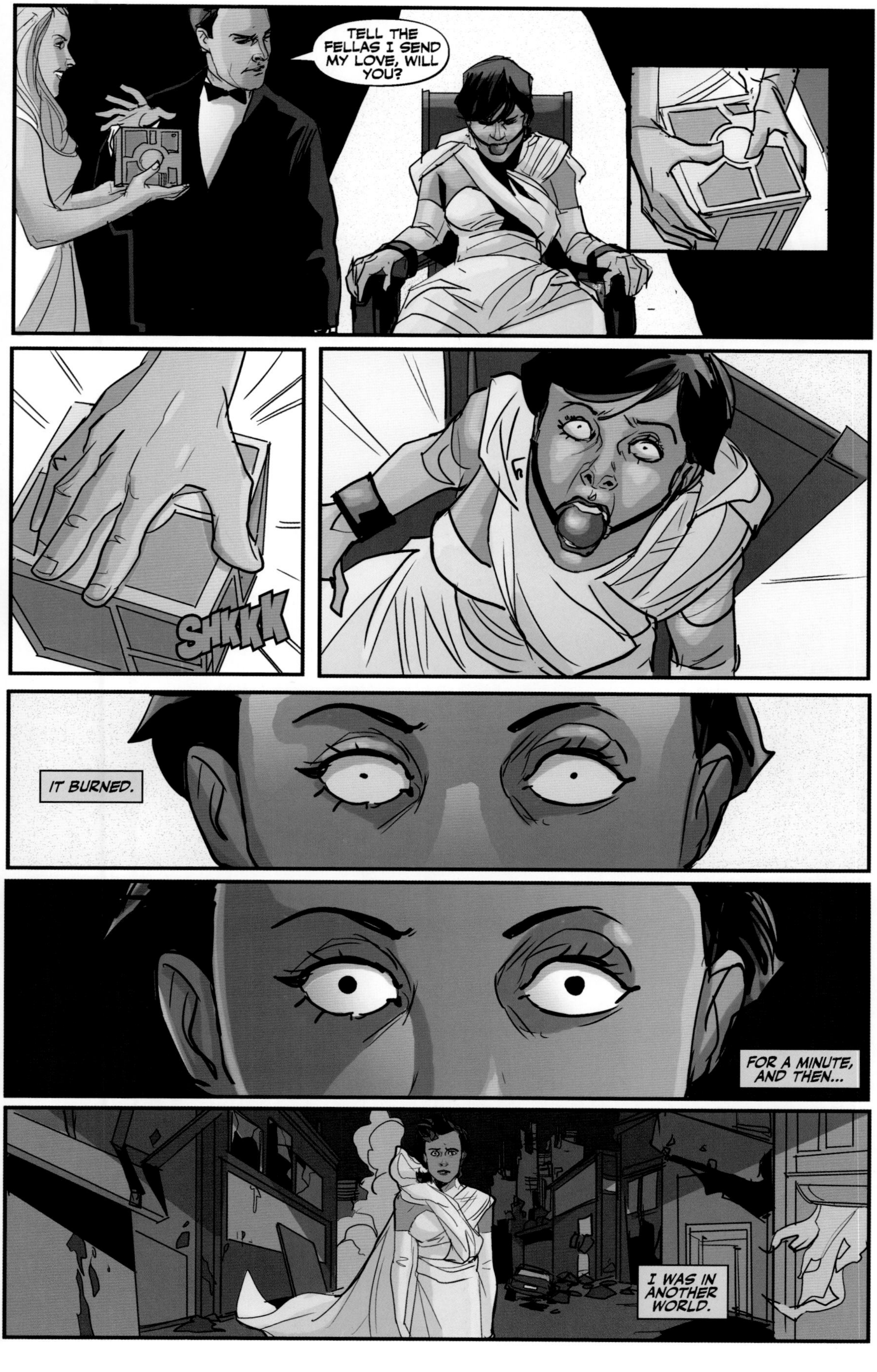
TELL THE FELLAS I SEND MY LOVE, WILL YOU?
SHKKK
IT BURNED.
FOR A MINUTE, AND THEN...
I WAS IN ANOTHER WORLD.

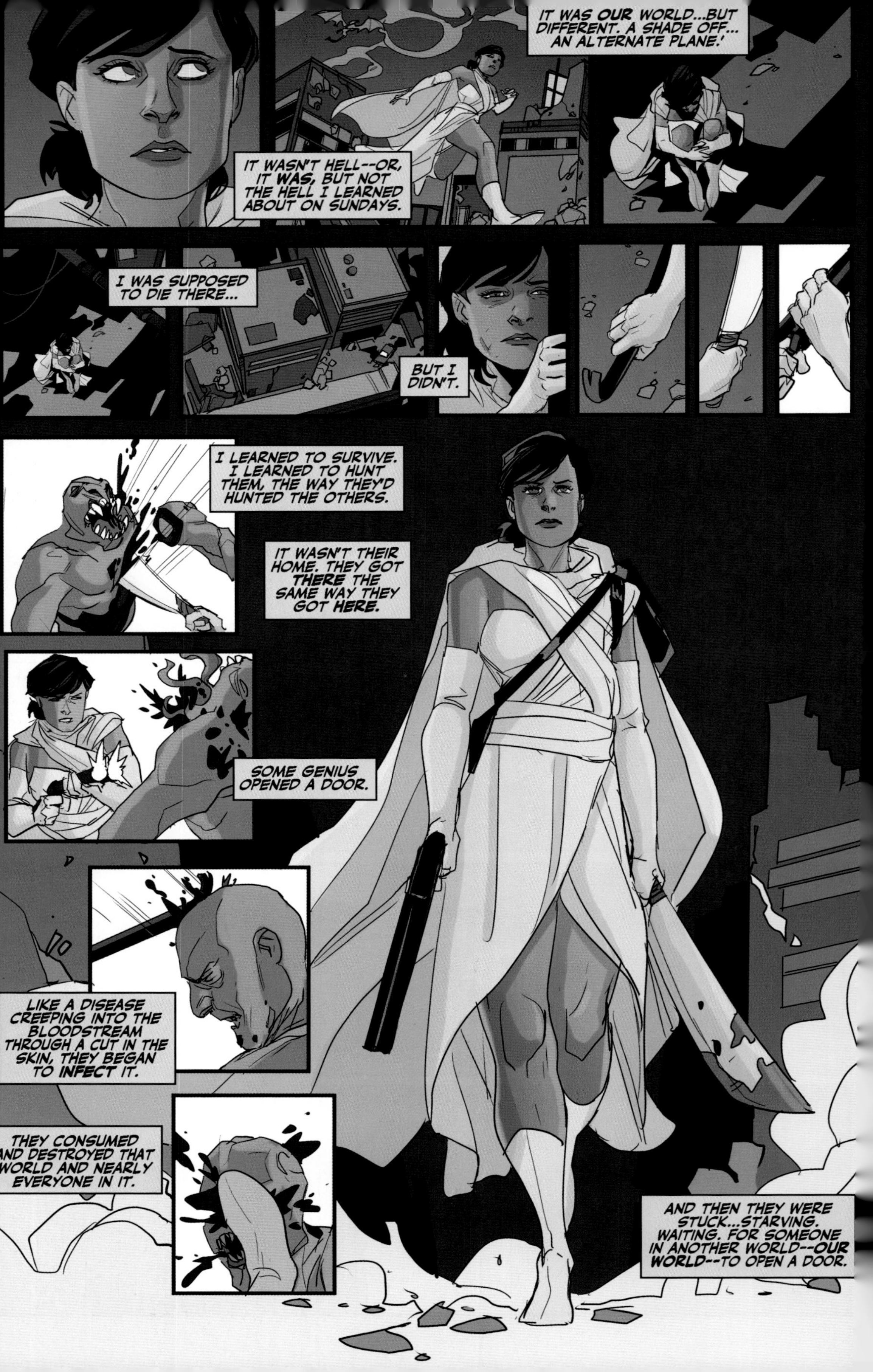
IT WASN'T HELL--OR, IT WAS, BUT NOT THE HELL I LEARNED ABOUT ON SUNDAYS.
IT WAS OUR WORLD...BUT DIFFERENT. A SHADE OFF... AN ALTERNATE PLANE.'
I WAS SUPPOSED TO DIE THERE...
BUT I DIDN'T.
I LEARNED TO SURVIVE. I LEARNED TO HUNT THEM, THE WAY THEY'D HUNTED THE OTHERS.
IT WASN'T THEIR HOME. THEY GOT THERE THE SAME WAY THEY GOT HERE.
SOME GENIUS OPENED A DOOR.
LIKE A DISEASE CREEPING INTO THE BLOODSTREAM THROUGH A CUT IN THE SKIN, THEY BEGAN TO INFECT IT.
THEY CONSUMED AND DESTROYED THAT WORLD AND NEARLY EVERYONE IN IT.
AND THEN THEY WERE STUCK...STARVING. WAITING. FOR SOMEONE IN ANOTHER WORLD--OUR WORLD--TO OPEN A DOOR.

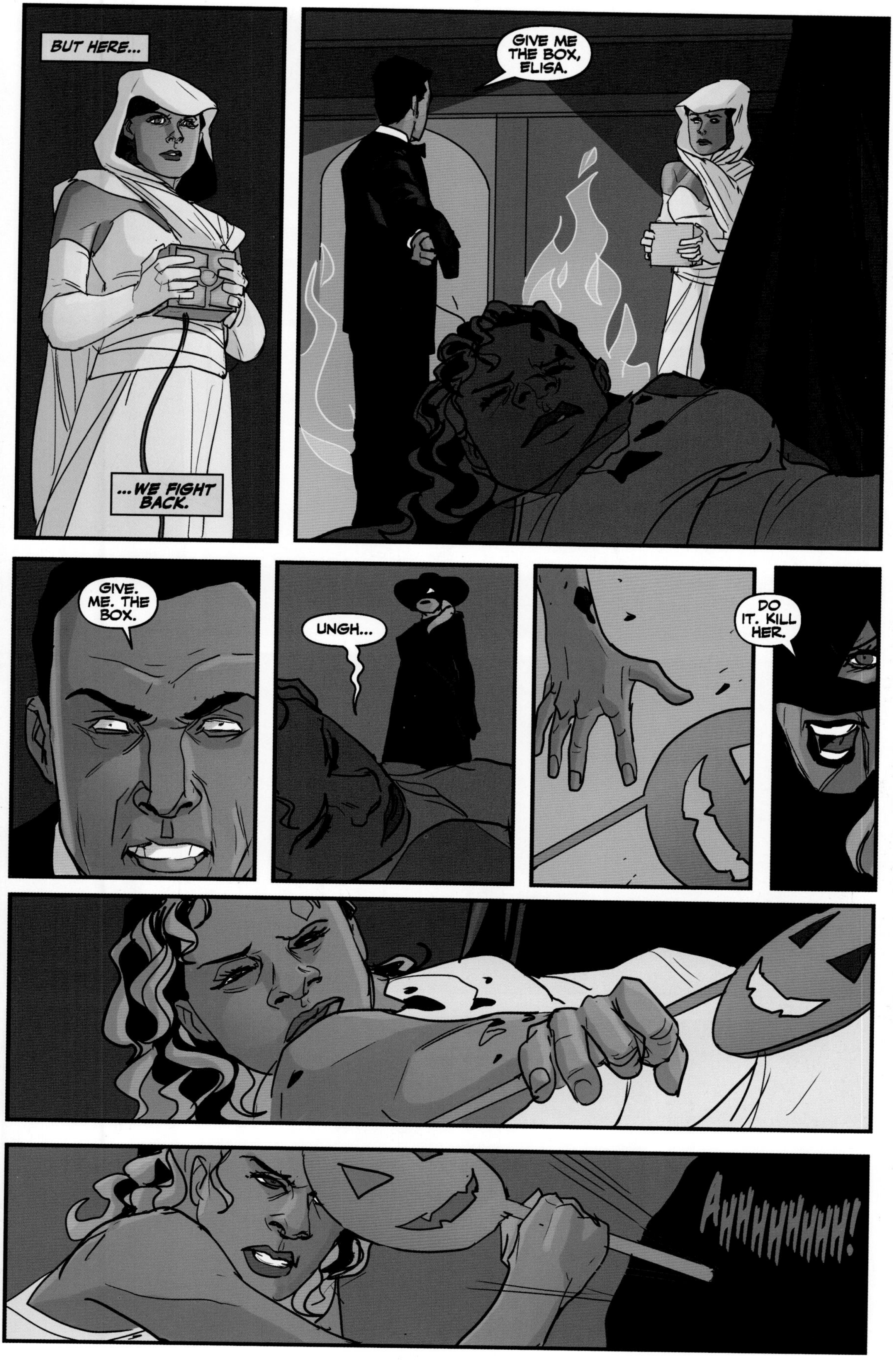
BUT HERE...
...WE FIGHT BACK.
GIVE ME THE BOX, ELISA.
GIVE. ME. THE BOX.
UNGH...
DO IT. KILL HER.
AHHHHHHHH!

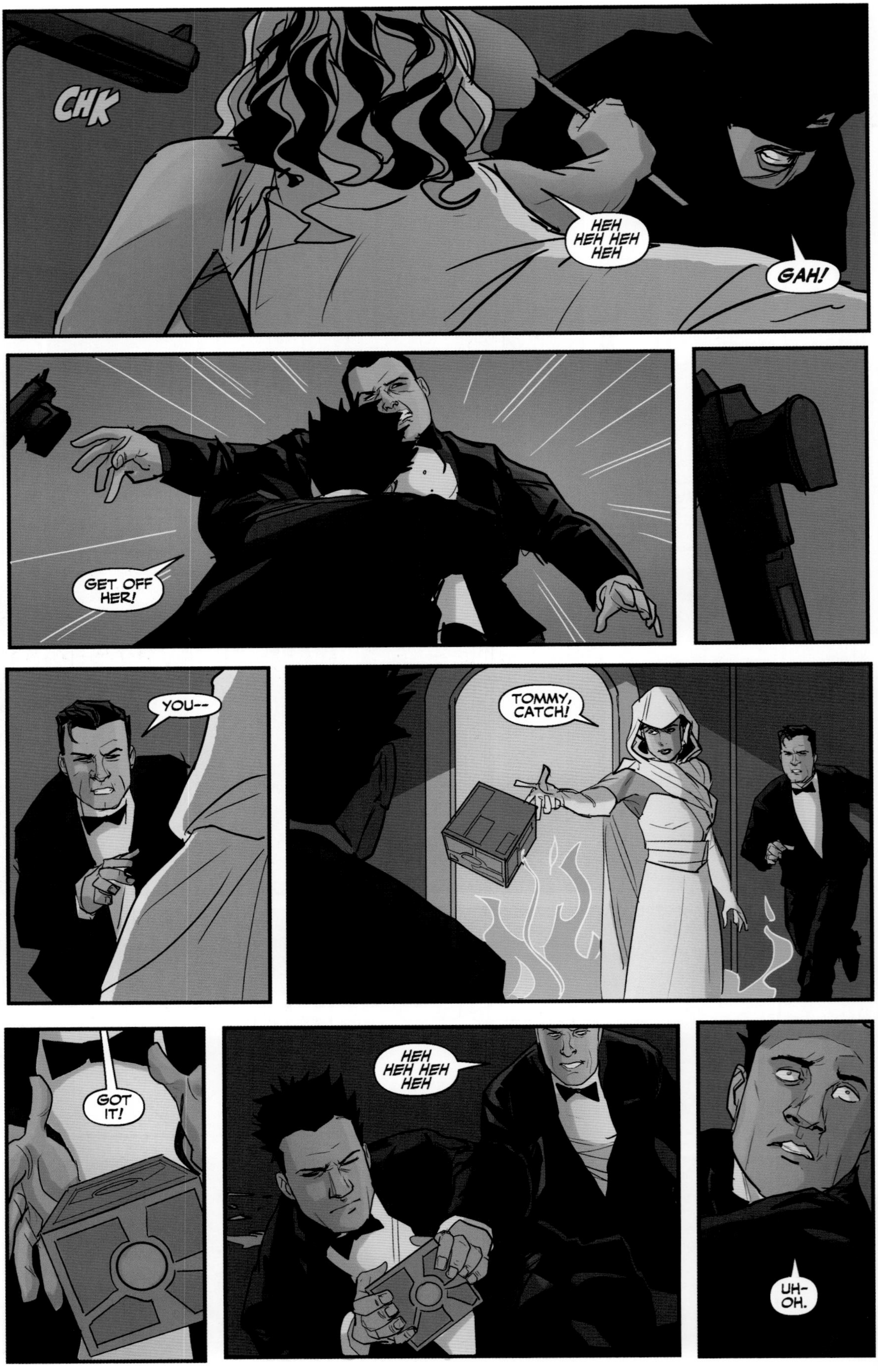
CHK
HEH HEH HEH HEH
GAH!
GET OFF HER!
YOU--
TOMMY, CATCH!
GOT IT!
HEH HEH HEH HEH
UH-OH.

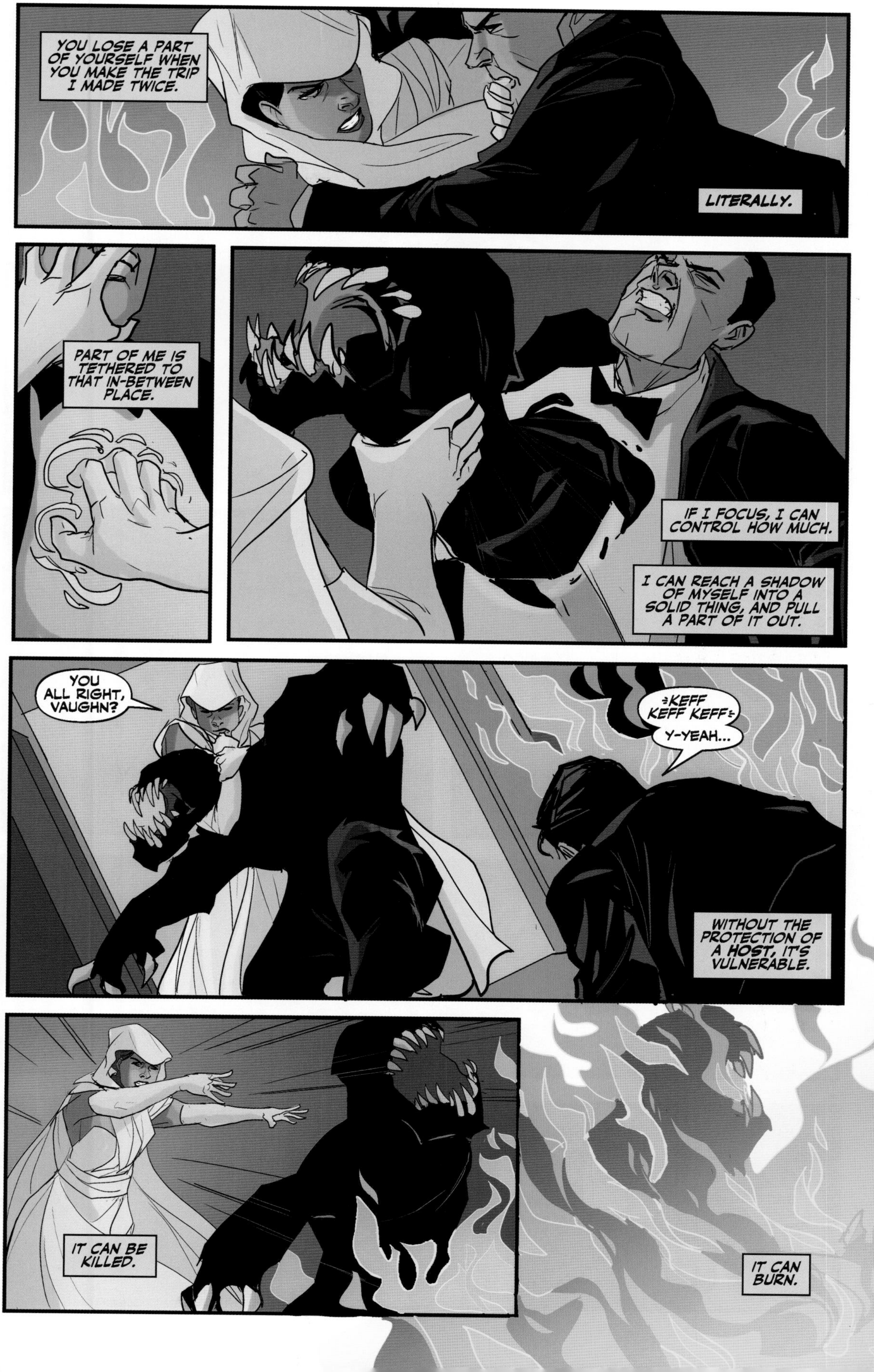

YOU LOSE A PART OF YOURSELF WHEN YOU MAKE THE TRIP I MADE TWICE.
LITERALLY.
PART OF ME IS TETHERED TO THAT IN-BETWEEN PLACE.
IF I FOCUS, I CAN CONTROL HOW MUCH.
I CAN REACH A SHADOW OF MYSELF INTO A SOLID THING, AND PULL A PART OF IT OUT.
YOU ALL RIGHT, VAUGHN?
KEFF KEFF KEFF
Y-YEAH...
WITHOUT THE PROTECTION OF A HOST, IT'S VULNERABLE.
IT CAN BE KILLED.
IT CAN BURN.

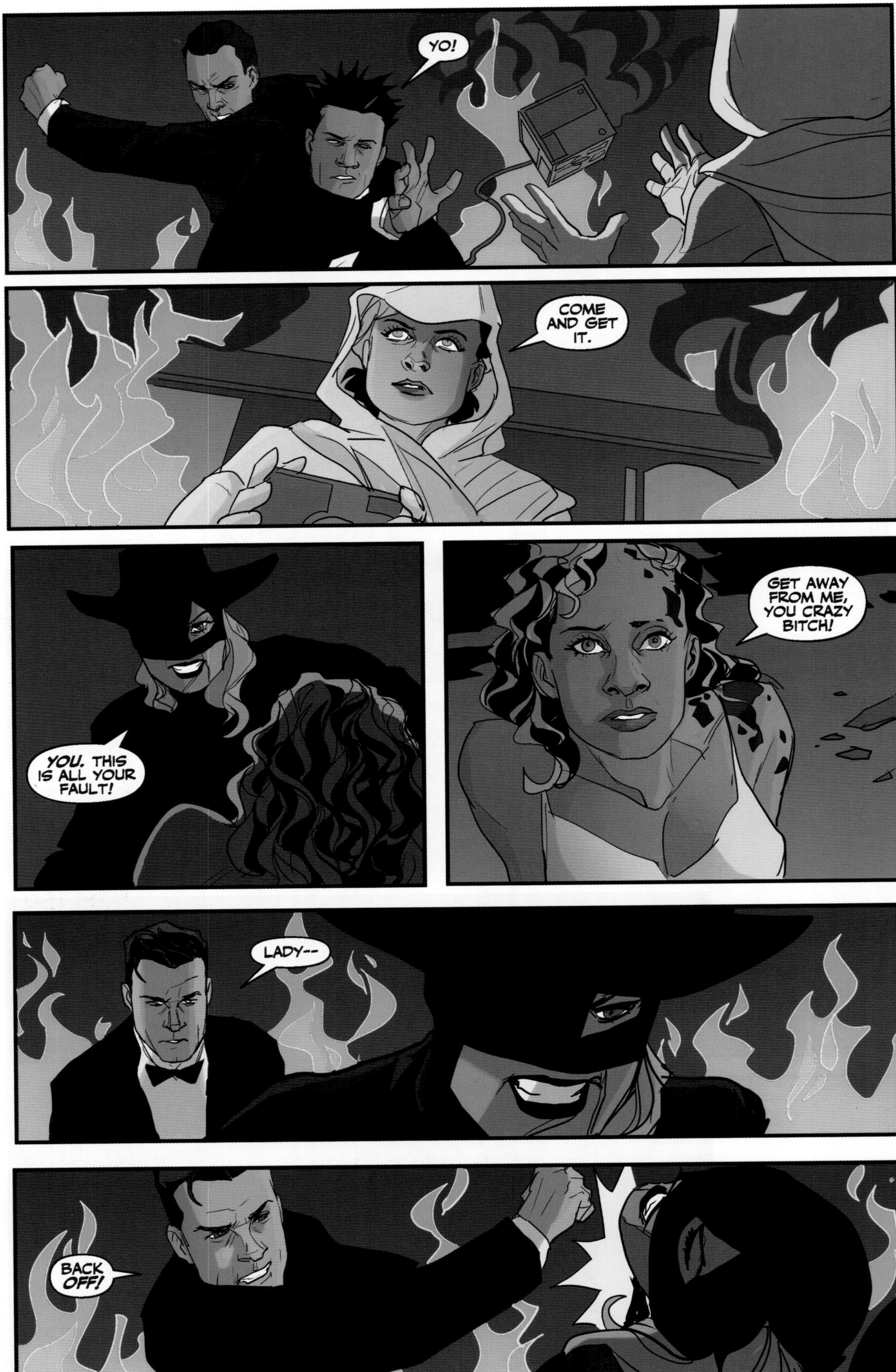
YO!
COME AND GET IT.
YOU. THIS IS ALL YOUR FAULT!
GET AWAY FROM ME, YOU CRAZY BITCH!
LADY--
BACK OFF!

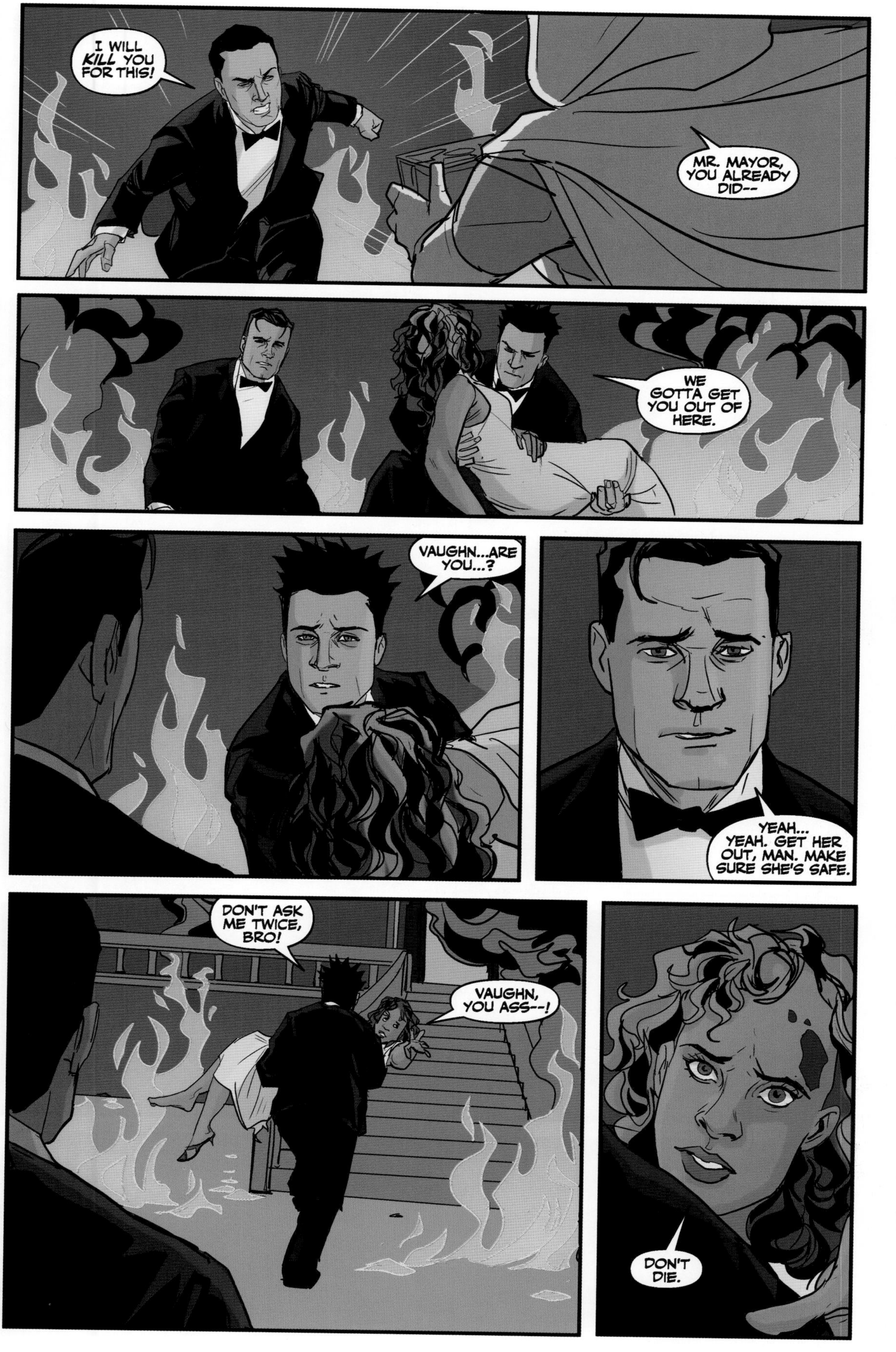
I WILL KILL YOU FOR THIS!
MR. MAYOR, YOU ALREADY DID--
WE GOTTA GET YOU OUT OF HERE.
VAUGHN...ARE YOU...?
YEAH... YEAH. GET HER OUT, MAN. MAKE SURE SHE'S SAFE.
DON'T ASK ME TWICE, BRO!
VAUGHN, YOU ASS--!
DON'T DIE.

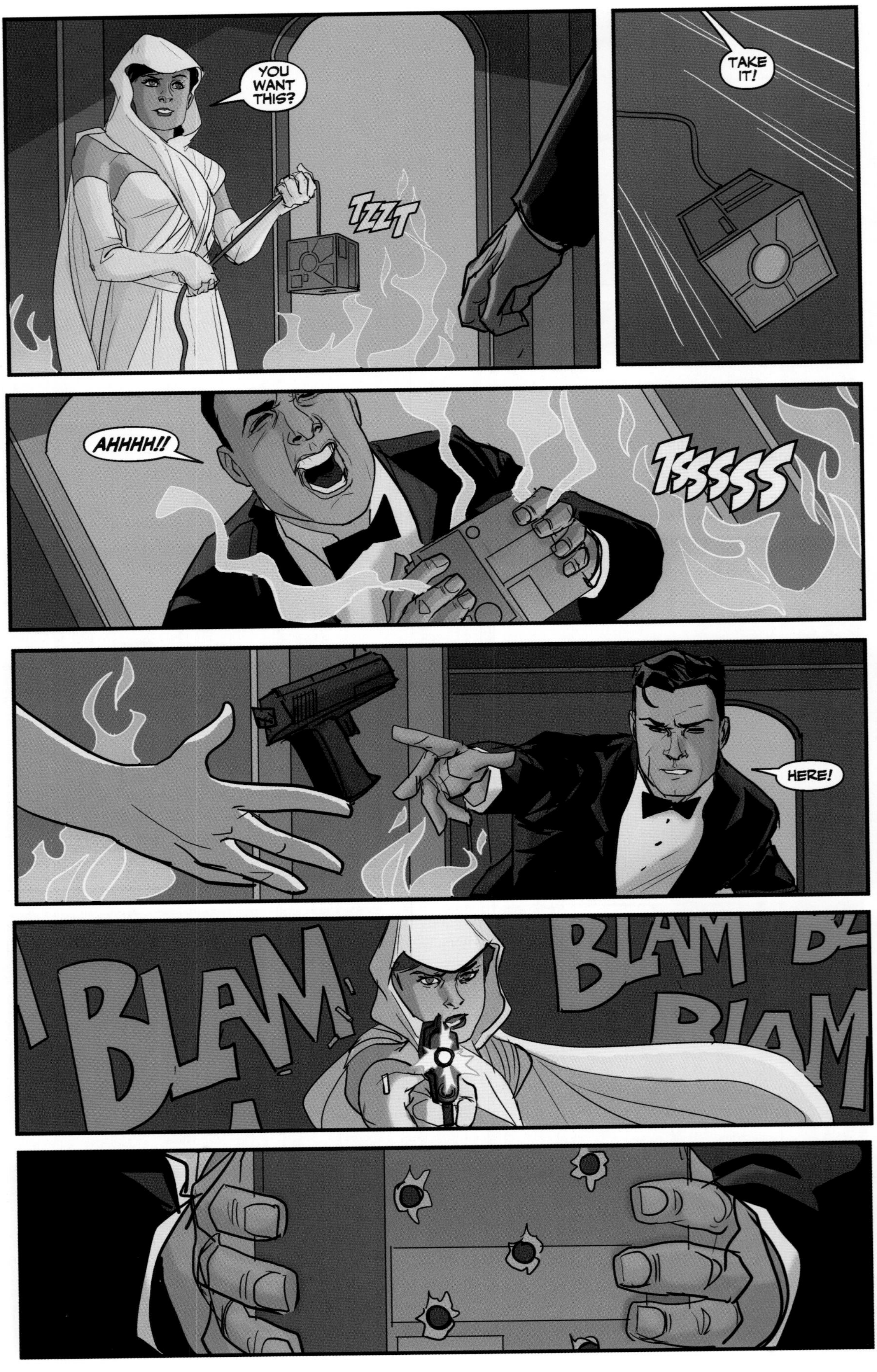
YOU WANT THIS?
TZZT
TAKE IT!
AHHHH!!
TSSSS
HERE!
BLAM
BLAM
BLAM

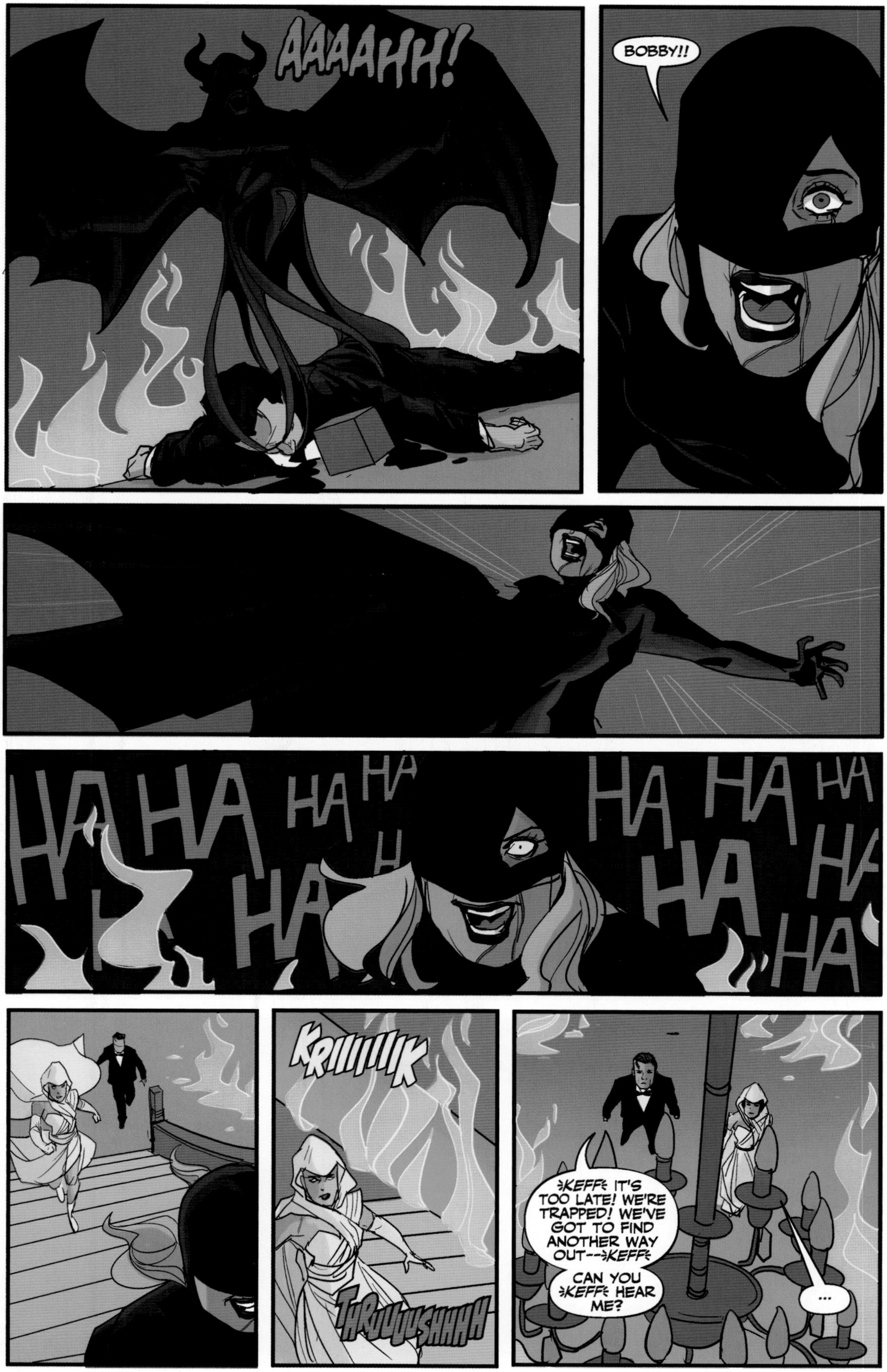
AAAAHH!
BOBBY!!
HA HA HA HA HA HA HA HA HA HA HA HA HA HA HA
KRIIIIIIK
THRUUUUSHHHH
KEFF IT'S TOO LATE! WE'RE TRAPPED! WE'VE GOT TO FIND ANOTHER WAY OUT-- *KEFF*
CAN YOU *KEFF* HEAR ME?
...

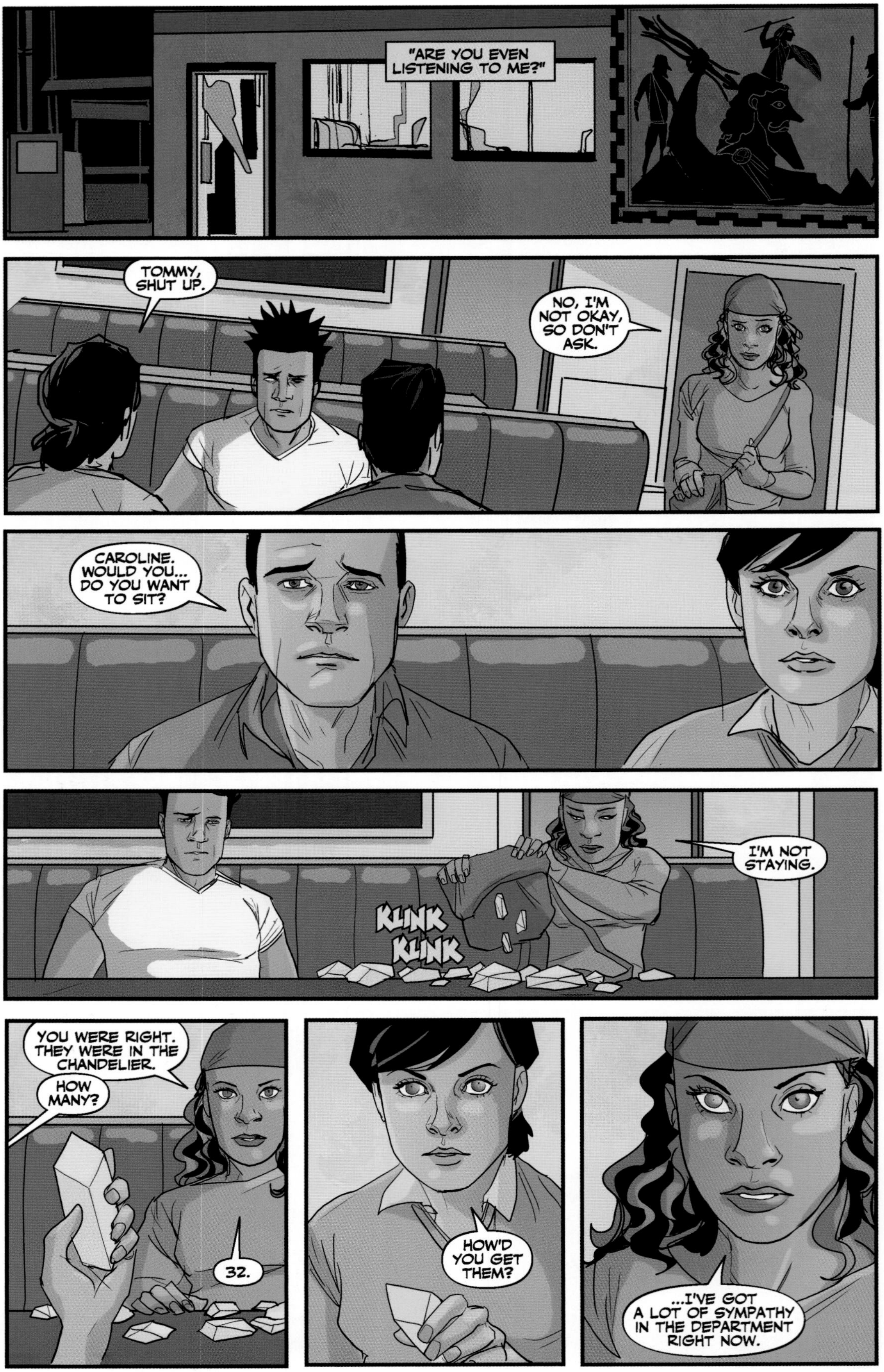
"ARE YOU EVEN LISTENING TO ME?"
TOMMY, SHUT UP.
NO, I'M NOT OKAY, SO DON'T ASK.
CAROLINE. WOULD YOU... DO YOU WANT TO SIT?
I'M NOT STAYING.
KLINK
KLINK
YOU WERE RIGHT. THEY WERE IN THE CHANDELIER.
HOW MANY?
32.
HOW'D YOU GET THEM?
...I'VE GOT A LOT OF SYMPATHY IN THE DEPARTMENT RIGHT NOW.

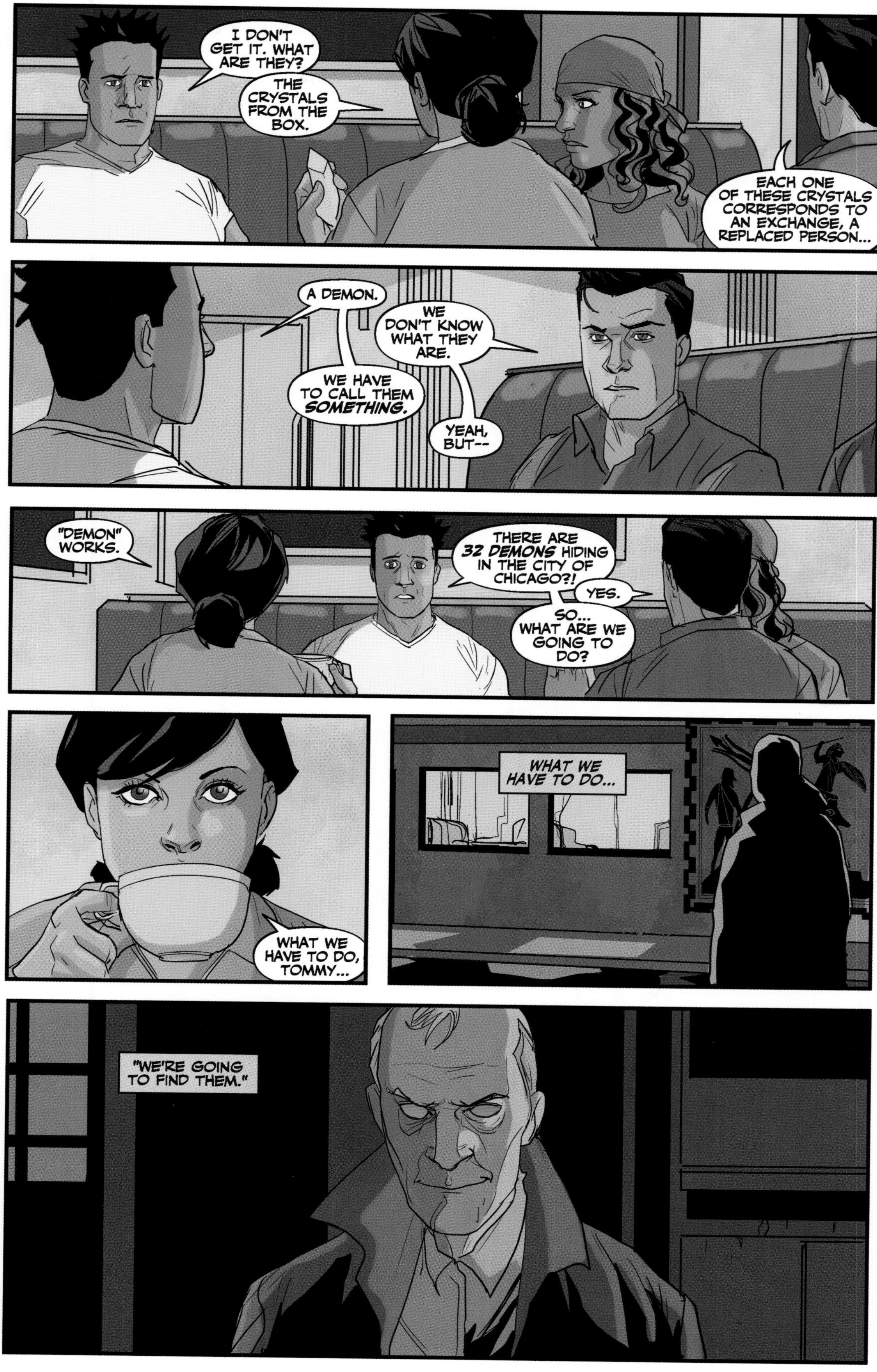
I DON'T GET IT. WHAT ARE THEY?
THE CRYSTALS FROM THE BOX.
EACH ONE OF THESE CRYSTALS CORRESPONDS TO AN EXCHANGE, A REPLACED PERSON...
A DEMON.
WE DON'T KNOW WHAT THEY ARE.
WE HAVE TO CALL THEM SOMETHING.
YEAH, BUT--
"DEMON" WORKS.
THERE ARE 32 DEMONS HIDING IN THE CITY OF CHICAGO?!
YES.
SO... WHAT ARE WE GOING TO DO?
WHAT WE HAVE TO DO, TOMMY...
WHAT WE HAVE TO DO...
"WE'RE GOING TO FIND THEM."

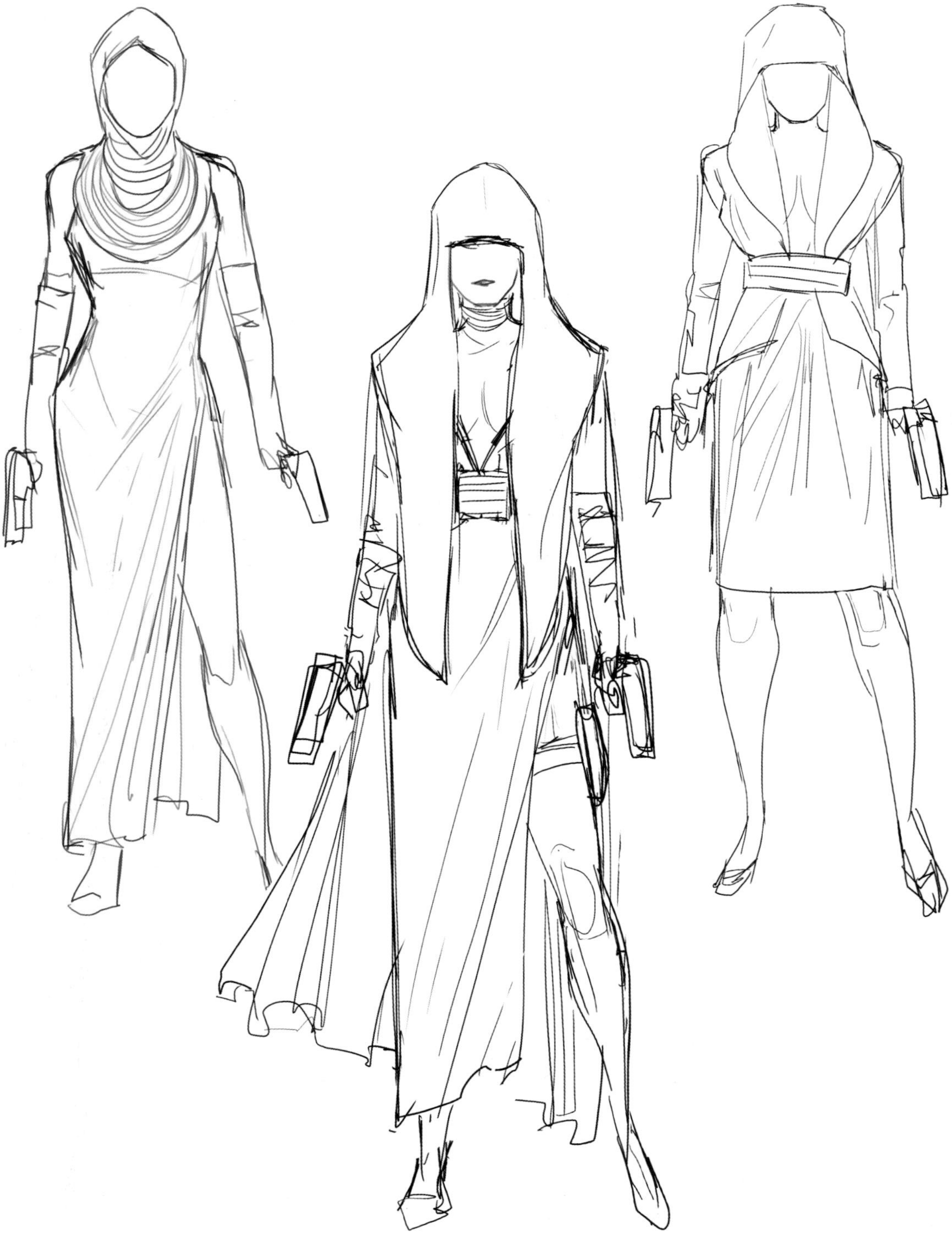

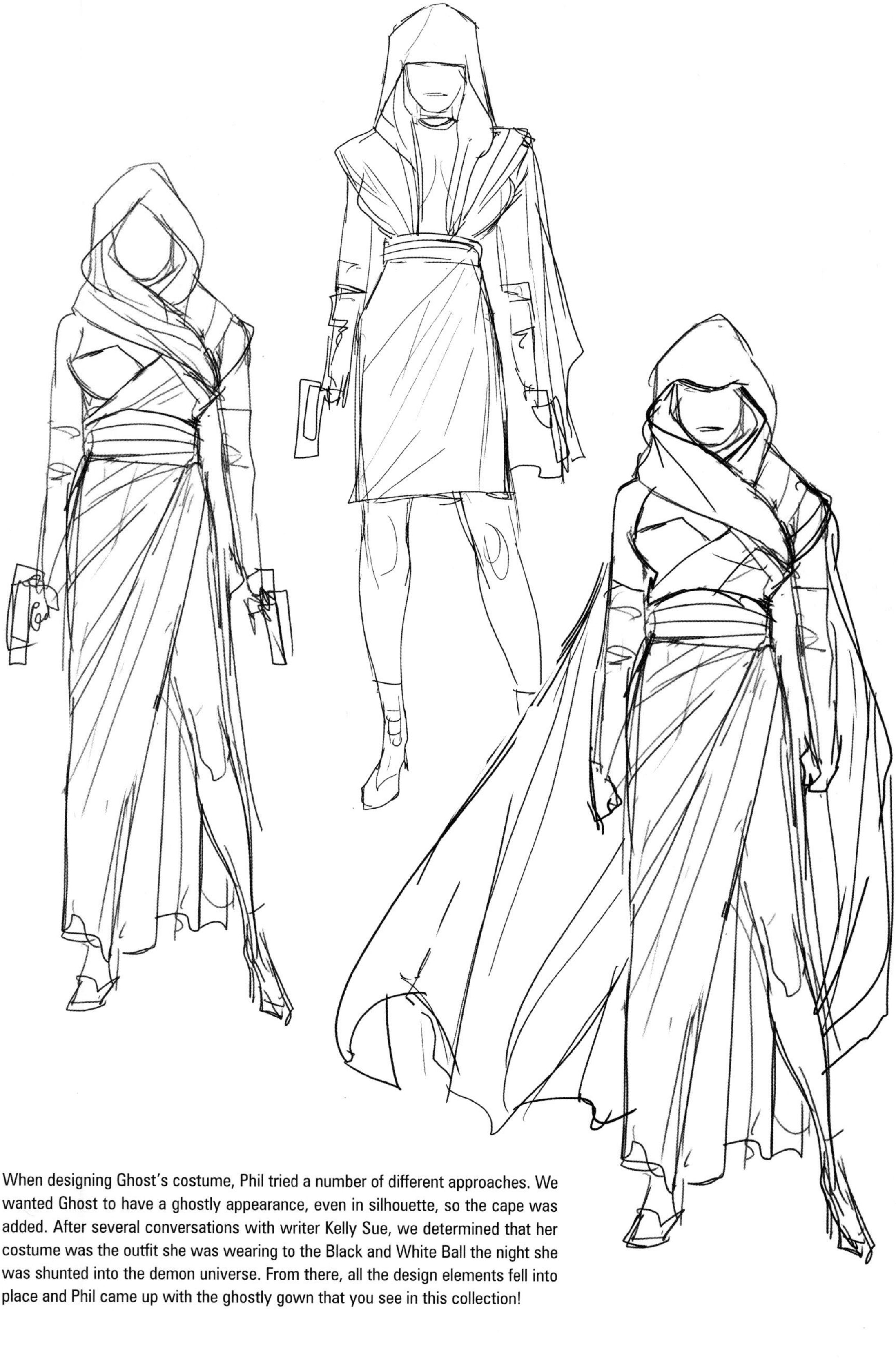

When designing Ghost's costume, Phil tried a number of different approaches. We wanted Ghost to have a ghostly appearance, even in silhouette, so the cape was added. After several conversations with writer Kelly Sue, we determined that her costume was the outfit she was wearing to the Black and White Ball the night she was shunted into the demon universe. From there, all the design elements fell into place and Phil came up with the ghostly gown that you see in this collection!

DARK HORSE PRESENTS #13 COVER BY **PHIL NOTO**.

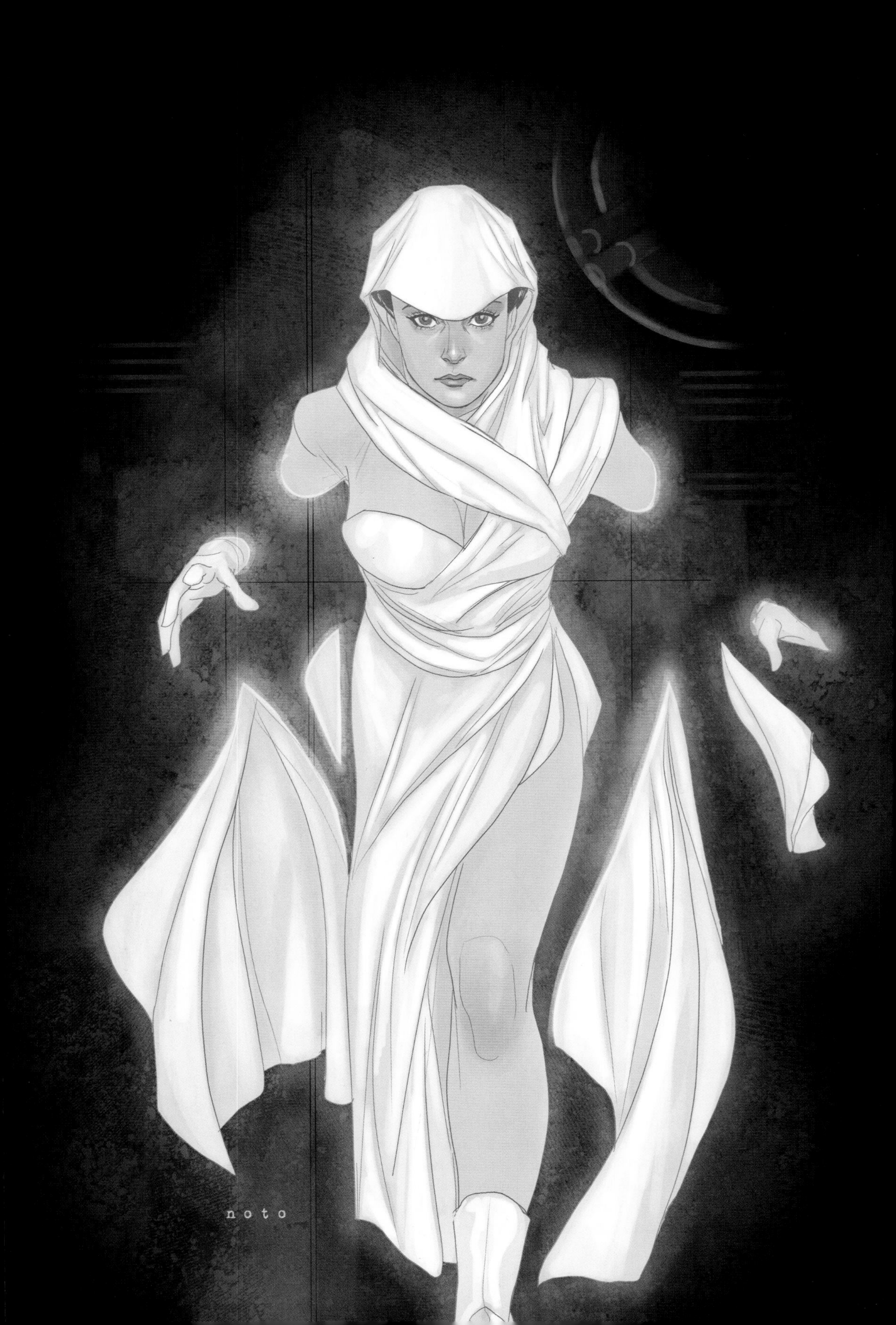
noto

PINUP BY **SIMON MYERS**. CHECK OUT MORE OF HIS STUFF AT PRETTYFUNKY.COM!

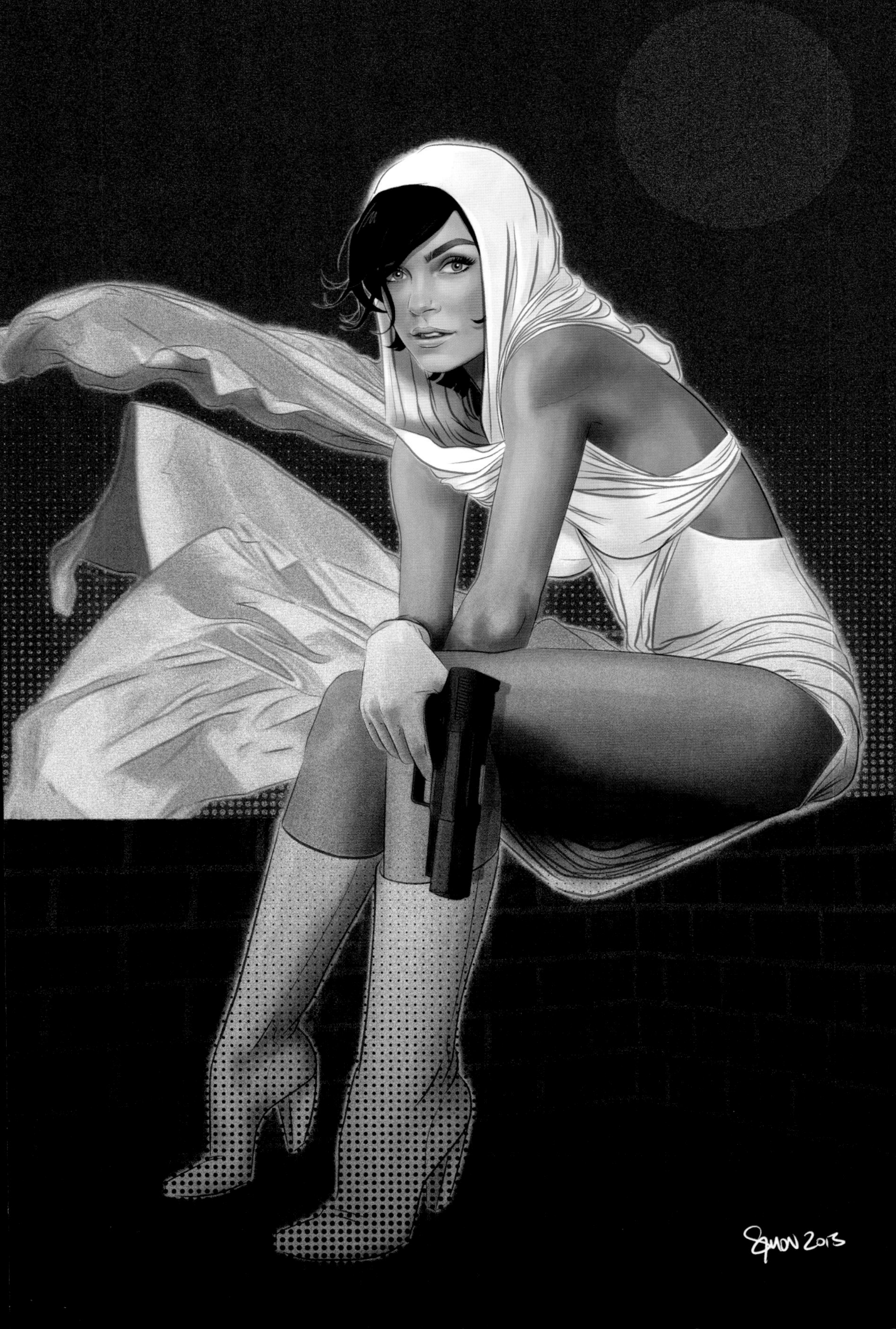
SIMON 2013

GHOST #1 VARIANT COVER BY **ALEX ROSS**.

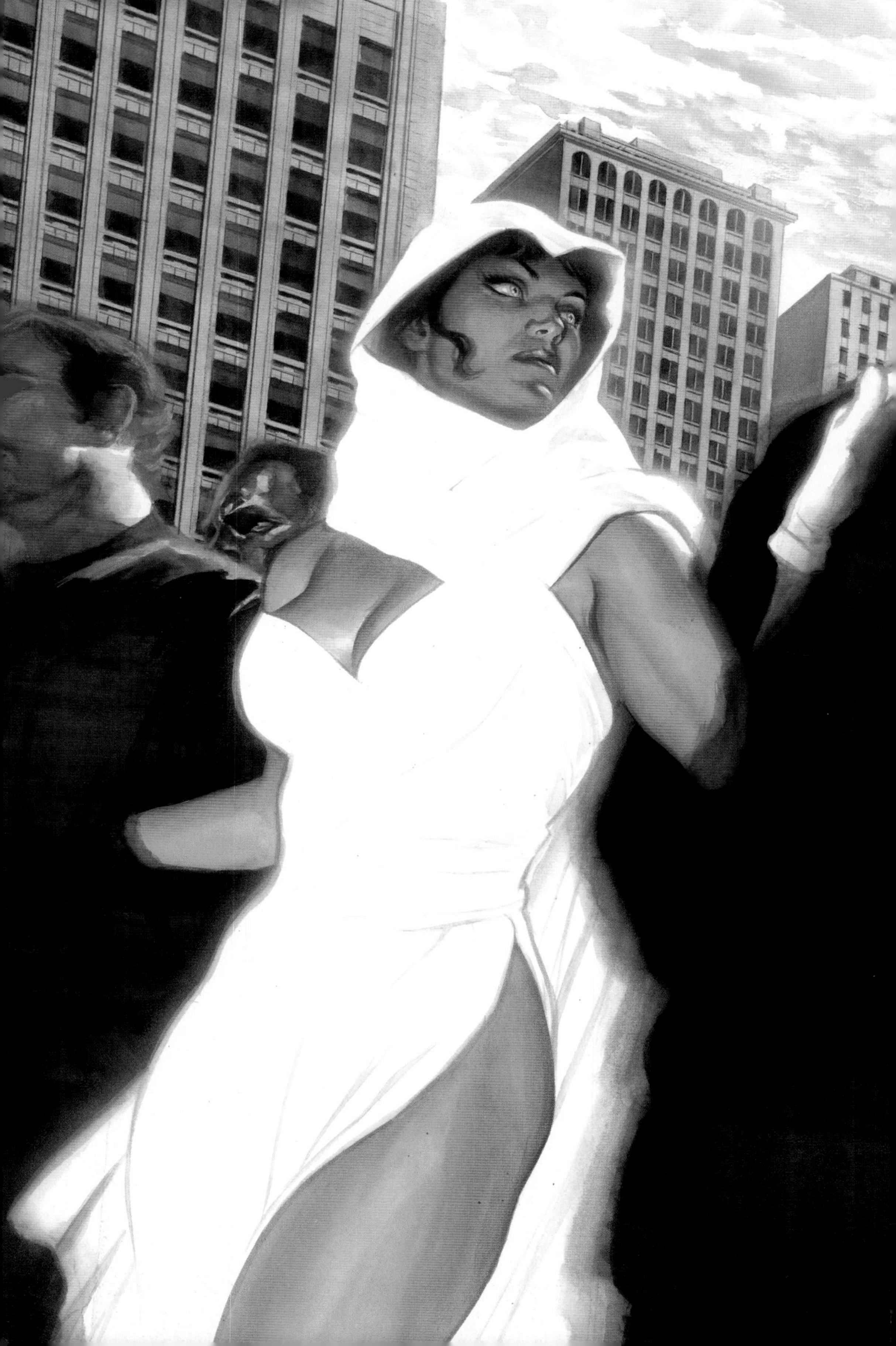

GHOST #2 VARIANT COVER BY **ALEX ROSS**.

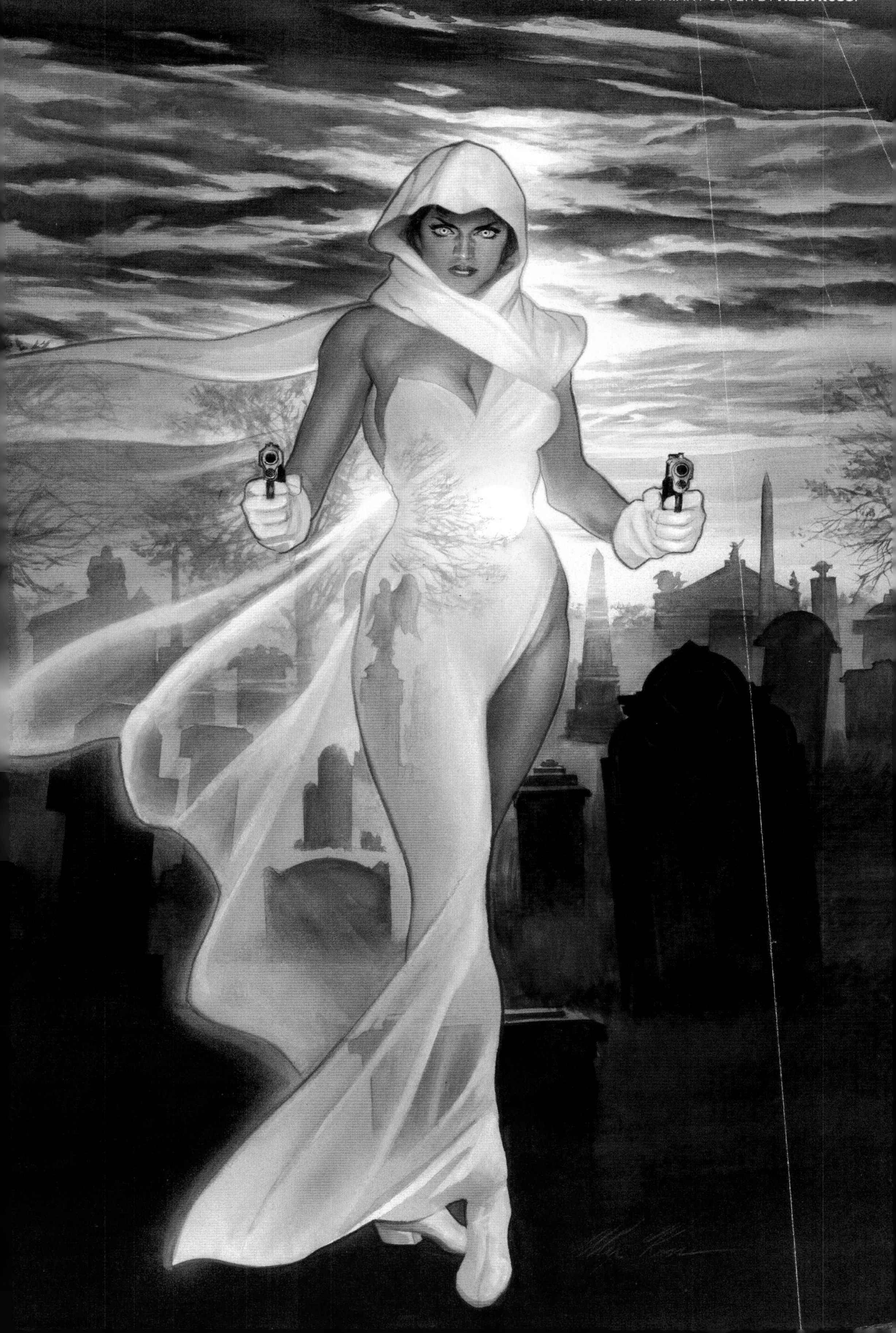

FROM JOSS WHEDON

CHECK OUT THESE OMNIBUS COLLECTIONS FEATURING CLASSIC DARK HORSE HEROES!

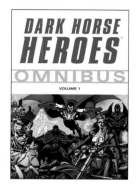

DARK HORSE HEROES OMNIBUS

Would a world populated by supermen become a battleground for good against bad . . . or bad against worse? *Dark Horse Heroes Omnibus* collects *Comics Greatest World* and *Will to Power*, the two hit maxiseries created by Dark Horse Comics that turned the concept of the superhero universe on its head, featuring the first appearances of Ghost, X, and Barb Wire, among others. This omnibus collection brings together an all-star team of the industry's top talents to forge a unique and exciting take on the superhero mythos.

Volume 1
ISBN 978-1-59307-734-1

Volume 2
ISBN 978-1-59307-928-4

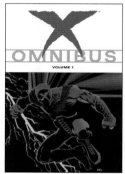

X OMNIBUS

X Omnibus collects the audacious, critically acclaimed Dark Horse series that made "grim and gritty" superheroes seem like cuddly plush toys. Violent and morally ambiguous, *X* walks the thin line between heroism and obsession and shows that sometimes the cure may be worse than the disease. The *X Omnibus* features incredible stories and arresting artwork from creators including Steven Grant, Doug Mahnke, Chris Warner, Jimmy Palmiotti, and Tim Bradstreet.

Volume 1
ISBN 978-1-59307-939-0

Volume 2
ISBN 978-1-59307-937-6

THE MASK OMNIBUS

It has all the makings of an epic adventure: an ancient artifact is rediscovered—a mask of unknown origin with unforeseen power. But who knew that after donning this mask even the wimpiest geek would become an indestructible shape-changing super-tornado with a mind for mischief and an appetite for destruction? Equally adept with gun, knife, bat, bomb, pie, or bat-knife-gun-pie-bomb, the Mask cuts a crazed swath of cartoon mayhem! This omnibus edition collects *The Mask*, *The Mask Returns*, and *The Mask Strikes Back* (long out-of-print) for the first time in one volume.

Volume 1
ISBN 978-1-59307-927-7

Volume 2
ISBN 978-1-59307-937-6

BARB WIRE OMNIBUS

Steel Harbor is a hell of a town, with the emphasis on *hell*, an urban wasteland of shuttered factories, decaying neighborhoods, and broken dreams. Crime and street violence are the soup of the day every day, but if you're a bounty hunter, every day in "Metal City" can be Christmas—assuming you survive, since the worst of the Harbor's most wanted can fly, summon up tornadoes, or tear cars in half with their bare hands. But manhunter Barb Wire is the best tracker in the business, and no super-gangster is too tough. Beautiful as she is lethal, Barb Wire really puts the "drop dead" in drop-dead gorgeous. The comics series that inspired the movie, *Barb Wire* is over-the-top action that opened doors for today's bad-girl characters.

ISBN 978-1-59307-993-2

$24.99 EACH

OMNIBUS

Someone brutally murdered reporter Elisa Cameron, but back from the grave as the spectral avenger Ghost, Elisa intends to find out who killed her and why . . . and grab a double dose of .45-caliber retribution. But Ghost's journey to the truth follows a dark, twisted path, and the revelations she unearths may lead not to redemption, but damnation.

Tales of the spectral avenger created by some of the top talents in comics, including screenwriter Eric Luke, Ivan Reis, Doug Braithwaite, Adam Hughes, John Cassaday, and others!

VOLUME ONE	VOLUME TWO	VOLUME THREE	VOLUME FOUR
ISBN 978-1-59307-992-5	ISBN 978-1-59582-213-0	ISBN 978-1-59582-374-8	ISBN 978-1-61655-080-6
$24.99	$24.99	$24.99	$24.99